PROGRAMMER PRODUCTIVITY

PROGRAMMER PRODUCTIVITY

Myths, Methods, and Murphology

A Guide for Managers, Analysts, and Programmers

LOWELL JAY ARTHUR

A Wiley-Interscience Publication

JOHN WILEY & SONS

New York   Chichester   Brisbane   Toronto   Singapore

Library of Congress Cataloging in Publication Data:

Arthur, Lowell Jay, 1951-
  Programmer productivity.

  "A Wiley-Interscience publication."
  Bibliography: p.
  Includes index.
  1. Computer programming management.   I. Title.

QA76.6.A767 1983   001.64′2′068   82-13417
ISBN 0-471-86434-X

Printed in the United States of America

10 9 8 7 6 5 4 3 2

To Paula Martin—my inspiration

Preface

There's no such thing as a free lunch

If you expect a simple, elegant, and inexpensive solution to your productivity problems, you have come to the wrong place. Crawling out of the unproductive mire will take time, money, resources, and dedication. But think of the gains that can be yours—productivity improvements of 100 to 1000%!

"A thousand percent!" you say. "That's impossible!" James Martin says it is possible today. Edward Yourdon will tell you that there is a 10:1 difference among programmers. Are the 10s that much smarter or do they just work smarter? And if they just work smarter, why not tap their knowledge and use it?

Everything has been thought of before, but the problem is to think of it again.

Johann W. von Goethe

Ever since my earliest experience with computers, I have felt there must be a better way to create programs. Years of experience and rubbing elbows with super-programmers has shown me the light. I wrote this book to help you and your company learn productivity and quality methods without having to think of them all by yourself. With experience and application, your productivity can double in no time at all.

You do pay a price for vastly improved productivity: your systems must be more generic, possibly less efficient, and less tailored to the business. But if you can build the first version of the system in a tenth of the time, you will still have plenty of time to find its deficiencies and build a better system. Programmers always erect the second system more quickly than the first, so productivity and quality may both exceed your expectations.

The transition from how you work now to how you should be working to improve productivity will exact a toll. The guts of this book will cost you money, time, and people. You will need retraining, new support systems, new methodology, and new programming tools. You will be forced to change how you think about programming. That's the kicker: you're finally being asked to join the computer revolution and change how you work. I want to automate your job. Do you feel threatened? You needn't be. Do you feel obsolete? Nonsense. Information processing is one of the few jobs that keeps getting more interesting. Think of your software shop as a factory that is being remodeled, retooled, and reworked.

The title of this book mentions mythology, methodology, and Murphology. Myths perpetrate the hoax that programmer productivity cannot increase dramatically. People in your organization will try to block changes that will disrupt their way of working. They use myths, witchcraft, and subversion to undermine the process of change. I'll expose these myths as they surface, disprove them, and show you ways of overcoming them.

Murphology reminds us of the ever-present Murphy's Law that threatens even the simplest software development activities. This law permeates the development process; anticipating it will help reduce its impact. The most important requirement is to beat the law as often as possible. If you expect productivity to improve without a lot of hard work, then you are functioning under one of my favorite corollaries. Don't believe in miracles—*rely on them.*

Methdology focuses on how you should change to improve productivity and quality in the Data Processing shop. The most important factors that affect productivity are methodology, technology, people, management, organization, and external influences.

The chapter on methodology examines how super-programmers work; the chapter on technology discusses what tools they use or build to support their needs. Super-programmers and analysts are just people. How do human needs affect productivity? What do the super-programmers require from a humanistic standpoint? The chapter on people answers these challenging questions. Management has the responsibilities of supporting changes for productivity growth and planning for the future. The organization of a Data Processing department can affect productivity either positively or negatively by imposing or eliminating roadblocks. The management and organization of a Data Processing shop require change and fine tuning to help improve productivity and quality.

These components of productivity mesh to form either a cohesive or confusing arena for program development and maintenance. I plan to guide you to the more productive environment known as the software factory.

Your current factory probably spends more time repairing old systems than building new ones. Qualities such as reliability, maintainability, and flexibility weigh heavily on your maintenance costs. The renovated software factory will depend heavily on quality improvements to increase productivity.

I plan to show you how to improve quality without affecting productivity negatively. I'll also show you how to ensure software quality through quality assurance and software measurement.

Knowing your concern with costs, I'll also recommend ways to buy software rather than build it, which can be both productive and cost effective. Some mix of home-grown and purchased software will optimize productivity for the money spent.

To achieve superior levels of productivity, quality, and cost benefits requires planning. Industrial manufacturers increase productivity by phasing out old hardware and methods. They substitute new technology and capital for labor costs. Implementing a software factory will require similar analysis and planning. I'll recommend ways to begin the development of your own software factory.

Finally, I'll examine the software factories of the future. Will software create software? What kind of new systems will appear? Without planning for the future, you will jeopardize the competitive position of your company.

Changing things is central to leadership, and changing them before anyone else is creativeness.

Creative thinking may mean simply the realization that there's no particular virtue in doing things the way they always have been done.

Rudolf Flesch

It's up to you. The rewards are great: you can produce entire systems in a month or two. You can capture information that will make your business more competitive. Channel your creativity into the development of your own software factory. Join the computer revolution!

LOWELL JAY ARTHUR

Denver, Colorado
December 1982

Contents

xi

PROGRAMMER PRODUCTIVITY

CHAPTER ONE

The Evolution of Software Engineering

In the early 1960s computerization became a growing factor in business. People suddenly feared that a machine would someday replace their jobs and careers, threatening their homes, families, and survival. At the same time, the national productivity level, which had been growing at 3.2% per year since World War II, suddenly started to drop; it has not regained its growth rate since, hitting bottom in 1967, at 0.7% per year.

Although many factors led to the decline in productivity, the computer, with its perfect accuracy, may have accelerated the descent. The computer's appearance on the horizon as the perfect replacement for many routine jobs alienated many workers. But in spite of the manufacturers' claims, the computer did not cause widespread unemployment. Instead, it allowed businesses to expand and grab a larger market share, and it enabled workers to move into more challenging jobs. The dawn of the Computer Age brought with it the most extensive set of new careers since the Industrial Revolution, creating thousands of jobs in the manufacture, maintenance, and programming of computers. Even now, there seems to be no end to the varied systems that need development. Without the advent of computers, national productivity would be far lower.

As with any new increase in productivity, some breakthrough in knowledge elevated people to the next level of understanding; the computer was that breakthrough. Tedious clerical jobs, requiring days or weeks to complete, were accomplished by the computer in just a few minutes.

In light of these productivity benefits, it is strange that programming hasn't changed greatly in the last 20 years. The computer allows people to do repetitive tasks quickly and efficiently, but its power hasn't been harnessed to enhance the development or maintenance of systems significantly. It handles predominately clerical jobs, and only a few management or professional tasks. Mechanizing white-collar jobs offers tremendous benefits, since over 60% of office costs, in a service economy, come from them.

Automating the programming task benefits the company by making programmers more productive, and it benefits programmers by expanding their creative horizons. To date, small productivity increases have come from a variety of methodologies and technologies, but they haven't been sufficient to meet the demands for new and enhanced systems. Most productivity enhancements have focused on hardware, not software development. Through constant advances in technology, significant hardware productivity gains have been made. The human portion of the software development task, however, has experienced only two major advances—one through technology and the other by way of methodology.

First, assembler languages replaced machine languages and then high-level language compilers removed the programmer from the intricacies of assembler language. F. P. Brooks, Jr., who was project manager on the IBM System 360 operating system project, said that he "cannot now conceive of a system, even operating system, that would be written in assembler language" (Brooks 1975). Industry comparisons of assembler language productivity to high-level languages has shown that assembler languages require up to five times more effort to implement or maintain a given program or system. Although this appears to be an exceptional gain in productivity, the language development affected only the coding portion of system development, which is only 10–20% of the total development time and cost. Between this breakthrough and the next lay many fallow years.

The next knowledge breakthrough involved a rigorous structuring of the design process. Structured Programming evolved as a means to direct programmers to the "right" program solution, despite their differing abilities. This methodology often prevented design errors, but it also burdened the programmer with overly graphic representations of the design, which required excessive time to draw and update. Very few, if any, tools exist even today to simplify the task of creating these graphics. Among the design methods that used graphics are data flow diagrams (DFD), HIPO or IPO (input, process, output) charts, structure charts, Nassi–Schneiderman diagrams, and Chapin charts. The burdens these methods carried often consumed the productivity benefits they were supposed to provide. And, more often than not, because of their complexity and the difficulty involved in correcting them, these documents were rarely maintained after the initial development process, so that documentation was relatively useless after the first program change. Up-to-date documentation facilitates the programming task, while out-of-date documentation inhibits it, often misdirecting the programmer and reducing productivity. Here again, Structured Programming affected only the design portion of all work being performed in a Data Processing shop. It failed to provide the kinds of breakthroughs that the hardware industry had enjoyed.

Competition is the prime motivator behind hardware's explosion. Faced with innovation or extinction, computer companies expanded their research and development to keep ahead of competitors. Software, however, hasn't experienced this competition except for operating systems and related software, and it is difficult to translate intangible software benefits into bottom-line savings or competitive ability. Until competition forces change, software development will continue to lag behind hardware productivity.

For every action, there is an equal and opposite criticism.

A large body of experience indicates that new methodology and technology could enhance software development productivity. But programmers quickly reject changes in technology and methodology, knowing that each change nibbles away at their job security, so programmer resistance to change will continue to slow innovation. History tells us that future changes will not displace programming jobs, but rather create new interesting and challenging ones.

1. THE PROBLEMS

A shortcut is the longest path between two points.

Why should you want to improve productivity, anyway? Well, these are trying times for the Data Processing manager and staff. Auditors often find a lack of controls and audit trails in delivered systems and documentation. Upper management complains about schedule overruns and overtime costs. Maintenance of existing systems accounts for 50-80% of the budget. The client needs more enhancements, more systems, and faster implementation. In the rush to get projects out, shortcuts are taken and the penalties are paid later—in maintenance. All these factors contribute to the declining quality of delivered systems, while productivity continually falls short of management's expectations. Change will occur only when existing problems cause more trouble than the solutions.

2. PRODUCTIVITY

Productivity is defined here as the ability to create a quality software product in a limited period with limited resources. Productivity improvements come from ways to shorten production time for the same product or ways to produce an improved product in the same amount of time. Often, if a discipline is in its infancy, it is possible to do both—produce a better product and do so in less time. This sort of potential has been obvious in the electronic chip industry, with the resulting advances in computers, TV games, and pocket calculators. The same must be true for software, since so few improvements have appeared since the industry's birth. Hardware breakthroughs came from technology; where will software's appear?

3. THE SOLUTIONS

Each company must analyze the five factors that affect productivity in meeting their software demands. They are methodology, technology, people, the company's management and organization, and external factors (such as legislation, government regulations, etc.). This book focuses on these factors and on ways to improve their interaction. Enhancing how they affect data processing will improve programmer productivity and the quality of your systems.

3.1. Methodology

Methodology embodies the "how" of program development and maintenance. What work habits and procedures enhance productivity? What effect do they have on quality?

In the beginning, Structured Programming was touted as the

cure for all software problems. It did improve the quality of programs, but its productivity gains were spent on hard to maintain documentation.

The methodology in this book builds on Structured Programming to create the basis for Structured Systems Engineering. When properly implemented, Structured Systems Engineering will allow any DP staff to create programs and systems in the same way that Japan creates cars. The software robot component orientation, almost an assembly line arrangement, of this methodology leads to the expression "software factory" to describe its implementation.

3.2. Technology

Once the proper methodology is implemented, the right tool kit can be created to support the programmer's and analyst's needs. Technology is the tool kit that substitutes capital and software for people in the software development environment. What tools do you need? Can you buy them ready-made or should you build them? How should they be designed to optimize their use? As you would expect craftspeople to be more productive with power tools, programmers and analysts will produce programs of better quality if they have the proper tools. In the rush to automate clerical jobs, however, programmers and analysts still use primitive hand tools to mechanize other jobs. It is possible to automate DP jobs to improve productivity, system quality, and the quality of work life.

3.3. The Human Factor

The human factor is often the most important ingredient in the productivity recipe and the most overlooked. The intangible human element puts methodology and technology to use in creating systems of varying complexity. The human factors involved in program development are complex and can have a great impact on productivity. Employee sabotage and computer crime come to mind as a few negative impacts of the human element.

Many different people maintain programs during a system's lifetime, and each person is unique, with diverse needs that can affect software development. These programmers leave their own indelible marks on the program, much as the publisher and editor will leave this book more readable and understandable. Unfortunately, the programmer's mark may add friction to a system that is already decaying.

The hidden flaw never remains hidden.

Nature always sides with the hidden flaw.

The human factor makes obtaining good, up-to-date documentation almost impossible, since this clerical task is the most feared and hated of all. It introduces logic errors in systems that even exhaustive testing won't uncover—errors that won't be found until years later, when processing volumes or input changes exercise the code in new and often fascinating ways. And yet, although many managers would dispute the statement, people enjoy being productive. Their jobs are enriched by using more productive tools and methods. Programming, unfortunately, has its own negative side effects.

Computer programming is one of the more mentally abusive jobs available. No matter what the programmer does, the computer constantly sits in judgment of his or her work. It traps even the smallest error and gives immediate feedback on mistakes. It never comments on a well-structured code or program efficiency: when a job is completed successfully, all the machine gives as encouragement is a zero return code and some output. The computer is a hard, authoritarian task master. With this cold, impartial judge, it is a wonder that computer people aren't completely crazy. What motivates these rare individuals? Most are self-motivated and enjoy being the best at what they do. They take secret pride in beating the computer by their logic and skill. The computer becomes a giant video game that programmers play to win. Give them the freedom and tools to conquer the vain and pompous computer, to be more productive, and they will take up their weapons and enter the crusade.

The underlying message is that people are the backbone of any productivity improvement. Support their needs and productivity will automatically improve. Supporting human needs is often the least expensive productivity solution. Who meets these needs? Management.

3.4. Management and Organization

Management and organization give structure and order to what would otherwise be a chaotic process. Management approves changes in the environment and the use of new technology, thereby directly or indirectly affecting the people in the system. Proper management of all information system resources, coupled with the proper development and maintenance organization, greatly improves productivity in any DP shop.

It is also time for management to derive the benefits of mechanization. This section of the book will describe not only optimal management and organizational techniques, but also computerized tools for management at all levels.

3.5. External Forces

It is impossible to control the external forces that affect your productivity. What can you do about the forces of nature that destroy your computer center or new laws and government decrees that place sudden demands on your programming staff? Nothing. Unless you have your own staff wizard or legislative lobby, there is little you can do.

4. MEASURING PRODUCTIVITY AND QUALITY

Once you begin to install new ways to improve productivity and quality, you will want to measure the impact of your changes. Although it has been widely debated, it is possible to begin measuring your software products. Chapter 6 invites your participation in the development of software measurement tools from the basic building blocks provided. These building blocks will allow you to begin analyses of your programs to identify "good" and "bad" qualities from the code. They will provide the basis for productivity measurements as well. Only through constant measurement can you be sure that you are building the best programs at lowest cost.

5. REQUIREMENTS CONSTRAINING PRODUCTIVITY

Obviously, DP shops can produce programs and systems that do not meet user specifications, rarely run to completion, cannot be easily maintained, and are subject to undetectable security breaches. Anyone can produce poor quality systems in a highly productive fashion. In fact, huge systems, requiring many hours of computer resources, can be generated quickly and easily to perform absolutely no useful function. Any program or system, however, that fails to meet the company's requirements for reliability, quality, maintenance, and ease of auditing is virtually worthless.

5.1. Reliability

Undetectable errors are infinite in variety, in contrast to detectable errors, which by definition are limited.

Software reliability implies that the system will always run to the end of the job, giving the user the results required. The software must be able to handle any kind of input, evaluate it, and produce error messages and output based on it, regardless of content. It can be observed from almost any system in existence that this kind of reliability is unlikely. Many systems, however, do approach this state of nirvana after an initial burn-in period. But at some point, the cautiously maintained parts of the system begin to fail, much as the parts of an automobile fail. The system atrophies until it finally expires. For some systems, this happens in a few years; for others, only after ten or more.

The key question the productivity analyst must examine is how to produce a system with relatively few errors in the shortest period. If the developed software kept aircraft airborne, with programmers depending on it to protect their lives, it would approach a zero fail rate—total reliability—and programmers would never introduce spurious changes into the system. But this is not the usual case. Programmers install changes knowing full well that in most instances they will incur little or no personal inconvenience from potential failures. Software failure is something management has come to expect.

There are trade-offs to make when dealing with development time frames and zero fail software. Chapter 7 will show you ways to insure fewer errors in the resulting systems. These methods also decrease the time needed to produce a system with an acceptable level of reliability. Furthermore, they reduce the possibility of errors entering the system from subsequent modifications.

5.2. Maintainability

Program complexity grows until it exceeds the capability of the programmer who must maintain it.

Maintainability measures a system's ability to change gracefully. As most maintenance programmers will explain, this utopia just doesn't exist. In fact, many projects require more maintenance personnel than were originally required for development.

With 50–80% of each DP department's budget allocated for maintaining existing software, huge returns may be garnered from improving maintenance productivity. This book, however, can tell you only how to maintain your existing programs in a somewhat more productive way. A system's maintainability is built in and cannot be added on. It can only be changed by rewriting portions of the system.

> *Twenty percent of the programs cause eighty percent of the costs.*
>
> *Pareto's Rule*

Historically, 80% of any cost savings can be obtained by modifying or rewriting 20% of the code. Chapter 8 will discuss numerous methods to identify this "problem" code and to insure that all new code and systems will be easier to maintain. Unfortunately, existing DP shops will have to wait from five to ten years before the dinosaurs are phased out and rewritten: it took 20 years to get into this mess, so don't expect immediate salvation.

5.3. Quality

Quality, in part, includes the reliability of the system. It also includes documentation and code. Without "good" quality system and program documentation, the system may be considered of poor quality, causing many late-night phone calls and a lot of overtime. The code must be structured according to the company's standards and have a very positive coding style to improve maintenance. It should also have in-line documentation to supplement the design documentation.

Quality also indicates levels of user satisfaction with the system. If the system doesn't meet the user's needs (not necessarily the requirements), it is of poor quality.

In short, the system's quality becomes imperative to the success or failure of each and every company. Chapter 9 will explore ways of improving the quality of systems while maintaining or decreasing the time required to deliver the system.

5.4. Ease of Auditing

Auditors used to be stereotyped as little people who ran around inspecting the company ledgers, looking for discrepancies. Back then, the ledgers were prepared by lots of people, with feather pens and inkwells, all of whom were capable of error. But people no longer toil over the company books; computers do. A large computer can do more additions in a second than the best accountant can do in a year, and at a substantially lower cost.

So with all this automation, why audit? Unfortunately, a few companies have been convicted of cheating on their financial statements and income tax and of hiding payments to foreign governments. These convictions led to legislation to prevent this kind of business ethics abuse. Now, anyone who knowingly allows such problems to enter or remain in their software is in violation of the law. The company's top management—not the programmer or analyst—are held personally responsible. The personal liability of the company's management has made audit trails a commandment, rather than a nicety.

To err is human. To really foul things up takes a computer.

If sufficient run controls and audit trails are nonexistent, security breaches may go undetected and result in stolen profits and pilfered information. There have been over 400 known cases of computer crime, which have resulted in the loss of over $200 million, at an average take of $500,000. It is doubtful that any firm can afford to lose this much money at any time. Information is becoming the key resource of many institutions, making its value equivalent to the company's survival. Imagine computer theft of special formulas, special designs, or data for use in court cases.

It should be obvious that almost every financial program should have some built-in audit trails to detect computer criminals in the act, but there are other reasons for requiring audit trails. As was mentioned before, the firm's financial status depends on the information systems. If data that cost your company thousands of dollars to collect can be stolen, those data should have had audit trails as well.

These audit trails don't just magically appear in code; someone must put them there. The most obvious choice for this task are the designers of the system and those who implement it. If DP productivity levels stay the same, fewer systems will be produced. It is significantly more cost effective, however, to build audit trails into the system than to try to add them later, and higher auditor productivity will also result. The chances of an extensive financial loss will decrease. Finally, management won't ever be surprised by its internal or external auditing staff or by the government.

It seems that, even without an increase in productivity, audit trails are worth every penny, but they are an additional burden. Chapter 10 will examine ways to insure both ease of auditing and improved productivity. How do you add more work and do everything in less time? It will require an initial investment of time and resources, but thereafter, auditing, like the rest of the process, will take its place among your routine daily tasks.

6. BUYING SOFTWARE TO IMPROVE PRODUCTIVITY

Chapter 11 discusses the approach a business should take in obtaining and implementing an off-the-shelf system. This chapter emphasizes using consultants and purchased hardware and software to support your needs. Faced with waiting from several months to several years for a software product, you may want to buy them from a vendor at a substantial savings in time and expense.

7. IMPLEMENTATION

Software development is like a giant jigsaw puzzle in a darkened box. How can it be put together to satisfy all of the organization's requirements and yet not cost more to implement than it's worth? How can people be convinced to move to new technology? How can management be convinced to open up the budget to insure long-term returns? How should changes be implemented to phase in software engineering while phasing out the old mystic programming ways?

The key here will be the people, both management and DP staff; without their support and guidance, all is lost. The evolution may take many years. Structured Programming has been around for more than five years, but is implemented only in limited ways. Those shops that have implemented it have reaped its gains and are thirsting for more. Don't expect that the mere reading of this book will convince even the most innovative managers to accept it.

In some political climates, the implementation may have to be done subversively: initially, management will not condone it, even though the company and employees will profit in the end. The situation is analogous to the television commercial in which the man tries to sell pancake mix from door to door. Until he forces people to taste the results, he fails. The only means of getting management interested may be to whip up some productivity improvements, install them, and see how management reacts.

Chapter 12 recommends a way of implementing Systems Engineering concepts. It speaks from a common sense base and leads you to the "software factory," a clear plan for implementing and realizing extensive productivity and quality improvements.

8. SUMMARY

The concerns of every DP department lie with the productivity of their people and the quality of their work. This book not only suggests ways to improve productivity, but also describes the positive effects on the company's profits and the morale of its employees. It may take only one person to form the snowball and roll it down the mountain. Out of each action comes a re-evaluation of many traditions, which often leads to problem solutions, regardless of the path taken.

The initial obstacle is inertia. Without the force to start the process, no one will ever begin. A body at rest tends to remain at rest; a body in motion tends to remain in motion. And it takes more force to put a body into motion than to keep it in motion. The force needed to change an organization's direction may come from a single person in management, or from a few innovative programmers. The groundswells of programmer change can reshape system development more meaningfully than all the organizational charts drawn in management's board rooms. There is no person too small to initiate this change. Top management exerts a greater force than a programmer, but even a single programmer or analyst can start an avalanche with just one snowball. Programmers will suggest that politics shouldn't be necessary to improve the programming environment, but that's like saying that life should be fair and everyone should live happily ever after. In real life, politics can be used most effectively to gain support for ideas that otherwise would fail. It will take all the skills that you can muster to apply the contents of this book. Don't expect instantaneous results, but look for the gradual changes that will begin. Recognize them: they mean success.

CHAPTER TWO

Methodology

Methodology defines how one performs each task that leads to a finished system and the order in which each of these tasks is accomplished. Methodology can hasten your success in reaching your goal, or it can lead you in circles. You can design methodology like any other system: overall work flow first, detail later. By breaking the process into smaller, manageable pieces, each can be examined, improved, and later integrated into the whole. This chapter delves into system development and maintenance as a whole, continuing into the detail of each subphase. Methodology can either hinder or advance productivity. No one solution will work for all organizations, so select those portions suitable to your organization and implement them. The benefits are yours for the taking.

1. PHASED SYSTEM DEVELOPMENT

If you don't already have a phased methodology for implementing software projects, you need one. Phasing your work breaks the development process into manageable work pieces. Phases provide meaningful checkpoints and specific interim products, allowing you to gain better control of your programming process, which will improve productivity. The phases most often referred to are the following:

1. *Proposal.* Why do we want to do this project? What problems will the system solve? What benefits will the company receive from its implementation?
2. *Feasibility.* Can it be done? Is it technically possible and economically justifiable to build this system?
3. *Definition.* What needs to be done? What does the user require?
4. *Design.* What are the people going to do and what is the computer supposed to do? How will each part do its job? How will the two interact? How do the programs work? What does the user documentation need to contain?
5. *Programming.* Coding, testing, and documenting
6. *Conversion.* System installation
7. *Performance Review.* Does the system work as we would like? Is the end user satisfied? Is it efficient? Can it be audited? Can it be maintained?

Without such a phased process, the system will always be "just about done" and you'll have another major cost overrun to deal with. Without intermediate products, the end user will have no idea what he or she is getting.

Table 2.1 shows the outputs of each phase and the suggested approval body. The user should review all outputs.

1.1. Phase Review

Each phase should serve as a project review. The project manager is responsible for producing the phase report. If a system becomes apparently impracticable, cancel it. If estimated costs exceed the value of the system, cancel it. Cancelling a system will upset the people working on it, but the system will already have cost a significant amount of money; continuing development burdens the company with unnecessary costs for years to come. Phase reviews also provide a yardstick of progress. Problems in the schedule can be resolved before continuing.

1.2. Estimates

At the end of each phase, estimates for all subsequent phases are reviewed and revised. The early estimates will probably be off by

50–100%, so don't base your plan on these estimates; update them at the end of each phase. By the end of the definition phase, estimates should approach ± 10% of the actual cost.

1.3. End-User Involvement

The most important person in the development or maintenance team is the end user. You can build the right system, from the ground up, but only with the end user's help. How should this person be involved? Usually someone from the client department assumes the role of project manager. Many books and courses describe the project manager's function in system development and maintenance, so it will suffice to say that this person is responsible for the proposal, feasibility, and definition phases of development and the activities of the user department during the remaining phases. The project manager also controls the changes made to the system after it goes into production.

> *The inevitable result of improved and enlarged communications between different levels in a hierarchy is a vastly increased area of misunderstanding.*

Having one person as the focus for this task improves productivity by reducing the number of communication channels between the end user and the DP department. Figure 2.1 shows the communication lines between the project manager and the development team. If information doesn't get to the DP or client department, the project manager is responsible. Figure 2.2 shows the network required without the project manager. Each additional communication link costs time and effort and represents a potential communication failure. If one of the developers fails to get needed information, no one knows where the break has occurred. These communication failures affect the final costs by increasing testing and possibly causing delay for redesign and reimplementation of portions of the system.

2. PROPOSAL

Are you doing the right projects? Do you have a current priority list of which projects are most beneficial to the company? If not, you are probably wasting valuable time developing the wrong applica-

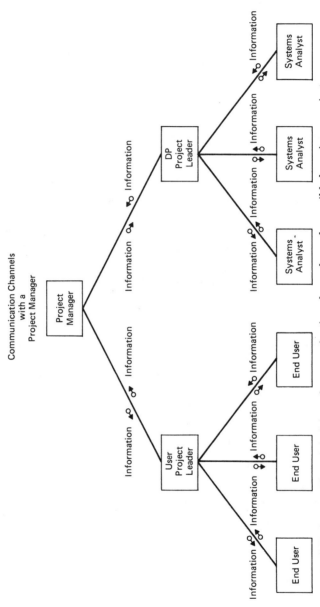

FIGURE 2.1. The minimizing of communication channels made possible by using a project manager.

tions. If the project won't buy the company the maximum benefit per dollar invested, you will lose not only productivity but the opportunities derived from more beneficial systems.

Will the project still have benefit when it is finally implemented? Surprisingly, many projects get started and then fail to meet the needs of the company. The average life span of a system is three years, so you must implement the system in time to get back your investment. Establish a formal committee that reviews, establishes priorities, and selects the projects for development. Once you have done so, you will eliminate the unnecessary work you've been doing, freeing people to handle more important work.

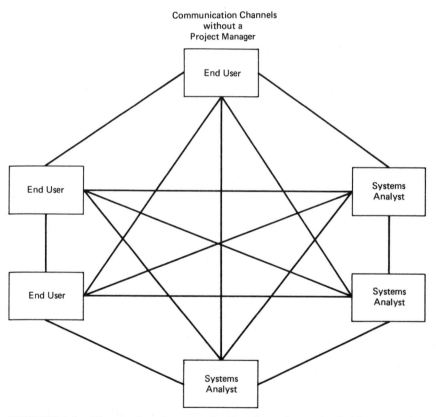

FIGURE 2.2. The number of communication channels required without a project manager.

3. FEASIBILITY

Is this project feasible? Can we do it with the resources we have? If not, why even start? Here the DP department gets involved in establishing the expected costs of the project. Economic analysis evaluates whether the project is justifiable, based on the cost and benefits. It may be too expensive to implement or technology may not support it, in which case the projects should be held until external changes make them possible. The project manager provides a detailed phase report, indicating the disposition of the project: should we cancel it, hold it, or proceed to the definition phase? At this point, phase estimates are updated, assuming that better information has come to light.

4. DEFINITION—REQUIREMENTS SPECIFICATION

Users must specify what they want. To understand what they want, you must first perform a task analysis: what do end users do? These tasks are then grouped into a position—a job that controls similar pieces of information. Some of these jobs are repetitive and best done by computer. Once these are identified, the problem becomes one of fueling the system with information to provide the needed outputs. Typically, the end user will see only the inputs and outputs of a system. Definition provides answers on how to provide input to the system and how to handle the output. Definition also answers the question of how the system should transform input into output.

The effort to change course increases geometrically with time.

On a phase-by-phase basis, it costs 10 times more to correct an error in the current phase than it would have to correct it in the previous phase. So if you discover a definition error in conversion, it will cost 1000 times more to correct it than if it is found during definition, which is why each phase is so important. Project delays happen one day and one error at a time.

There's never enough time to do it right, but there's always time to do it over.

There always seems to be a mad rush to start coding and testing. I recommend that you quell those urges and make sure that you have done your planning, definition, and requirement specification home-work before proceeding to design.

5. DESIGN

5.1. *Preliminary Design*

This phase in the development process separates the system into the parts done by people—the personnel system—and those done by the computer—the computer system.

If you want a track team to win a high jump, you find one person who can jump seven feet, not seven people who can jump a foot.

First, you'll need a system architect or two. I recommend that you follow Brooks' suggestion here and have a small architectural team—the fewer the better. In *The Mythical Man-Month* (Brooks 1975) he describes his experience with OS/360, which caused him to choose a large design team instead of a smaller one. That choice caused the design to be late. He also feels that it lengthened the development cycle by a year or more.

Any system can and will take longer than expected.

In the OS/360 project, the lateness of the design can be traced to the lines of communication among the 120 engineers that designed the system, compared to the original architect group of 10. Portions of the design task are not divisible; as Brooks so aptly puts it, "the bearing of a child takes nine months, no matter how many women are assigned." These activities are typically on the critical path, meaning that they set the schedule. Attempting to do these tasks by committee takes longer and provides a result of lower quality.

Information necessitating a change of design will be conveyed to the designer after—and only after—the plans are complete.

Communication failures among the larger group probably initiated design errors that caused slippages in the schedule. Too much information gets lost in such a large organization. Information is the roadmap of system development: without it, wrong turns are taken, resulting in hours of backtracking and redirection.

Clearly, you should have a minimum number of people involved in the architecture—one, if possible. One person has no external communication links. Two people working closely are also an excellent choice; they have only one link. Three people, however, have three links, four people, six links, and the number grows geometrically. A good example of the success of a small architectural team is the UNIX™ operating system. Dennis Ritchie and Ken Thompson designed and built the original system in one year. Through extensive modification and expansion, the operating system and all of its facilities have remained simple and easy to use. The operating system is only 11,000 lines of "C" code, a language similar to PL 1 and PASCAL. This operating system is smaller than many COBOL business programs.

Another creative approach to system design involves looking around to see if you can buy the system. Purchased systems cost less than developing them yourself. You can install these systems in short order, putting the information where it's needed, when it's needed. Chapter 11 talks about this option in depth.

5.2. Detailed Design

5.2.1. End User. The user should actively participate in designing input/output screens and reports. Typically, working with the user and a screen or report design tool, the DP department can save itself a lot of headaches. These tools will be discussed in the next chapter.

5.2.2. Information Systems. There are three ways to improve job performance.

1. Eliminate unproductive time—time spent doing things that don't put programs into production. But, you say, everything you do culminates with the release of programs. True, but there are always better ways to accomplish the same tasks.
2. Eliminate delay. Delays are caused by roadblocks, whether the roadblocks are people or machines.
3. Find ways to insure the accuracy, quality and maintainability of systems.

5.2.3. Standards. Properly implemented design standards insure consistent documentation, which pays off handsomely in either system development or maintenance. Programmers need not understand many different techniques to implement or maintain the code. Standards should require certain tools, such as IPOs, pseudocode, structure charts, or data flow diagrams, for each specific design task, allowing us to communicate in structured ways about system design. Without such a structured design standard, productivity and quality will suffer.

Selection of the design tools should restrict the use of graphic methods. Graphical design tools, such as data flow diagrams, structure charts, Nassi-Schneiderman diagrams, and IPOs should be used only at a high level. They are not easily maintained and will not be updated. Data flow diagrams and structure charts are good for high-level design, while pseudocode adequately covers module logic. Design standards set the stage for standard program designs.

5.2.4. Generic Designs. Structured Programming, the panacea of the 1970s, turned out small increases in productivity. It did, however, help insure the quality of the systems developed, which enhanced productivity. But structured programming also imposed some roadblocks that negated many of its gains. Structured documentation is much more graphical in nature and therefore harder to update, since it must be completely redrawn. This kind of documentation remains hard to automate and impedes productivity.

There are a few things that no one has mentioned about Structured Programming: everyone designing the same program should get the same design, and once you have a good design, you should use it over and over again. That's how productivity can multiply with the use of Structured Programming. But are you following these guidelines? Probably not. Each new programmer or analyst redesigns programs for which there are perfectly good designs. A fledgling programmer I knew was given the job of writing an update program. Following all the design methodologies, she took three weeks. Then, in the walk-through, the participants tore her design apart. Not for pleasure, not for fun, but because they all knew what a well-designed update program should look like. What excuse did they use for wasting everyone's time? "We're developing her skills," they said.

Imagine a new writer, a six-year-old. Do you ask him or her to write like Leon Uris or Kurt Vonnegut? No, you take the child slowly through Dick and Jane and then on to more sophisticated writing. The writer learns from reading well-written literature. Why not have programmers and analysts learn good design techniques from copying good designs? Reinvention of the wheel invariably costs more and takes longer than copying good designs.

One study (Kapur 1980) of productivity and maintenance problems found that fewer than 40% of all designs of a simple master file update program were error-free; the other 60% contained errors. The logic errors found were inherent to the design of the update program. These were classified as *generic* logic errors. Only 35 of 465 study participants copied a standard design model. Design techniques varied widely, as did the resulting documentation. This study also found little correlation between years of experience and the ability to produce an error-free design. It served to redirect the efforts of the department. Standard generic designs and code were developed, and the staff now uses these designs extensively, logging a productivity boost of 50–80%. Unfortunately, most of us are still grappling with the previous situation. The solution? Develop those generic designs for ourselves.

Figure 2.3 shows a list of the most common generic program designs. Use Structured Programming to design them in a common way, instruct everyone in their use, and be done with all those otherwise wasted hours of design and walk-through.

Figure 2.4 shows the current method for designing a program. First you think about the design, conceptualizing how it will work. Then you put it on paper, using whatever technique you prefer, designing the logic first and the data transforms second. Next, you have the dreaded design walk-through, where everyone does his or her best to shoot down your design. Then you revise it, possibly requiring logic or data redesign, have another walk-through, and so on, until you get it right.

Do you think General Motors spends a lot of time reinventing steering mechanisms, drive trains, or transmissions? No, they just grab a design off the shelf and modify it slightly to fit their needs. How does this apply to you? Well, if you have all these generic programs at your disposal, why redesign them? Copy 'em. That's easy enough. Then you can easily fill in the nongeneric information relating to the specific design you're after.

Figure 2.5 shows this improved way to work. You never have to worry about logic design, only the data transformation. First, the analyst considers which generic functions are needed to implement the program. If the analyst needs an edit, update, or report design, he or she copies them from a generic design. The analyst then inserts the necessary nongeneric information, such as field validations, update validations, and report format. Next, the analyst

Logic Problems

1. Reporting (generic design)
   a. Headings (common subroutine)
   b. Footings (common subroutine)
   c. Pagination (common control logic)
   d. Control breaks (common control logic)
   e. Accumulating totals (common control logic)
   f. Margin control (common subroutine)
   g. Writing groups of lines on one page (common subroutine)
2. Edit/data validation (generic design)
3. Table handling (generic design)
   a. Table loading
   b. Table deloading
   c. Table searching and interrogation
   d. Table sorting
4. File processing
   a. Sequential input/output (generic design/code)
   b. Temporary work file (generic design/code)
      i. Output first then input only
      ii. Output/input alternating
      iii. Output of sort and then input only
   c. File matching (generic design/code)
      i. Two input update (generic design/code)
      ii. Two input file smash to create a file (generic design)
      iii. Two input data selection to drive report processing
5. Advanced file processing (generic design)
   a. Three or more sequential file control (generic design/code) indexed access, vsam access (generic design/code)
   b. Direct access
   c. Data base management system interface (generic design/code)
6. On-line (generic design/code)
   a. Data collection (generic design)
   b. Data validation (generic design/code)
   c. Inquiry/update of the data base (generic design/code)

FIGURE 2.3. Potential generic program logic designs that can be translated into common designs and code.

holds a walk-through of the nongeneric code. It takes less time to review the design when the logic is impeccable. The analyst then revises and submits the design to the programmer.

So where is the challenge, you ask? There isn't as much of the old kind of challenge, but now there is a new one: analysts must think in terms of functions, instead of logic structures. It is analogous to thinking in COBOL instead of assembler language. You don't have to know the nuts and bolts of the COBOL compiler to code pro-

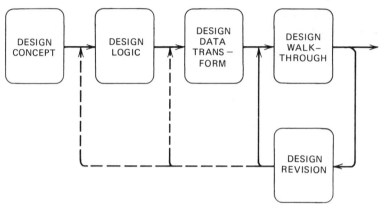

FIGURE 2.4. Work flow for the current design process. It includes one more path than that shown in Figure 2.5.

grams. COBOL programmers generally are faster and produce more maintainable programs. With generic designs, you can produce program designs faster than anyone working in the old way. That affects your rating, raises, and promotions. It also affects your company's profits. Generic designs also aid the programmer. In the good old days, each design looked different, causing coding delays; programmers had to learn each new and varied design. Programmers who work from the standard design have a much easier time coding and testing the program because they know and understand the basic design.

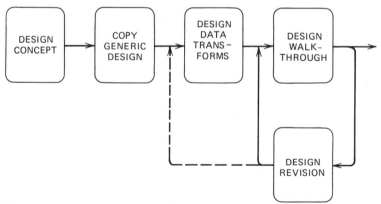

FIGURE 2.5. Work flow for the generic design process. It eliminates logic review and revision.

One book that discusses this generic philosophy in detail is *The Structured Programming Cookbook*, by Paul Noll. Cookbook programming has been bandied about by everyone and popularized by the great minds of our profession. So what? Do something about it. Build those libraries of designs. Train your people and stop wasting their valuable time. Generic program designs provide the following benefits.

1. Analysts can create designs in hours instead of days, eliminating unproductive time.
2. Generic designs decrease design costs and time spent in walk-throughs. Walk-throughs are limited to evaluation of the code that transforms the data; the logic is already error-free.
3. A faster design process fuels the programmer with timely designs, eliminating delay between design and coding, thereby improving productivity.
4. Generic designs do not vary in style, so they are easier to understand, implement, and maintain, further improving productivity.
5. Generic designs are modular and more maintainable, insuring the accuracy, maintainability, and quality of the design and program.

6. PROGRAMMING

6.1. End User

The user should develop a training, conversion, and installation plan with assistance from the project team. Installing today's systems requires coordination of hardware ordering, networking, training, and installation.

6.2. Coding

Coding accounts for only 10-20% of the total cost of developing a system, yet programmers rush through coding in their panic to begin testing. That's the first problem. The way programs are coded cements the future maintenance of the program. The "goodness" or "badness" of the code fixes the maintenance costs of the program.

Programs are often coded in the wrong language. If an assembler language programmer is free, let's write the application in assembler. This is the second problem.

6.2.1. Language Selection. To quote Brooks, the project manager of OS/360, again, "I cannot easily conceive of a programming system I would build in assembly language." Assembler language is five times more costly to maintain. Some modules may require assembler, but you should restrict its use as much as possible. Write a higher level program first, and tune it. Then, if efficiency dictates, rewrite it in assembler. No one can predict a program's efficiency before it is written.

Now, some reasons to choose one language over another.

1. *Modularity.*   The ability to code independent functions and link them together, rather than coding monstrous single modules.

2. *Structure.*   The ability to implement the five Structured Programming logic constructs: sequential, IF–THEN–ELSE, CASE, DOWHILE, and DOUNTIL.

3. *Data Structure.*   The ability to group data together logically. The language should interface with data base management facilities.

4. *Clarity.*   The capability to be read easily, listing control, clear data naming, and self-documentation. The language should allow blank spaces or pages to separate portions of code. It should also allow a significant number of alphanumeric characters for a data name. COBOL and PL/1 both provide acceptable data names; FORTRAN does not. The language should not structure the code; it should allow indentation for nesting data items or procedure statements. The language should allow in-line comments.

5. *Concision and Function.*   Concise statement format improves the reading and maintenance of code. For example, COBOL and PL/1 provide preprogrammed functions to eliminate costly development time. One such facility is the Report Writer feature of IBM's COBOL. The standard math and string subroutines of PL/1 are another example of preprogrammed functions that concisely state a larger amount of code.

6. *Flexibility.*   How easily can the program language be changed? For example, compare COBOL to assembler, or a report generator language to an actual report program. Two

such report generators are Informatic's MARKIV™ and Pan-sophic's EASYTRIEVE™.

7. *Robust Support.* COBOL, PL/1, FORTRAN, and BASIC seem to be everywhere. Also look for optimizing compilers to improve efficiency. Investigate report generators such as MARKIV and EASYTRIEVE. Consider prototyping systems such as IBM's ADF—the Automated Development Facility for IMS. Nonprocedural languages are also expanding their capabilities and support.

6.2.2. Standards

Those who write clearly have readers; those who write obscurely have commentators.

Albert Camus

Before the first line of code enters the machine, I recommend that you prepare coding standards. I recommend *The Elements of Programming Style*, by Brian Kernighan and P. J. Plauger, as a starting point. This succinct reference work is to programming as E. B. White's *The Elements of Style* is to writing. It gives many good pointers on programming style that come from years of experience.

Standards are needed for several reasons.

1. To restrict poorly designed features of the language, such as the ALTER statement of COBOL.

2. To enhance clarity and the self-documenting style of the program, which improves maintenance.

3. To provide a uniform implementation of the Structured Programming logic structures: Sequential, IF-THEN-ELSE, CASE, DOWHILE, and DOUNTIL. Figure 2.6 shows a suggested implementation, which further enhances the reading and maintenance of code.

4. To reduce the possibility of interface problems by identifying guidelines for module coupling. Module coupling refers to the way two modules share data. As defined by G. J. Myers (Myers 1975), the types of coupling are as follows:

a. *Content Coupling.* One module refers directly to data inside another module. This is the worst type of coupling; nothing is sacred and any module can violate another.

```
Sequential

        MOVE ...

        ADD ...

        PERFORM ...

IF-THEN-ELSE

        IF condition THEN
              sequential statements
        ELSE
              sequential statements.

CASE

        IF A = 1
              sequential statements
        ELSE IF A = 2
              sequential statements
        ELSE IF A = 3
              sequential statements
        ELSE
              default statements.

DOWHILE

        PERFORM PARAGRAPH-NAME
            VARYING something
            UNTIL condition.


DOUNTIL

        PERFORM PARAGRAPH-NAME.
        PERFORM PARAGRAPH-NAME
            UNTIL condition.
```

FIGURE 2.6. Indenting programming logic constructs enhances readability.

28

b. *Common Coupling.* Both modules refer to the same global data structure, such as the COMMON statement in FORTRAN. This type of coupling allows any module to modify the global data, making maintenance more difficult by expanding the number of places a programmer must check for data modification.

c. *External Coupling.* Both modules refer to the same global data item, such as a data item defined as EXTERNAL in PL/1 or C. It reduces the module's access from all data items to only specific ones.

d. *Stamp Coupling.* One module passes the other module an entire data structure rather than just the necessary data item. A module that reads a file and returns a record would be stamp coupled.

e. *Data Coupling.* Only the required data are passed by means of parameters. This is considered the best form of coupling. Interfaces between modules are concise and can be tested easily.

5. To insure the modularity of the program design; guidelines also provide direction for module strength. G. J. Myers defines the types of module strength as follows:

a. *Coincidental Strength.* There is no relationship among the different functions of the module. This is the worst form of strength. Functions with nothing in common should not co-exist. A future maintenance programmer will surely try to mate them, producing varied mutant offspring.

b. *Logical Strength.* This module contains many related functions, but it executes only one function per call. The common example is an input/output module that handles all the files.

c. *Classical Strength.* This module executes many related functions in sequence. Any COBOL module with PERFORM paragraphs has classical strength.

d. *Procedural Strength.* This module performs many related functions in a logical sequence.

e. *Communicational Strength.* This module performs many functions that are related by their use of data.

f. *Functional Strength.* This module performs a single function. This is the best form of module strength because it is easy to identify when it fails or needs modification. The programmer can go directly to the module without tripping over several other functions on the way.

g. *Informational Strength.* This module performs several functions that operate on the same data. Each function is characterized by a unique entry point. For example, a module that updates a data base may collect statistics on records added, changed, or deleted. A separate entry point may be useful for retrieving those statistics.

6. To specify a module's size. Figure 2.7 shows the mean time to repair or enhance a module, based on its size. There are two types of change to a module—the simple and the complex. The former takes little time, regardless of module size. Complex fixes and enhancements, on the other hand, take exponentially more time, based on the size of the module. The maximum size typically should not exceed 100 executable lines of code. Chapter 6 will explain how to evaluate larger modules for their inherent ability to be maintained.

7. To prevent bizarre abbreviations and insure consistency throughout a system.

8. To insure proper in-line documentation—the only kind that seems to be maintained.

9. To specify performance goals or the use of efficiency-related features of the language. In COBOL, specify the use of COMP and COMP-3 data items and the use of SEARCH versus SEARCH ALL verbs.

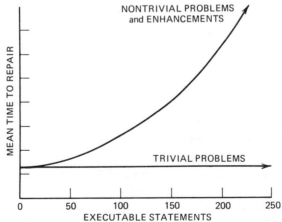

FIGURE 2.7. Program maintainability decreases as program size—measured in executable statements—increases.

10. To guarantee uniform style and appearance. Standards encourage a simple, easily readable style in writing programs. They suggest a way of formatting your code so that it can be scanned and understood easily, ultimately making the programs easier to modify and reducing maintenance costs.

Walk-throughs serve as the vehicle to enforce standards. When encouraged to enhance program maintainability, programmers will meet those needs. With standards available, coding styles are no longer a matter of personal taste, but a matter of cost savings to the department.

6.2.3. Generic Programs.   Now that you have generic program designs and standards to live by, you can code programs that are as generic as each of the program designs. There are many different ways to code the same program; I suggest that you pick one and make it standard. Standard code provides programmers with error-free starting code. When first developed, these generic programs will require extra testing to insure their reliability, but the payback in development and maintenance productivity will return this investment a hundredfold.

In a development environment, programmers familiar with these designs can produce working programs in a day or two, instead of weeks. They first copy the code, then insert the portions of the program that are specific to the program design. Walk-throughs of these programs need only examine the specific application code, thereby reducing the time spent in meetings. There will be no more arguing over personal preferences in regard to coding styles or implementation choices.

You are probably saying, "But this eliminates much of the creativity of the programming job." Yes, that's true, but your other option saddles the company with a severe maintenance burden. It will become clearer that programming is repetitious; automation is the only way to overcome the productivity gap.

Appendix A contains an example of a generic update program. It provides the programmer with 400 lines of documented, structured code. The programmer inserts only the data structures and actual update code. Given a time-sharing development tool like TSO, UNIX, or GCOS, the programmer can enter the code in one terminal session without the need for coding sheets. The programmer's productivity is improved so much that a design may be coded in hours instead of days. The biggest payoff of generic programs, however, is in maintenance.

Once familiar with these generic programs, maintenance programmers have little trouble finding functional parts of any program. For example, if they know they have to make an enhancement in the edit program, they know where and how to find the code. They don't have to spend days reading the program, trying to divine where to put the changes. Generic programs improve the maintenance programmer's productivity in that most changes are trivial and can be accomplished in a few hours. If you want to reduce the 50–80% of the budget spent for maintenance, try coding programs in a generic way.

6.3. Common Code

Common code—such as file descriptions, record layouts, linkage sections and working storage macros—can be maintained in COPY libraries to minimize duplication of code and to enforce data naming standards. The value of COPY libraries to reduce maintenance has been overlooked and underrated.

Use of common code and subroutines eliminates redesign, coding, and testing of similar routines. For example, if a system has 50 reports with common headers, it is worthwhile to write a more complicated common subroutine than to write 50 different header routines. Otherwise, these 50 would look entirely different and would be potentially unreliable.

Common code philosophy extends the generic program idea into the specific. Functions that are generic to the system are coded, tested, and reused throughout the system. I have designed and worked on systems where common code was over 50% of the delivered code. It is a thrill to write and test a program in a single day: without generic designs, code, and liberal quantities of common code, it would not have been even remotely possible.

Common code improves maintenance productivity by focusing coding and testing on one module instead of many. If the common function has to change, only one module need change, not 50; programs are then relinked and tested. To gain additional productivity, spend time considering what code can be developed and reused. It will provide productivity improvements once the common code has been developed.

6.4. Testing

This phase strikes fear into the hearts and minds of everyone, but it shouldn't. Testing consists of three parts.

1. *Unit Test.* Making sure that each module does what it should.
2. *Integration Test.* Making sure each module talks to its neighbors as it should.
3. *System test.* Making sure the programs work together to produce the correct output.

Top-down testing forms these three parts into a continuous, overlapping process.

When programmers take on unit, integration, and system testing as one huge task, it becomes too complex. No wonder testing takes over 40% of the development cycle. Structuring testing into these three parts breaks the process into understandable pieces, thereby improving the productivity and quality of the test.

6.4.1. Unit Test. If each module functions correctly by itself, it should integrate easily into the system. Path analysis, also known as graph or vector analysis, provides the means to structure the testing of each module. Figure 2.8 shows the path analysis of an

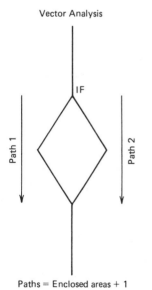

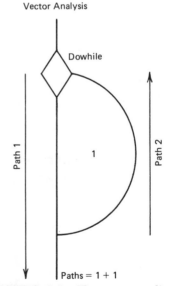

FIGURE 2.8. The vector or directed graph for an IF-THEN-ELSE statement, showing the two possible paths through the code.

FIGURE 2.9. The vector or directed graph for a DOWHILE statement, showing the two possible paths through the code.

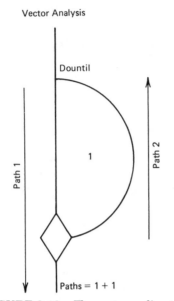

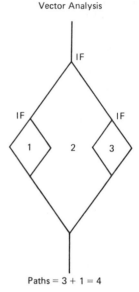

FIGURE 2.10. The vector or directed graph for a DOUNTIL statement, showing the two possible paths through the code.

FIGURE 2.11. The vector or directed graph for a CASE statement, showing the calculation of the paths through the code.

IF-THEN-ELSE statement. There are two possible paths that may be taken, so two test cases are needed—one to exercise the code on one side of the IF, another to exercise the other path.

Figures 2.9 through 2.11 show the paths for DOWHILE, DOUNTIL, and CASE statements. If a program module is well structured and modular, you can easily draw the path chart of the module. With the path chart in hand, test cases are easily created for each path. Figure 2.12 shows the path chart for an update driver module. This simple chart shows each possible test case—a total of 10.

Test	1	While not at end of-file
Test	2	Master less than transaction
Test	3	Master equal to transaction
Test	4	Add transaction?
Test	5	Change transaction?
Test	6	Delete transaction?
Test	7	Master greater than transaction

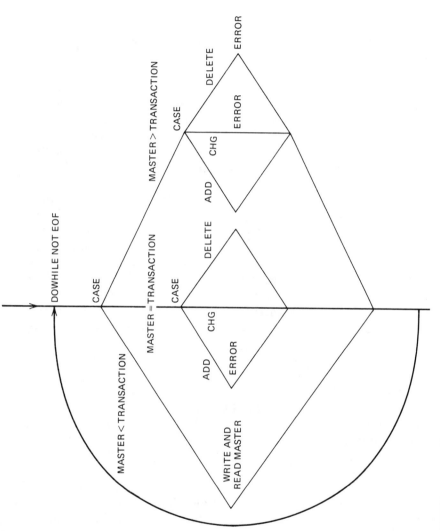

FIGURE 2.12. The vector analysis of an update program, showing the possible paths through the code.

Test 8	Add transaction?
Test 9	Change transaction?
Test 10	Delete transaction?

With so few test cases, testing becomes simple. Module verification is easy. Path analysis breaks testing into manageable pieces, making error detection much easier. The result—more reliable code.

6.4.2. Integration Testing. Once it has been determined that each module performs its functions correctly, integration testing continues the process. There is no reason to test the module's functions, only its interfaces. The number of test cases for verifying the module's links to other modules is therefore reduced, which further simplifies testing and improves productivity.

6.4.3. System Testing. Since each function and its interfaces have all been tested, system testing becomes a process of verifying the output. Test cases already exist for each module and interface, so system testing need only pull these together into a compact testing base. The path charts, developed for unit testing, document the processing flow in each module and can be pulled together to form documentation of each program in the entire system. Documentation assists the test group in pinpointing trouble areas, thereby improving the productivity of the developers who must make the program change.

6.4.4. Top-Down Testing. This type of testing requires many small test runs. It allows a slow accumulation of test data, rather than requiring one massive build-up. Each test must be repeatable; this is known as regression testing. Procedures must be built to automate much of the regression testing.

Top-down testing begins by coding the driver module for each program and unit-testing them. Then submodules, called stubs, are coded by means of the generic program concept. The driver module is integration-tested with its stubs. Next, the system test group validates the workings of this early structural system to begin balancing the test load, allowing a continuous flow of modules into system testing. The users get immediate feedback and a look at their future systems. Their comments allow for design and requirement correction long before the system is released.

This testing process iterates, building layers of submodules, while unit-, integration-, and system-testing each subsequent version. Design errors are found early. The user gets incremental systems to validate. Top-down testing provides meaningful milestones in the development and insures a better tested, higher quality system. Best of all, it cuts the costs of testing by simplifying what is usually the most brutal portion of the development cycle.

7. CONVERSION

Two further tests are performed at the beginning of conversion: environmental testing (Does it work in the field?) and acceptance testing (Does the user like the way it works?). These tests provide an opportunity to test the system operationally, validating it before putting it into production. The system should not be installed until it has been vigorously abused by end users. If the system doesn't work properly, the user dissatisfaction will create a negative environment that is difficult to change. It's tough enough to replace a manual system with a mechanized system without having to deal with the additional resistance to a poorly engineered system.

If it took 30 people to build the system, but it will affect 400 end users, you should spend some time touching the system up before conversion. The loss of user productivity is much greater than the cost of additional programmer hours. You may also find that, as originally conceived, the system does not meet today's business needs. If so, there's no reason to install the system; it will only cost you more money without providing any benefits.

8. PERFORMANCE REVIEW

After six months or more, the system should be reexamined. If you can quantify what is right or wrong with it, you can encourage future system designs to include the good and avoid the bad. Evaluate the system on the following criteria:

Effectiveness	Did the system provide the benefits expected? Did it provide unexpected benefits? Why or why not?
Performance	Does the system operate well and at a reasonable cost? Do the user documentation and training meet the system's needs?

Development Evaluation	What techniques and methodologies aided or hindered the development cycle? What was the productivity of the development group? What was the quality of the resulting system?
User Evaluation	How does the user like the inputs, outputs, system response, system security and overall assistance of the development organization?

The answers to these questions will help streamline the development process and avoid future errors.

9.   QUALITY ASSURANCE

One of many ways to insure quality is to control the development process with the seven phases described earlier. Each of these phases has an output, shown in Table 2.1, that should be verified. One of the best ways to validate a system output is by means of group review. Depending on the output, this group is the quality assurance organization (as discussed in Chapter 9), the system review committee, or a peer group.

9.1.   Quality Assurance Group

This autonomous group reviews all system outputs for quality. If no such group exists, peer groups should perform this function.

9.2.   System Review Committee

This separate approval body should review phase reports to decide on the fate of the project. Some projects should be cancelled, others accelerated. This group of managers should provide direction to the DP department.

9.3.   Walk-throughs

Walkthroughs provide benefits by

TABLE 2.1. System Development Phases

Phase	Output	Verification
Proposal	System proposal	Quality assurance System Review Committee
Feasibility	Feasibility report Project Manager's report	Quality assurance System Review Committee
Definition	Requirements definition	Quality assurance
	Project Manager's report	System Review Committee
Design	System architecture	Quality assurance
	Computer system design	Quality assurance
	Personnel system design	Quality assurance
	Project Manager's report	System Review Committee
	Program designs	Quality assurance
	Documentation and training design	Quality assurance
	Project Manager's report	System Review Committee
Programming	Program code	Walk-throughs Quality assurance
	Testing plans and documentation	Walk-throughs Quality assurance
	Project Manager's report	System Review Committee
Conversion	Environmental test Acceptance test	Quality assurance User Quality assurance
	Project Manager's report	System Review Committee
Performance review	Performance analysis Project Manager's report	Quality assurance System Review Committee

1. identifying problems when they are easiest to fix;
2. stimulating "ego-less" programming and teamwork;
3. providing a forum for sharing better design and coding techniques;
4. improving quality of the designs and code; and
5. improving communication.

Walk-throughs by peer groups are similar to Japanese quality control circles. They can benefit everyone connected with system development while improving the system's maintenance.

10. MAINTENANCE

What is the first thing that happens to your beautiful new system once it's installed? It starts to change. Errors are found. The user requests enhancements. The system has entered the maintenance phase.

Just like a kid with a new car, the user will want whitewalls, a sunroof, a custom paint job, and a well-tuned engine. When it doesn't run properly, it will be brought to the garage for repair. The corporation faces the problem of justifying these changes in relation to the benefits they will provide. How do you justify and control change to information systems?

10.1. Change Management

There are two kinds of change—program repair and program enhancement. The first is the result of a program failure, incorrect function, or incorrect output. The second requires changes to the function of the program.

Program errors may be classified into error categories.

1. *Severity 1.* The system cannot be used until program is repaired. A program has ended abnormally or the payroll system is writing checks for a million dollars.
2. *Severity 2.* The system can be used, but a change must be made by a specific date. If not implemented by then, the change satisfies the criteria of severity 1. For example, if the federal government requires a change to the payroll system for increases in Social Security payments, this enhancement must be in effect by January 1.
3. *Severity 3.* Not critical. The change may be implemented as time permits.

Once detected, the user and the DP department should classify these errors by their origin. For example, which program caused the error? Was the error due to a problem in the definition, design, or programming phase? When did the error occur? Who is assigned to correct the error? When is the correction due? Who must approve the correction before its release?

If you develop a methodology for tracking and reporting your errors, the benefits may seem obscure, but it provides better control and improves productivity and quality. If the users report the same error several times, the errors may be combined into just one work activity.

After significant reworking, programmers often discover that a change has already been done. If an error sounds familiar, the programmer can investigate past changes to look for a similar problem. If found, the computer center may be running an old version of the program, a problem that is easily fixed. Without this historical information, the programmer may spend days searching for an error that has already been corrected.

If the department tracks all of its errors, knowing where they occur helps prevent future errors of a similar type. If the frequency of occurrence of a definition error is known, it can be identified and specifically checked in future projects. This historical data base helps the department evolve toward zero fail software.

10.2. Enhancements

Besides finding errors, the user also finds new and creative requirements for the system's operation. These changes are enhancements to the system and are treated similarly to errors. Once again, duplicate enhancements may be combined to reduce reworking and improve productivity. Are maintenance enhancements arranged according to priority? They should be. If you have 20 enhancements and time to do only 10, the user must establish the priorities and you select the top 10. Otherwise, the top priority work will not get done. Programmers will do the most technically challenging or the easiest enhancements first. If they're not doing the most beneficial work, the company's productivity is being reduced.

Develop a formal change management procedure. Require a change request (CR) for each system enhancement or repair. This is the time to involve the users and let them originate the CR and justify doing the work. The DP department estimates the cost of making the change. Then, the user establishes the priorities for the requested changes.

Establish a formal committee that authorizes all maintenance work. It is possible that one project may be of higher priority than the others. This application should receive more resources since it is more beneficial to the company.

10.3. Controlling Documents

System definition, design, and requirements documents should be controlled by some form of change management. If system or program documentation changes haphazardly, errors can be propagated throughout the system. Any document modification should require a change request. Chapter 3 will discuss ways of automating document management.

10.4. Release Scheduling

Once a change management system exists, errors and enhancements can be combined into releases. Releases may occur two or more times a year, depending on the needs of the project. Release Scheduling has many benefits.

Planning	Planning creates priorities for work in each release. The top priorities that can be accomplished with the available work force are selected. This control prevents schedule slippages and improves relations with users by allowing their participation in the change process. The users know what each release will contain and the business reasons for the choice. Establishing work priorities gives them control of the enhancements worked. If insufficient resources are being applied to their projects, they can lead the fight for staffing or support.
Grouping Work	Many different enhancements may affect a single module. By combining them into a group, a single programmer may accomplish all changes to that module at one time. In a typical scenario, programmers must spend time learning the workings of

the module to be fixed. Then they correct or enhance the module and test it. Often, learning the module takes longer than making the fix. By grouping work, the repetition of the learning process is eliminated, improving overall productivity.

System Test Grouping changes into releases allows the formation of a system test group, whose sole function is to verify the system before each release. Every error it catches saves the company money. The time spent testing may be planned for and this responsibility is removed from the programmers, which is advantageous because programmers still have ego links to their programs. They do not necessarily want to find errors in their own programs. The system test group is evaluated on finding errors, so it is much more efficient at error detection than programmers.

Quality Assurance Unit and system test results for a release can be reviewed by an independent quality assurance team. Its function verifies the quality of the documentation, programs, and tests, and ascertains that the system is ready for release.

Operations The staff running the system can gear up for a new release. They can handle installing new JCL and programs, running environmental tests, and coordinating overtime for special work. They can prepare backout procedures as well. This ability to plan for change improves productivity in the operations center. Compare this to an environment in which the computer operation center receives new modules every day, which causes unscheduled JCL changes and module installation. This atmosphere creates confusion and causes failures in production—unnecessary failures, all of which cost the company time and money.

11. TASK ANALYSIS

You can't force people to work harder to improve productivity, but you can eliminate some of the steps they take in producing a product. Task analysis gives you a tool to analyze work flow and improve productivity. It involves four simple steps.

1. Identify every process that happens in a given work flow.
2. Identify every person involved in each process.
3. Identify each document or product of each process.
4. Change the work flow by eliminating redundant processes, unnecessary interim products, and unnecessary personnel. Each reduction is accomplished either by complete elimination or the substitution of technology and capital.

Task analysis is much like data flow diagraming. Figure 2.13 shows

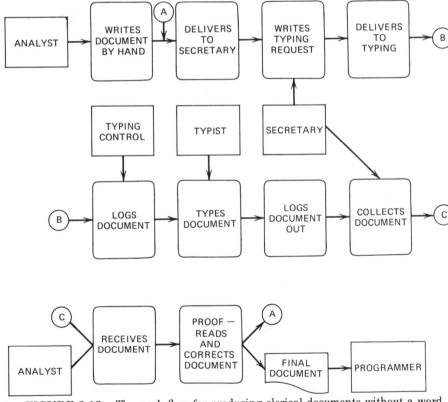

FIGURE 2.13. The work flow for producing clerical documents without a word processor.

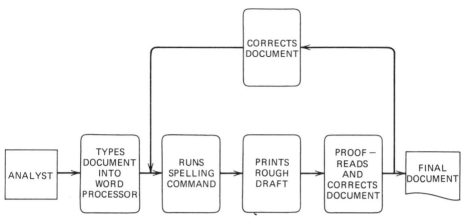

FIGURE 2.14. The work flow for producing documents with office automation, which reduces the number of people and steps involved.

the task analysis for submitting a document to a word processing group or secretary for typing. Chapter 3 covers office automation— putting word processors in the hands of the analysts and programmers. Figure 2.14 shows how the substitution of technology and capital will change the work flow. Instead of ten processes, there are only five. Instead of four people, there is only one. Instead of several administrative documents, there are none.

By analyzing how new technology and methodology will affect the current work process, you can predict the productivity benefits that will be derived. If the task analysis increases the number of processes, people, or intermediate products, the system may not meet your requirements. Task analysis can diagram either existing or future work flows. It serves as both a design and analysis tool. Once your work flow is streamlined, your productivity will increase.

12. SUMMARY

This chapter has covered various methodologies that control system maintenance and development and improve productivity. It presented the "work smarter" methods employed by super-programmers to enhance their productivity by 100% or more. By implementing these methods selectively, your programmers and analysts can realize these benefits, while providing the company with new and enhanced systems in less time. Your company benefits from reduced program cost and improved ability to compete in the marketplace. Implementing the software factory methodology is up to you.

CHAPTER THREE

Technology

In 20 years, software development has evolved from wired boards to machine code, to assembler code, to high-level procedural and nonprocedural languages. The input devices have changed from cards to interactive terminals. Outputs range from cards and print-out to magnetic media, such as disk and tape, to visual media, such as terminals. In the face of this technical explosion, tools have developed to support every facet of today's development process.

This chapter delves into those tools and their application. The question is, how and where should you automate the development process to assure maximum productivity and quality?

1. OFFICE AUTOMATION TOOLS

The 1980 Booz and Allen study of white collar workers indicated that a 15% improvement in productivity could be obtained by implementing office automation systems, and by 1990, a nationwide opportunity benefit of $300 billion could be realized.

Figure 3.1 shows the composition of the nation's work force: 65% is white collar. Before 1950, the United States had a primarily agricultural and manufacturing economy. Since then, automation has displaced many of these laborers, who have been retrained and have entered the white-collar community. Booz and Allen refer to these people as "knowledge workers"—they work with information.

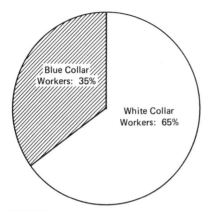

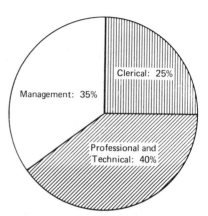

FIGURE 3.1. A pie chart depicting the current makeup of the nation's work force.

FIGURE 3.2. A pie chart showing the current profile of the nation's white collar workers.

Of these knowledge workers, 40% are professional or technical workers (see Figure 3.2). Many are computer programmers, analysts, and managers. Others use computers in their jobs—engineers use computer-aided design, doctors rely on computer analysis, bankers depend on electronic funds, and the list goes on and on. Another 35% are management. Managers also handle large quantities of information. Unfortunately, most of them handle the information manually—reading and writing—just as has been done for years.

Faced with a growing administrative and professional work force, industry turns to mechanization to improve white-collar jobs. The tools currently available are as follows:

1. word processing
2. electronic mail
3. teleconferencing
4. information retrieval
5. personal time management.

1.1. Word Processing

Documentation is the castor oil of programming.

If the act of producing the document has no value to the programmer, the job will always be done in the minimum possible way; but if producing the document has demonstrable good effects, there will be no way of **preventing** *reasonably good documentation.*

Gerald M. Weinberg (Weinberg 1971)

Word processors automate virtually every kind of typed documentation. Some even provide capabilities for graphics. They provide direct access to documents, allowing easy corrections and reproduction.

Although virtually everyone will argue that $25,000-a-year programmers shouldn't be spending their time typing, it is far less expensive than you might think. These people have been typing ever since they first encountered a card punch. Their keying skills may not be equivalent to those of a good typist, but remember that they are thinking about what they write and then typing instead of writing. Of course, if they write something out in longhand first, they should not type it in. The clerk should do that. The Booz and Allen study showed that some employees simply will not key their own documents. My experience has been that most people will learn to use the keyboard rather than delay information. Knowledge workers, like programmers, who already have the keying skills will gladly shed the clerical duties of handwriting and proofreading a document.

In the past, the first step would be writing a rough draft. But because of the time required for revision, the worker would rarely edit and revise the draft. The result was the production of inferior documents—rough drafts presented as final papers. With a word processor, major and minor changes can be made in minutes, without laborious notes to direct the typist. The quality of final documents improves by 100% or more, and time and money are saved. Word processing also satisfies many humanistic needs. Programmers work with a machine, their favorite tool, not with pen and paper. As Dr. Weinberg tells us, when they enjoy their work and recognize its benefits, programmers will provide good documentation.

It is important that word processing integrate with the program development environment. Obviously, you don't want to train people on more than one machine if possible. UNIX™ provides excellent benefits in this regard: word processing (WP) and data processing (DP) combine in one operating system to provide a standard development system. Other manufacturers are also integrating WP and DP. In an integrated environment, programmers can place documents under change control just as they do with programs. Analysts can store and retrieve documents from source maintenance systems for better control. Change control is the only way to patrol the tendency to neglect documentation.

Up-to-date documentation will improve the maintenance task significantly. Your people will be able to go to the program and systems documents and actually learn about the current system, not the one built five years or two months ago.

1.1.1. Document Preparation.

You can make document preparation easy by creating skeletons of the design and maintenance documents. In any system that has a command language, these skeletons can be copied and created interactively with the copy command. The programmer or analyst may then fill in the basic skeleton. This system has certain advantages.

1. Forms can be standardized, not retyped each time, which saves 300 or more key strokes—several minutes of typing. Key words placed in the text are easy to find and change.

2. Standard forms improve readability. Everyone will learn where to extract required information. Programmers often overlook information in the document; now they won't.

3. The quality assurance group or an automated standards checker can easily review these forms for completeness and accuracy.

Automating these forms provides a user with friendly interface to the word processing system. Some systems provide the ability to set up these forms and select them from a menu, or you can write your own command procedures. A typical command procedure would ask the programmer, "What type of document? (IPO, Programspec, etc.)" The programmer selects the required format and the computer moves a fresh copy of that document into the file. (See Appendix B for examples of skeletons and the command procedures to create them.) Next, through the magic of full-screen editing, the analyst fills in the blanks, changes the key words, and presto—a finished document. Store this document under your source management system and suddenly you have a completely auditable change process; the documents should change whenever the source code changes.

1.1.2. Word Processing Benefits.

Normally, a person writes a document by hand, gives it to a typist, proofreads the document, and submits revisions until it is in final form. This process, shown in Figure 2.13, can take days or weeks. Figure 2.14 shows how a word processor modifies this work flow. A word processing facility, in the hands of programmers and analysts, reduces the process to just a few hours. Eliminating typists and the usual roadblocks creates an environment where the analyst is sole master. But this isn't the only reason that productivity improves. Programmers cannot start to work before they have a design from which to work. How many times have you heard programmers complain that they're waiting for an analyst's specification? All too often? Chop out delays in the document work flow and you will see immediate improvements in productivity.

The most immutable barrier in nature is between one man's thoughts and another's.

William James

Any simple idea will be worded in the most complicated way.

Software metrics (see Chapter 6) explains how to analyze your documents mechanically to determine ease of reading and size. These measurements will help your workers write more clearly. If they improve their writing, there will be fewer errors caused by misinterpretation and you will have a product of better quality. Avoiding interpretation errors improves productivity by preventing design, code, and test errors that require extensive rework. Word processing is not just a tool for clerks, but a powerful tool for technicians and managers too. If you want better documentation and higher productivity, give your people a facility that makes good documentation easy and fun.

1.2. Electronic Mail

"Out of sight, out of mind," when translated into Russian [by computer] then back again into English, became "invisible maniac."

Imagine the office of the future. A manager sits in front of a row of terminals and calls to the secretary, "What is this piece of paper doing on my desk?" Farfetched, you say? Not in the least. The technology already exists to create it. The problem is to get people to change how they work, a formidable task indeed. Figures 3.3, 3.4, and 3.5 show the current work flows for delivering or requesting information. Figure 3.6 shows the work flow for the same information requests and delivery, this time by electronic mail.

52   *Technology*

FACE-TO-FACE COMMUNICATION

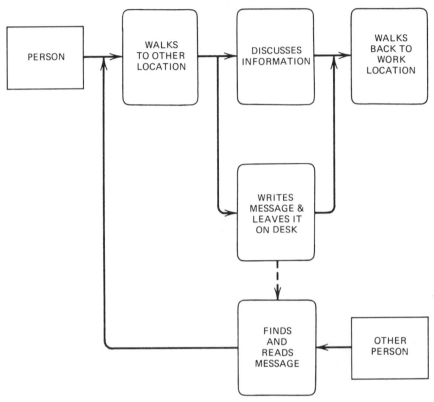

FIGURE 3.3. The work flow for face-to-face communication, showing potential loss of information and delay in its delivery.

Why go through the hassle of writing a document and having it typed, copied, and sent through company mail? Why not just mail your information electronically, directly to the persons involved? Why try to call someone, seesawing back and forth, just missing one another, wasting valuable time, when all you have to do is send mail. The person can then answer your mail at his/her leisure.

The Booz and Allen study found that telephone calls reach the intended person less than half the time. Incomplete telephone calls take an average of 45 seconds—time that could be spent productively elsewhere. These calls also consume the secretary's time in taking messages. The person returning your call has less than a 50% chance of catching you, so more time will be wasted. How many

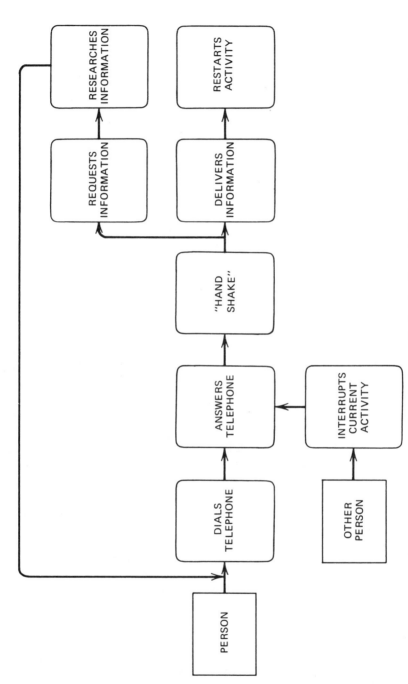

COMPLETED TELEPHONE CALLS

FIGURE 3.4. The work flow for making a complete telephone call, showing the potential interruptions in other work processes that it can cause.

INCOMPLETE TELEPHONE CALLS

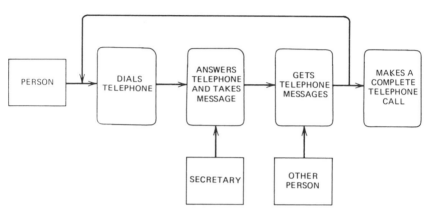

FIGURE 3.5. The work flow for incomplete phone calls, showing the secretary's involvement and delay in returning the call.

times have you tried for several days to make contact with someone? Booz and Allen also found that when a call is completed, it invokes several "shadow functions," which include the interruption of the phone's ringing, the usual "handshake" of identifying and greeting each other, the start of your conversation, and restarting your previous activity. Up to five minutes of shadow functions can be involved in each phone call.

Booz and Allen identified two types of phone call—one that passes information and one that requests information. Often, the information request requires research and another call to return the information. How can you avoid much of this telephone madness? Install electronic mail. Coupling a word processor to electronic mail enables informational documents to be sent to the proper people without any delays for typing, mailing, or telephone calls. The people receiving your mail can store it electronically for later retrieval.

Programmers, analysts, and managers can send project-related information or information requests without interrupting the receiving party, eliminating shadow functions. Those receiving "mail" can read it when it fits in with their other activities. They can answer information requests when they finish researching the problem, without interrupting the person who requested the data. Data exchange happens in seconds instead of hours or days, and since time is your major resource, eliminating delay increases your productivity. Booz and Allen found that a typical manager can waste

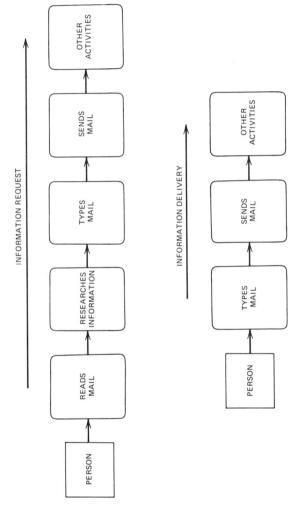

FIGURE 3.6. The work flow for information exchange using electronic mail, showing the delivery and receipt of mail that eliminates interruptions and secretarial involvement.

30 minutes a day on incomplete telephone calls and shadow functions. Electronic mail will get that time back. Assuming an eight-hour day, it can mean at least a 5% savings, possibly more.

This savings doesn't include the value of timely documentation. If your user needs to make a change in the system definition, it will affect everyone working on the implementation. If someone fails to get the revised information, all hell breaks loose when the system is being tested or converted. Electronic mail insures timely, accurate delivery. Nor does it include the resolution of such problems as loss of company mail, loss of notes left on your desk, and the time wasted running around to leave those little notes. Electronic mail eliminates these intangible but frustrating problems.

On the human side, electronic mail improves communication and productivity, which programmers and analysts find beneficial. Technicians are also people, with social needs. Electronic mail allows them to communicate personal information without interrupting their fellow workers. Although this is not a strictly businesslike use of the computer, the alternative forces them to interrupt their friends. The shadow functions invoked are far more costly than the machine use. Although electronic mail is the most frequently used command, it consumes few system resources, while providing significant productivity improvements.

If you explain so clearly that nobody can misunderstand, somebody will.

Be obscure clearly.

E. B. White

Electronic mail does have a negative side. People tend to write more cryptically than they talk. Face-to-face conversations provide a faster information flow. Electronic mail does not allow the study of body language. If your boss leaves you an electronic message that should convey an urgent tone—"GET IT DONE NOW!"—you might interpret it as saying, "When you get around to it, please take care of this." Electronic mail is not good for all human communications, but it can improve many interactions significantly. If you want to improve productivity, save time, and reduce the number of errors caused by information lag, install electronic mail. This facility exists in a variety of word processors.

1.3. Teleconferencing

Booz and Allen found that professionals and managers waste a lot of time going to and returning from meetings, especially if the rooms are in remote locations. The obvious solution to this waste is to create an electronic conference room—teleconferencing. This application is still evolving; look for future vendor announcements.

1.4. Information Retrieval

Quick access to information can spell the difference between a timely, profitable decision and a missed opportunity. Most office automation systems provide some form of information retrieval capability, but the most important information in the company resides in data bases on mainframe computers. Distributing this information into the smaller office machines delays your access to the data. The current alternative requires using nonprocedural languages to extract the data from the mainframe and then distributing that information into office machines if required. Distributed data processing is taking great strides in providing data base management systems and inquiry or nonprocedural language support. As these progress, the office will become truly automated.

1.5. Personal Time Management

An electronic calendar and reminder facility? Why not? The computer may remind you of meetings or lunch or that it's time to go home. An automated meeting scheduler? Again, why not? Scheduling meetings among a group of people is always a troublesome task. Normally you spend time organizing a meeting only to find that the last person can't make it. More scheduling and shuffling around are required. An automated scheduler eliminates these problems.

Quite literally, a man's memory is what he forgets with.
Odell Shepard

Although not a major impact on productivity, future time management tools will aid managers in accomplishing this day-to-day task, substituting electronic memory for the ever-fallible human one.

1.6. Future Tools

Because there is so little known about automating the work of white collar workers, expect management tools to expand and evolve to meet unforeseen needs. Anticipate "decision support systems" that will help managers in the search for the "right" decision. Budgeting systems, time reporting systems, and the like provide productivity benefits in the office. Start now to collect your share of the $300 billion savings from office automation.

2. REQUIREMENTS DEFINITION TOOLS

One of the few tools that exists to structure the definition of requirements is the Problem Statement Language/Problem Statement Analyzer (PSL/PSA) from the University of Michigan. This system uses its own language (PSL) to define the requirements for the system, producing documentation and reports that cover all aspects of the system definition and design. The analyzer (PSA) examines your input for missing information and requirements. Since major systems are often difficult to define properly, this system assists you in insuring that nothing is overlooked.

Perhaps five years in the future, this kind of system will be sufficiently friendly to the user to require little DP intervention. It should also produce design documentation for the programs to be written. By then, it may even produce source code from the detailed requirements. Programmers will have to tune the resulting programs and enhance them to meet more specific user needs, but the vast majority of the system should be created directly from the requirements definition.

PSL/PSA shows promise of structuring the user's definition job such that designs and code can be produced automatically from the requirements process without programmer intervention. This potential signals a dramatic leap in productivity and quality over the existing development process. The question is when and how will this change take place.

3. DESIGN TOOLS

Numerous automated tools that aid the analyst exist. They include office automation tools, screen design, report generation, and application development systems.

3.1. Word Processing

The most obvious design tool is a word processor with graphics capabilities. Because of the proliferation of design documents required by today's structured methodologies, an office automation system would greatly enhance your analyst's productivity.

3.2. Screen Design

Before the first line of code is created, the analyst needs ways of showing users what their input and output will look like. By examining various input and output designs, the user and analyst insure that the human–machine interface is correctly designed. There are a variety of tools to support these needs.

On the input side, hardware vendors offer packages that simplify CRT screen design. Using these tools to iron out the user's input screen format can save a lot of later enhancements. It also encourages the user to take responsibility for proper system design. Well-designed human interfaces will increase the system's acceptance, thereby improving the end users' productivity. Normally, they don't know what they want until they see it. Now you can show them the terminal in action. They will know immediately what they dislike. Continuing the interaction, the user and analyst modify and enhance the inputs until they satisfy all user requirements.

3.3. Application Generators

> *A complex system that works is invariably found to have evolved from a simple system that works. A complex system designed from scratch never works and cannot be patched up to make it work. You have to start over, beginning with a simple system that works.*

Similarly, application generators, like IBM's Application Development Facility (ADF), provide the analyst with the opportunity to make a prototype of the user's entire system in a short period. Starting with a simple working system, the user and analyst can work together to expand the system's design and capabilities.

3.4. *Report Generators*

Finally, the analyst can combine test data generators with report generators to create simulated reports. Test data generators include products such as DATAMACS™ (Management and Computer Services) and PRO/TEST™ (Synergetics Corp.). Report generators include such products as MARKIV™ (Informatics) and EASY-TRIEVE™ (Pansophic).

Working with the user, the analyst refines the output design to meet the specific needs of the end user, again improving user acceptance of the system and providing the user with a sense of ownership and responsibility towards his or her system. If the outputs include CRT screens, the analyst can use the screen-oriented tools described previously.

If you subscribe to the Jackson design methodology, you know that the design of the black box between the inputs and outputs results from the organization of the data. Since the input screens and output reports have been properly designed with the user's involvement, the system design should naturally reflect the transformation of the data. In effect, the proper design of the human interface will streamline the design and operation of the entire system, reducing the amount of rework normally required to enhance the system to meet the user's real needs. Productivity and quality naturally improve from the use of these tools.

4. CODING TOOLS

In an inflationary environment, where the demand for information systems exceeds the ability to supply them, significant productivity gains can be obtained by managers and organizations willing to support development and implementation of program generators. These tools can improve the productivity of the system developers by 50 to 100%, so more work can be done to satisfy the corporation's demands for new systems. This improved productivity is not only more cost-effective, but also improves the corporation's ability to compete by providing timely information for better decision-making.

In today's environment of higher personnel costs, DP managers are looking for new ways of improving productivity. Unfortunately, many simply keep adding people to the staff, rather than implementing alternatives. If the corporation had 50 ditch diggers, would you hire 50 more to double productivity, or would you buy machinery to double productivity? The decision to improve productivity is always a proper balance of tools and personnel.

To fill the productivity gap, many software firms are now offering program generators—power tools for programmers. Two such COBOL program preprocessors and generators are METACOBOL™ (Applied Data Research) and SCOPE™ (H & M Systems Software, Inc.). A variety exists for the FORTRAN language as well. For those of you using IBM's IMS, there is the Application Development Facility™ (ADF) for developing IMS application programs, or you can choose Series 80 MANTIS™ (CINCOM Systems). As software and hardware companies reach further insights into design generation, more program and application development systems to support the programming backlog will appear. Because these packages are all designed for a generic market, they have several specific problems.

Problems	Programmers must, unfortunately, be trained to use program generators as well as the COBOL source code they produce.
	Most program generators concentrate on only a subset of all program designs, such as reports or simple sequential programs. They don't produce the perfectly polished programs that the user wants, only some subset of their real needs.
	These packages can cost thousands of dollars and may or may not meet the requirements of a particular DP shop for programming standards or style.
	They are typically inflexible, so they cannot bend to the needs of a corporation.
	The programs produced are often less efficient than an equivalent custom program.
Opportunities	These generators provide productivity benefits that are especially attractive in an environment where more than 80% of all DP costs are for personnel.
Cost Benefits	Figure 3.7 shows how the hardware and personnel cost trends have reversed in the last 20 years. Considering this trend, the majority of all cost savings can be derived during a program's de-

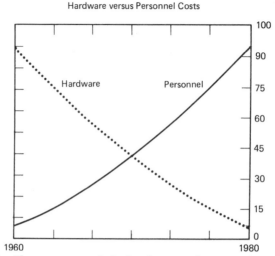

FIGURE 3.7. The current trends for hardware and personnel costs, as a percentage of all EDP dollars, have made considering human productivity as the most important cost factor erroneous.

velopment, not from its operating efficiencies.

Hardware will continue to get cheaper, while personnel costs continue to inflate. This is why businesses are focusing on program generators to provide productivity and cost improvements.

Alternatives

There is an alternative to hiring more programmers or buying program generators. For those programming staffs operating in a time-sharing environment with a command language, such as IBM's TSO or UNIX's Shell, it is possible to build flexible, expandable program generators using the features of the command language and libraries of skeletal program code. They adapt easily to fit varying standards, expand to encompass new designs and applications, and are relatively inexpensive to develop.

4.1. Program Generators

It was said as far back as 1969 that the key to programming productivity is to build on the work of others—to stand on each other's shoulders. To do so requires an investment in new methodology and building the tools to support it.

To begin to analyze how to build these tools, it is first necessary to examine programming languages. Every programming language consists of some required and some optional statements. Optional statements include input and output declarations, data definitions, control logic, and data transformation statements. In COBOL, required statements include the IDENTIFICATION, ENVIRONMENT, DATA, and PROCEDURE DIVISION clauses. The I/O declarations include the SELECT and FD statements. The data definitions include the realm of possibilities for the DATA DIVISION. Control logic includes the IF-THEN-ELSE, GOTO, and PERFORM statements. Finally, data transformation statements ADD, COMPUTE, MOVE, or SET values in the program.

Keeping in mind the various required and optional statements, let's examine how a programmer typically creates a new program. To do this, any programmer with some common sense copies an existing program and deletes the old data definition and transformation code and inserts the new. In doing so, they have used a basic form of program generator. This process, however, has some problems.

Problems   No two programmers copy the same program.
            Deleting code takes time.

```
PROC 0 PROTO()

        SET &COB = COB

        SET &COBMAIN = COBMAIN

        SET &COBSUB = COBSUB

        SET &TYPE = COBOL

        WRITE ENTER PROTOTYPE NAME (COBMAIN OR COBSUB)

        READ &PROTONAME

        WRITE ENTER PROGRAM NAME

        READ &PGMNAME

        COPY SKELETON(&PROTONAME) &PGMNAME..&TYPE RENUM

        WRITE &PROTONAME PROTOTYPE CREATED HAS BEEN CREATED AS &PGMNAME..&TYPE
```

FIGURE 3.8. A simple TSO CLIST to copy generic program skeletons for programmer use.

Copying old code possibly propagates errors from old to new programs.

Solution   Have all programmers copy the same program, which can be done by means of any command language through copying an existing program skeleton (one without data or data transformation code) into the programmer's directory.

Suppose that a library existed, called SKELETON(member), containing COBOL main and subroutine skeleton modules. A simple TSO command procedure (CLIST) to provide all programmers with access could then be developed, as is shown in Figure 3.8. For COBOL skeletons they could be several hundred lines of fully tested, error-free code, depending on what your organization requires. A simple example is shown in Figure 3.9. A more complex sequential update program is shown in Appendix A. The command language prompts the programmer for optional statements, inserts them in the required statements, and generates a compilable program module. The programmer may then edit the program, filling in appropriate data as needed. For those who may wish to edit automatically, the CLIST may be enhanced as is shown in Figure 3.10. Use of command language statements in concert with "clean" code eliminates the possibility of typing errors, since data substitution is always done by the computer. If audit trails are required, they can be embedded in the skeletons, as is shown in Figure 3.11, insuring that the required trails are provided automatically in all new code. Adding a required program description or other "installation standard" code is no problem either.

These are just some basic ideas on how the reader might tailor program skeletons to the organization. Aside from these basic skeletons, there are also input, output, data definition, control logic and data transformation statements.

4.1.1. Input-Output. If the command language has a "DO WHILE" statement, all I/O statements may be added to the skeleton. For example, using UNIX Shell, Figure 3.12 shows how to prompt for input, input-output, output, and sort files, building groups of SELECT and FD source statements to be included in the program. For IBM shops, the command language procedure can also create JCL, during the I/O stage, providing correct test JCL. JCL has long been the most difficult programming language, so automated generation of JCL improves productivity.

```
IDENTIFICATION DIVISION.
PROGRAM-ID. 'PGIDOAAO'.
AUTHOR. YOUR NAME.
DATE-WRITTEN. MM/DD/YY.
REMARKS.
    ****************************************************************
    *                                                            *
    *   MAIN PROGRAM: PGIDOAAO                                    *
    *                                                            *
    *   PROGRAM DESCRIPTION:                                      *
    *                                                            *
    *   SUBROUTINES CALLED OR REQUIRED:                          *
    *                                                            *
    *   REFERENCE: (JOB DEFINITION, IPO, ETC)                    *
    *                                                            *
    ****************************************************************
EJECT
ENVIRONMENT DIVISION.
CONFIGURATION SECTION.
SOURCE-COMPUTER. IBM-370.
OBJECT-COMPUTER. IBM-370.
SPECIAL-NAMES.
SKIP3
INPUT-OUTPUT SECTION.
SKIP2
FILE-CONTROL.
SKIP2
********************************************************************
*                                                                *
*    SELECT STATEMENTS                                           *
*                                                                *
*        INPUT, INPUT/OUTPUT, OUTPUT, SORT                       *
*                                                                *
********************************************************************
SKIP1
**** NONE
EJECT
DATA DIVISION.
SKIP2
FILE SECTION.
SKIP2
********************************************************************
*                                                                *
*    FILE DESCRIPTIONS                                           *
*                                                                *
********************************************************************
SKIP2
**** NONE
EJECT
WORKING-STORAGE SECTION.
SKIP2
```

FIGURE 3.9. A simple COBOL program skeleton for programmer use.

(*Continued on p. 66*)

```
****************************************************************
*                                                              *
*   CONSTANTS                                                  *
*                                                              *
****************************************************************
SKIP2
01  CONSTANTS.
SKIP2
01  PGID-VERSION-INFORMATION.
     05  MODULE-ID                  PIC X(8)  VALUE 'PGIDOAAO'.
     05  SOURCE-CODE-LEVEL          PIC X(6)  VALUE 'RR.LLL'.
     05  VERSION-DATE               PIC X(8)
             VALUE 'MM/DD/YY'.
SKIP2
****************************************************************
*                                                              *
*   WORKING STORAGE -------- TABLES                           *
*                                                              *
****************************************************************
SKIP1
*  NONE
SKIP3
****************************************************************
*                                                              *
*   WORKING STORAGE --------  REPORT HEADERS AND FOOTERS      *
*                                                              *
****************************************************************
SKIP1
*  NONE
SKIP3
****************************************************************
*                                                              *
*   WORKING STORAGE -------- ERROR MESSAGES AND CODES         *
*                                                              *
****************************************************************
SKIP1
* NONE
SKIP3
****************************************************************
*                                                              *
*   WORKING STORAGE  -----  RECORD STRUCTURES                 *
*                                                              *
****************************************************************
SKIP2
EJECT
```

FIGURE 3.9. (*continued*)

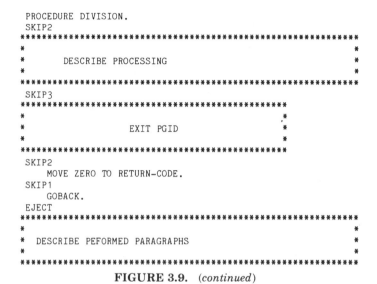

```
PROCEDURE DIVISION.
SKIP2
*************************************************************
*                                                           *
*         DESCRIBE PROCESSING                               *
*                                                           *
*************************************************************
SKIP3
*****************************************************
*                                                 *
*                     EXIT PGID                   *
*                                                 *
*****************************************************
SKIP2
      MOVE ZERO TO RETURN-CODE.
SKIP1
      GOBACK.
EJECT
*************************************************************
*                                                           *
*  DESCRIBE PEFORMED PARAGRAPHS                             *
*                                                           *
*************************************************************
```

FIGURE 3.9. (*continued*)

It is also trivial to add data definition statements by means of command language. If your standards require all data sets to have their record descriptions in COPY libraries, they could be added to the skeleton at the same time as the file descriptions. This same philosophy applies to anyone using a data base management system. System calls and data definition statements can be added in the same way.

4.1.2. Data Definition. The command procedure can also prompt for tables, linkage data, or whatever is frequently used, adding them to the skeleton. The command procedure can build record structures interactively, positioning data names and values according to local coding standards. It can align structure levels, PIC, and VALUE clauses automatically. The depth of your command procedure depends on the needs of your programmers.

4.1.3. Control Logic. What if an organization wanted audit records written during the execution of a program? It would be fairly simple to write the routines for use by the entire company, include them in the skeletons, and interface them with the aforementioned audit data definitions. Appendix A has an example that

```
PROC 0 PROTO()

        SET &COB = COB

        SET &COBMAIN = COBMAIN

        SET &COBSUB = COBSUB

        SET &TYPE = COBOL

        WRITE ENTER PROTOTYPE NAME (COBMAIN OR COBSUB)

        READ &PROTONAME

        WRITE ENTER PROGRAM NAME

        READ &PGMNAME

        COPY SKELETON(&PROTONAME) &PGMNAME..&TYPE RENUM

        WRITE &PROTONAME PROTOTYPE CREATED HAS BEEN CREATED AS &PGMNAME..&TYPE

        DATA

                EDIT &PGMNAME..&TYPE

                C 1,999999 /PGIDOAAO/&PGMNAME/ ALL

                C 1,999999 /PGID/&SUBSTR(1:4,&PGMNAME)/ ALL

                C 1,999999 $MM/DD/YY$&SYSDATE$ ALL

                C 1,999999 /RR.LLL/  1.1 / ALL

                END SAVE

        ENDDATA
```

FIGURE 3.10.   Another simple TSO clist to generate generic program code with some minor editing performed by the computer.

calls a standard message routine with the module name, date compiled, and the release and level number of the source code.

Further, if record counts are kept for all files, it would also be easy to add the appropriate READ and WRITE statements, combined with record-counting logic to the skeletons when creating the I/O statements. Including this auditing logic provides more main-

```
01  PGID-VERSION-INFORMATION.
    05  MODULE-ID              PIC X(8)  VALUE 'PGIDOAAO'.
    05  SOURCE-CODE-LEVEL      PIC X(6)  VALUE 'RR.LLL'.
    05  VERSION-DATE           PIC X(8)
            VALUE 'MM/DD/YY'.
```

FIGURE 3.11.   Sample audit trails that can be added to the generic code to make auditing easier.

```
echo "Input file name?"
read filename
while [ ! -z "${filename}" ]
do
        sed -e "s/fdname/${filename}/g" < select >> /tmp/tmp$$
        sed -e "s/fdname/${filename}/g" < fd >> /tmp/tmp1$$
        echo "Enter another name or a carraige return."
        read filename
done
cat inout >> /tmp/tmp$$
cat inout >> /tmp/tmp1$$
echo "Input/output file name?"
read filename
while [ ! -z "${filename}" ]
do
        sed -e "s/fdname/${filename}/g" < select >> /tmp/tmp$$
        sed -e "s/fdname/${filename}/g" < fd >> /tmp/tmp1$$
        echo "Enter another name or a carraige return."
        read filename
done
cat output >> /tmp/tmp$$
cat output >> /tmp/tmp1$$
echo "Output file name?"
read filename
while [ ! -z "${filename}" ]
do
        sed -e "s/fdname/${filename}/g" < select >> /tmp/tmp$$
        sed -e "s/fdname/${filename}/g" < fd >> /tmp/tmp1$$
        echo "Enter another name or a carraige return."
        read filename
done
cat sort >> /tmp/tmp$$
cat sort >> /tmp/tmp1$$
echo "Sort file name?"
read filename
while [ ! -z "${filename}" ]
do
        sed -e "s/fdname/${filename}/g" < sortsel >> /tmp/tmp$$
        sed -e "s/fdname/${filename}/g" < sd >> /tmp/tmp1$$
        echo "Enter another name or a carraige return."
        read filename
done
```

FIGURE 3.12. A sample UNIX shell procedure to create input and output files for the generic programs interactively.

tainable code and saves coding and testing costs while providing a common audit interface for Operations.

For maximum productivity improvement, you will need to use generic "types" of program logic designs. Each has a generic design and logic flow. Only the data transformation statements differ from program to program, so the control logic is independent of application. Figure 2.3 lists the potential generic logic designs that can be built and used by all programmers. One can gain access to, manipulate, edit, and produce each in compilable form by means of the command language. These generic skeletons provide flexibility that is not possible with marketed program generators. This flexibility improves productivity by tailoring the code to your local standards and needs. If your organization stresses modularity, these generic programs can be built in a modular way. If many different programming languages are used, generic programs can also be created for each language.

4.1.4. Implementation. Obviously, in the course of this discussion you have been led to a complex command procedure, a formidable development task. It could, however, be implemented in the following stages, to spread the development effort and to provide a smooth conversion.

1. Basic skeletons
2. Basic skeletons and I/O
3. Basic skeletons and I/O and data definitions
4. Basic skeletons and I/O and data definitions and control logic
5. Generic logic skeletons and JCL
6. Design documents
7. Operational documents

Starting from the ground up builds confidence in the use of program generators. As people use them, they will suggest enhancements to increase their ownership and acceptance of the system.

4.1.5. Benefits. Because these skeletons eliminate redundancy, redesign, recoding, walk-throughs, and retesting, they can provide productivity improvements of 50% or more. Given that 20-50% of staff is involved in development, it means you would have the equivalent of 10-25% more staff, or that you will complete projects in half the usual time.

Use of document, as well as code, generators eliminates the possibility of translation errors between the design and code. Linked into the office automation system, with its own document skeletons, your development staff can easily increase productivity by 100%.

Maintenance personnel are also affected by these generators, but not so directly as development personnel. Program generators give maintenance personnel the freedom to rewrite error-prone programs in the same time it would take to correct or enhance them, cutting maintenance costs and providing more resources for enhancements or new development. Since these generators use only tested, error-free program logic, they reduce errors in the delivered product as well as testing and maintenance costs. Should an error ever be discovered in one of these designs, it is simple to change all existing programs based on that design. This simplicity further decreases the potential maintenance work load.

These generators also insure the commonality of the program's code and logic, allowing personnel trained in update programs to move from application to application with ease. Maintenance is extremely simplified since all programs of one design will have the same structure. This situation is similar to automobile repair. Mechanics trained in fixing Chevrolets can fix any Chevy. But hand-crafted cars typically require more time to repair, even though the mechanic knows how to repair automobiles. The same is true of programmers. Programs from a program generator assembly line are like Chevrolets, while uniquely programmed designs are like Ferraris.

Because of the obvious cost benefits of these program generators, building them can be justified easily. They can also be produced economically as the byproducts of actual development projects. The selected development project can design and code a variety of the generic programs that would be needed for the project, and the resultant generic design and code libraries could be shared with the rest of the department.

Generators also allow a simple means of assuring a common audit, security, and run control philosophy by providing them automatically in the code. This factor prevents exclusion of this necessary code—enhancing productivity.

Finally, generators are an inexpensive way to show new programmers "good" programming and to make them more productive on the job. The Kapur study (Kapur 1980) showed that program generators provide productivity benefits of 50–80%. Such improvements are necessary to cut costs and meet the needs of a competitive marketplace.

5. TESTING TOOLS

These tools come in an assortment of sizes and shapes to fit virtually any testing environment. Such tools include program documenters, cross-reference lists, debugging compilers, execution analyzers, data generators, on-line testing packages, and a variety of miscellaneous software enhancers.

5.1. *Program Documenters*

Some documentation is generated in the form of flow charts. Unless you are fond of flow charts, avoid them: they provide less documentation than the actual program.

If a program is useless, it will have to be documented.

Other software documenters provide varied output that you may or may not find useful. The unfortunate problem about after-the-fact documentation is that it means there was no documentation to begin with, which probably indicates a poor analysis job, leading to a poor program that is difficult to maintain and enhance. No amount of follow-up documentation will cure a poor program, so the value of program documenters is questionable.

5.2. Cross-Reference Listings

You always find something in the last place you look.

Cross references can improve maintenance and testing productivity. These processors examine source code, indicating where each data name is used or modified. They simplify the inevitable search for data names that have been modified incorrectly. They help the programmer spot potential errors. Cross-reference listings are not especially useful with small modular programs that contain all of their code on one or two pages, but with the existing thousand-line dinosaurs, they can substantially ease the programmer's burden.

5.3. Debugging Compilers

Most compilers offer some sort of logic trace that analyzes program execution. A few compilers, like the CAPEX Optimizer III™ (CAPEX Corp.), offers additional facilities. It not only optimizes the source code for efficiency improvements of 25% or more, but also allows the programmer to analyze the program's execution in detail. By using the analyzer feature, the programmer obtains an execution listing that shows how many times each statement was executed, how much of the program's run time was consumed by each statement, and how much each module of the program contributed to the overall run time.

For simple efficiency analysis, the programmer can zero in on just those modules that consume the largest amount of CPU or run time. Then, using the statement-by-statement execution analysis, he or she can determine which statements cause the efficiency problems and correct them. For testing, programmers can discover from the execution counts if the test data exercised all of the code. If not, additional test cases are needed to support proper structural testing. Further, they can tell how many times a loop was executed. A common problem involves incrementing a counter or subscript outside its range. From the CAPEX analysis, such errors are easily found and corrected. Programmers can also tell if they have too many test cases. If all the statements were executed 2000 times, they could reduce their test data for faster tests, minimizing the load on the machine.

These debugging compilers exist for most languages and machines. Using them can improve the programmer's confidence in program tests and the program's efficiency. Compilers can indicate execution errors that program traces can't. Debugging compilers can substantially improve the testing process and the reliability of the programs tested. Install them, train for them, and see your productivity improve.

5.4. Execution Analyzers

Like the CAPEX analyzer, execution analyzers examine the program's run time, reporting where the majority of the time is spent so that the programmer can focus on a few sections of the code to improve efficiency.

Old-timers have some hang-up about efficiency. They live in a bygone period when the machine had only 16K. They often code a program with all kinds of strange tricks in them to improve efficiency. The tricks tend to make the program difficult to maintain. The efficiency gains are only slightly better than a structured program compiled by an optimizer.

Structured programs should be written modularly and should be examined for efficiency only after testing. Only programs with extensive run times should be examined in the first place, since a programmer's time is more valuable than the computer's. Only major inefficiencies should be corrected; further effort only wastes the company's valuable programmer resource. Execution analyzers are the only reliable means of examining and identifying run-time inefficiencies.

5.5. Test Data Generators

Numerous test data generators exist for a wide variety of hardware. They provide a simple means of generating the test data needed for unit and system testing and help eliminate the need for scaffold code to support intermediate tests. Test data generators will benefit new development projects more than maintenance projects. Maintenance groups tend to have entire test case libraries that satisfy their needs already, so they will not need to generate extensive test data. Productivity benefits will vary, based on the application being tested. Quality benefits derived from test data generation are questionable, since programmers will use data generators to create test cases in the image of their own programs. It is no different than it has always been—test data will exercise the code only in ways that the programmer expects, not in ways that find errors. You should examine the needs of your development process and determine if a data generator would help. If so, use it.

5.6. On-line Testing

On-line compilers and debugging facilities, such as IBM's TSO On-line Symbolic Debug, can significantly enhance the productivity of programmers engaged in testing. By allowing the programmer to compile and interactively test a module in one terminal session, these methods provide error feedback without delay. Contrast this situation to a batch environment where programmers have to wait for compiles and batch tests. Delays range from a few minutes to several hours, and even though they can use some of this time for other activities, programmers often waste time waiting for batch jobs to run. When a batch job finally prints, programmers are forced to spend some time remembering where they were and what they were testing. These refresher periods further degrade productivity.

On-line, programmers experience no such delays. They can, however, experience response time delays. Response times over a few seconds invoke "shadow functions." The human mind wanders if the machine doesn't answer promptly; delays mean that the person must refresh his or her memory to interpret the computer's response. Then a new command must be composed. The time between the computer's response and the programmer's next command is known as "think time."

Think time increases twice as fast as a computer response time. With a two-second response time, user response will take four seconds; with 15-second response, user response takes 30 seconds. The efficiency of the machine and the network carrying the information has a direct impact on the programmer's productivity. Tuning the machine or adding additional resources will improve response time and reduce think time, a major waste of programmer time.

Compiling modules that are larger than a few hundred lines takes several minutes rather than a few seconds, which constitutes a further argument for modularity. The minutes programmers wait for a larger module to compile are typically nonproductive. On-line debugging can be either productive or nonproductive, depending on the size of module being compiled and executed. Typically, on-line testing will be faster than batch testing. As machine speeds increase, on-line testing will be the only productive means to unit and system test programs.

Machines should work; people should think.
IBM's Pollyanna Principle

Because interactive testing allows the programmer to concentrate on testing without interruptions or batch delays, the quality of tests will improve. The machine does more of the work, giving the programmer more time to think and analyze the results. The result—a better quality of tests and programs.

5.7. Miscellaneous Tools

Some tools, such as ABEND-AID (Compuware Corp.), analyze IBM dumps and place the information into formats for easier programmer understanding and retrieval. These tools only improve the programmer's productivity in analyzing dumps, which makes up a fairly insignificant portion of their time, so the benefits may not warrant the costs.

A variety of tools to beautify source code exists. Older programs were written without regard for structuring and indenting the code for simplifying reading. Use of these tools to improve program clarity will improve the productivity of your maintenance groups.

6. NONPROCEDURAL LANGUAGES— THE INFORMATION CENTER

Letting someone else do your work dramatically improves productivity. Tom Sawyer formulated this principle over a hundred years ago. Nonprocedural languages provide just such an opportunity.

Although they are still evolving, nonprocedural languages provide a user-friendly, nontechnical interface to the computer. Languages such as NOMAD, RAMIS, and FOCUS fall into this category.

IBM originated the "Information Center Concept"—the DP department extracts data, provides them to the user in a data base to which access can be obtained with a nonprocedural language, and then leaves the user alone to develop his or her own programs and systems. Productivity is improved in numerous ways.

1. You don't have to spend time developing one-shot "what-if?" programs and systems. The user can develop them easily. You don't have to spend time with trivial enhancements. You let the user monkey around with minor report heading changes and creating summaries. You can spend your time on large systems of major importance to the company.

2. The users don't have to go through a lot of paperwork to get some programming done. They log onto the system and use the nonprocedural language to extract the reports they need interactively. Or they may create more extensive programs, cross-referencing several databases for other information needs. They can generate new reports and programs in hours, bypassing the usual delay of going through the systems department. Their ability to make decisions is improved, and the company is steered through the competition's blockade. The competitive advantages of nonprocedural languages will swing the user and the company to these fourth-generation tools.

3. The programmers and analysts can use these languages to create a prototype of a major system in just a few weeks. This ability to start with a working system and develop it to meet the user's needs will greatly improve productivity and quality. Future systems may be entirely of nonprocedural language, with only a few "coded" modules for the sake of efficiency.

Once again, these languages are generic. They will not perform as specifically as programs written in COBOL or PL/1. Fourth-generation languages will evolve to meet more specific needs, however. In the interim, productivity increases of 100–1000% will pay back the corporate investment and any losses caused by the generic properties of the programs. These languages are the wave of the future. Old assembler and COBOL systems that are prohibitively expensive to rewrite in their native language will be inexpensively rewritten in nonprocedural languages.

The future marketability of computers depends upon the vendors' ability to make their software so friendly that virtually anyone can program and use the machine. It happened with telephones and pocket calculators; it will happen with computers. Information will invade every household by way of cable and telephone networks, giving every household the information necessary to make the most of their hard-earned dollars. Nonprocedural languages will bridge the gap between the professional and nontechnical computer user. Corporations will provide the laboratory for trying and refining many of these languages.

Nonprocedural languages will benefit the user and the data processing groups, improving productivity and quality while providing timely information for management decision making. You can't afford to get behind in this race. Productivity gains of 1000% don't leave you much room to catch up when you fall behind. These languages will someday make everyone in the organization into a computer programmer and analyst. Controlling how that change takes place could make the difference between your company's survival and its demise. Your existing staff will still be needed for development of major applications, but they may have to use nonprocedural languages to meet the information demand. Retraining and innovation will be required, but the evolution to a software factory demands competent personnel—your existing staff—to handle these changes.

Keep in mind that company-wide productivity increases of up to 1000% are possible from these new languages. Not just your department, but all departments will benefit. They may comprise the single most important development in the evolution of software engineering. Since prior productivity boosts have been the result of changes in programming language, it is safe to assume that nonprocedural languages will provide similar benefits.

7. SUMMARY

Civilization advances by extending the number of important operations we can perform without thinking of them.
Alfred North Whitehead

Technology provides a myriad of tools to support every phase of software development and maintenance. The productivity and qual-

ity benefits of these tools vary widely. Maximum productivity benefits come from office automation, program generators, application
development systems, and nonprocedural languages.

Since organizations are not all alike, you will have to arrive at
priorities in implementing the tools you need. With the burgeoning
mass of software companies that design and build new tools, you
will have to search out new technology constantly.

Programmer productivity will double or triple, but not without
exacting its price: you will need new hardware, software, and a
staff to implement the new tools. Technology will require retraining
and a change in your staff's willingness to use unconventional tools.
The tools to transform your shop into a software factory are at your
fingertips. Reach out and grasp them. They will reduce costs in the
long run and improve your competitive position. Without them, you
will be lost.

CHAPTER FOUR

People

The last century has seen an explosion in information production. A hundred years ago, the total amount of information in the world doubled every 50 years; now it doubles every five. Information is the lifeblood of an organization. It flows through the organization, feeding the varied needs of each department. The conventional methods of conveyance will not work with the amount of information circulated and digested throughout a company in today's environment. So computers have taken over the assimilation of this data, reducing it to a volume that humans can handle. But as useful as computers are for compiling information, the volumes of data produced are impossible to deal with. We have yet to learn how to use the tidal wave of information the computer provides. Often, this problem arises from a failure to engineer the system properly for the people it serves.

Every solution causes new problems.

As capital grows scarcer, management should begin to suspect that the human contribution to production could be more fully understood. Businesses view the computer from a typically economic or political standpoint. Vendors originally sold the computer as a way to reduce staff and cut costs, but although computers solved many problems, they did not reduce expenses. They provided new opportunities and intangible benefits and made business expansion possible through the enhanced ability to process information. Imagine the telephone company trying to bill 100 million customers with only a clerical work force. Imagine the IRS trying to audit 120 million tax forms.

1. COMPUTERIZATION

Why do you want to computerize, anyway? First, economic and competitive pressures argue for the greater efficiency provided by new technology, which has been the major selling point of computers since their introduction. Second, there are political pressures to stay ahead of foreign powers. The Japanese introduction of robots has caused a formidable imbalance between American and Japanese manufacturing efficiency and productivity. As leaders in computers, America must continuously advance hardware and software design or provide their foreign competitors with an opportunity to overrun them. Third, technology promises to help solve many of our social problems, but it is a two-edged sword. The atom, with its infinite energy, is a terrible weapon, but it may provide energy independence. The same is true of the computer; could artificial intelligence someday replace human intelligence?

Fourth, the presence of technology creates an environment where someone will figure out how to use it. Give someone a hammer and the person will treat the whole world as if it were a nail; give the person a computer and he or she will devise ways to make it fit the needs of the world. Fifth, government and industry have a vested stake in new technology. They have the means to urge its installation and use regardless of public need or benefit.

It is impossible to install new computer systems without evoking changes in work flow, jobs, and organization. The business typically installs these systems in the same way that Hitler marched into Poland—a *Blitzkrieg* that creates fear, feelings of inadequacy, and alienation in those affected by the new system. For such a system to be installed properly, it must achieve a balance between technological innovation and the human's ability to adapt to the change.

Computers and their systems invoke the following changes.

The danger of the past was that men became slaves. The danger of the future is that men may become robots.

Erich Fromm

1. Systems may make jobs more routine. System design can relegate the meat of the job to the computer and leave the person only a few crumbs, reducing the individual's control over the approach to the job. The computer, by nature of its ability to perform repetitious operations, can make the human a slave to routine activities. On the other hand, a system can also be designed to enlarge people's responsibilities, providing more meaningful work and job satisfaction.

2. Because computers react so quickly, human communication will have to improve to keep up. There will be more time spent communicating with the machine instead of with other people. The computer will have to become more proficient at talking to people.

3. Computers will absorb many routine management tasks in white-collar jobs, which are predominantly unmechanized. Management information systems will provide time for planning and increased devotion to managing people. The resulting humanistic management will further improve productivity.

4. Human skills will change. In 50 years, the computer will be as common as the telephone. Everyone will know how to use one. As operators were once needed to make phone calls, programmers are needed to build programs. Computer software will become easier to use. "Program the computer" may become as common as an expression as "Answer the phone."

5. The computer will have psychological impacts. Because the computer is a relative newcomer to our environment, it will cause unexpected disruptions in workers, work environments, the organization, and possibly the survival of the company.

In the corporation, clerks work with application systems, programmers with programming systems, and managers with decision support systems. What do all of these systems have in common? They are poorly engineered in terms of human factors. The computer technician who built these systems was concerned with data and processes and often failed to take the human factors into account. Current computer systems use human adaptability to support their needs, rather than the other way around. The results are job boredom, reduced motivation, and lower productivity. Machines should adapt to the way humans work.

Lo! Men have become the tools of their tools.
Henry David Thoreau

It's no wonder that the computer plays the villain, since it works the person, instead of the person working the tool. Why do we design such systems? The most obvious reason is that programmers and analysts have not yet learned how to build systems that are compatible with the user.

People learn good and bad from studying examples of each. Analysts and programmers have dealt with computer operating systems and compilers that are cryptic at best. Consider the IBM completion code OC7. With a little human engineering, the system could explain that the program attempts to divide by zero and that the two fields in question are DAYS-WORKED and TOTAL-DAYS. Or it could explain that the program had blanks in one field and that the error occurred after packing the invalid data. Why do these systems produce enormous dumps of the program's core image rather than extracting relevant pieces of information? These are all carryovers from the golden age of assembler language programs and small computers, that only hinder the programmer in today's environment. They are examples of poor human engineering that teach programmers poor habits, which they pass on to each new application system.

Consider a program that terminates normally. The computer lets you know that your program has been completed by its condition code, 0000. No "Atta boy," no "Job well done," but a simple "Yeah, your job ran." The computer has all the compassion of a waitress in a New Jersey diner. A zero condition code doesn't necessarily mean that the output is correct, but at least the test paths executed without failure, something deserving of congratulations. And what about job control language (JCL)? Why can't a big, strong operation system be intelligent enough to figure out record lengths from the module it executes and calculate the best block size for the storage medium being used? Why can't the machine conclude that if an output file doesn't exist it must be new, and then have the operating system create it? Poor human engineering. Programmers have more trouble with JCL than with any other. These human engineering deficiencies waste countless years of human and machine effort.

Programmers have learned poor human engineering from the systems they work with. They propagate these atrocities in the application and management information systems they build. For example, consider systems that reject input transactions on the first invalid field without checking the rest of the fields, error reports that give poorly documented error codes, systems that lack the intelligence to determine correct default actions, or systems that require complete re-entry of erroneous transactions. Some systems provide piles of data for the user to wade through. The computer should screen the data, producing only exception reports, thereby reducing the information to be handled.

These systems have several fundamental things in common.

1. They do not incorporate the ideas and knowledge of the end user.

2. They emphasize the technical and economic aspects of the system and de-emphasize the human ones, forcing the human to work for the tool, a classic case of the tail wagging the dog.

3. They solve only a simplified version of the problem. Because there is a rush to begin coding, requirements are often ill-defined and the true problem and solution are overlooked.

4. These systems are typically inflexible, unable to meet the needs of a changing environment. This rigidity causes user dissatisfaction, overworks system maintenance groups, and expands costs beyond acceptable limits.

5. They focus on only one problem, ignoring the dynamic flow of information around the corporation. In solving one problem they may create others.

6. Information systems filter out information that cannot be expressed in language or numbers. For example, electronic mail can transfer only words or sentences. Without subtle body language clues or changes in tone, the reader can never know if a message conveys cynicism, irony, or humor.

The systems currently in use also cause problems among their users.

1. *Anxiety.* The machine seems a threat to one's job. Poor response time, computer down time, and program failures cause impatience and frustration.
2. *Depression.* Systems can increase job boredom, reduce responsibility, and the like, implying that the corporation no longer needs or trusts this individual.
3. *Depersonalization.* Some workers feel that a baboon could do their jobs. What was once challenging is now done by a box of wires. They no longer feel important to the corporation.
4. *Aggression.* People will become angry with the computer and organization for taking away their jobs. The results can be subversion and possible attempts to sabotage the system's

operation. The usual comment is, "See? I told you it wouldn't work."

5. *Avoidance.* People may choose to avoid using the new system and stay with their manual system.

6. *Resistance.* The new system, being only a partial solution, will necessitate the development of manual procedures to augment the computer or to verify its results. It may create extra work rather than reducing the work load.

7. *Personnel Problems.* Turnover, absenteeism, errors, and strikes are all possible actions. Unionization may occur to prevent mechanization.

8. *Reduced Motivation.* Productivity drops.

9. *Violence.* People may actually take action against the company or the computer.

Information systems should be designed to combat these problems. Here are a few of the ways in which a system can help.

1. Select only the information that is relevant to the specific job being done. The system should eliminate excess information and support incomplete or inadequate information with details.

2. Systems should compare actual data with estimates and flag significant differences for corrective action.

3. Management information systems should provide quick access to information that will support decision-making in a changing environment.

4. The system should be designed to deliver timely information; the value of information declines with time, decaying like radioactive material. The half-life of information may be a few days or only a few hours. The stock and commodity markets are prime examples of how timely information affects profit and loss.

5. The system must insure delivery of the information to all affected parties.

In summary, systems can cause many problems among the people they are supposed to serve. These problems, which are rooted in the constant change brought about by computers, can have far-reaching effects on the corporation in both tangible and intangible ways. Systems can be designed, however, to prevent these problems and to improve system acceptance and overall productivity.

2. HUMAN NEEDS

Society is a mule, not a car. If pressed too hard, it will kick and throw off its rider.

Introduction of the computer into the work environment changes how work is done. Clerks who worked with pen, paper, typewriters, and file cabinets now work with terminals and data bases. Programmers who worked at the computer console or with remote job entry now work from remote locations using terminals and software. Managers who once made decisions based on intuition and a few known variables now rely on operations research software and computers to analyze data for many decisions.

Managing this change and motivating people to work towards it is a challenge. To manage change requires understanding the needs of our vast human resource and what it takes to meet them. There are two prevalent views of human needs—Maslow's and Herzberg's. Reviewing their theories and relating them to humans working with computer systems may serve to enlighten or recharge those of you who use them consciously or unconsciously.

2.1. Maslow's Hierarchy of Needs

Maslow contributed the often quoted hierarchy of needs. He defines human needs as follows.

1. *Physiological Needs.* Food and shelter needs are fulfilled by the pay received, but money quickly ceases to motivate people. Once they have achieved a comfortable level of income, employees shift to new need levels.

2. *Safety, Security, and Stability Needs.* Benefit programs and a feeling of job security meet these needs. People in advertising may never rise above this level, because their jobs are always on the line. Programmers and analysts typically feel safe, unless they are involved in government contracts or branches of the aviation industry, because of the tremendous demand for skilled DP technicians. Should the supply ever exceed the demand, however, DP professionals might unionize to shore up their job security. Once they feel secure, employees shift to more social needs.

3. *Affiliation and Love Needs.* People need to work with other people. They strive for acceptance in their work groups. The

concepts of programmer teams and egoless programming help create this feeling of affiliation and teamwork. Poorly designed computer systems can dehumanize jobs and reduce these feelings. Poor design enforces the feeling of being just another cog in the machine. Fulfillment of social needs leads programmers to a sense of self-worth and a need for recognition.

4. *Self-Esteem and Social Recognition Needs.* At this stage, people rely on management and their peers to supply them with feedback. They need to know whether they are doing a good or a bad job. This need level can be fulfilled only by the people around them.

5. *Self-Actualization Needs.* Each person needs personal growth and skill improvement, new and more challenging work. From these increased responsibilities, one develops a sense of self-worth and self-motivation. One develops and strives for personal goals.

The computer systems people deal with must reduce the amount of boring work and provide new opportunities to perform in ways not previously possible. The self-actualized level is the pinnacle of Maslow's hierarchy, which implies that people are motivated for different reasons. By examining your employees' individual needs, you can provide the proper environment for maximum productivity. By ignoring employee motivation, you set up roadblocks to productivity and quality growth.

2.2. Herzberg's Theory

One of Herzberg's early excursions into human needs and motivation introduced the term KITA (*Kick In The Pants*). Both positive and negative KITA exert pressure on employees to make them produce. Negative KITA implies that the manager kicks the programmers in the pants, thereby motivating them to produce code. This is called negative physical KITA. Negative psychological KITA involves using mental games to kick the programmers. In either case, the manager—not the programmer—is the one motivated. The manager is motivated to make the programmer do his or her job. The programmer remains unmotivated because motivation comes from internal forces, never external.

Positive KITA, on the other hand, involves holding carrots, such as money or promotions, in front of the programmer to encourage movement. Is this motivation? Many managers will say yes. Once again, however, the manager is motivated to move the programmer; the programmer is not motivated to move on his or her own. "Negative KITA is rape, and positive KITA is seduction. But it is infinitely worse to be seduced than to be raped; the latter is an unfortunate occurrence, while the former signifies that you were a party to your own downfall. The organization does not have to kick you; you kick yourself." Providing the employee with meaningful work, in which he can assume responsibility, is the only way to motivate a programmer or analyst.

The KITA theory was later refined to indicate two mutually exclusive catalytic agents in humans—motivators and de-motivators, the latter also called "hygiene factors." These two operate independently to motivate or de-motivate people. De-motivators actually cause worker dissatisfaction by their absence. A low level of salary and benefits combined with a poor company policy, supervision, working conditions, and interpersonal relations de-motivates the employee. These factors coincide with the lower needs on Maslow's hierarchy. One of the major motivational problems involves recognition and feedback. Annual salary reviews, for example, do not follow performance closely enough to formulate an actual cause-and-effect relationship between work and rewards. People cannot understand how day-to-day behavior correlates with annual salary reviews and cannot improve without timely constructive feedback. Managers should recognize both superior and inadequate performance, dealing with them immediately.

Motivators, on the other hand, include achievement, recognition, work itself, responsibility, advancement, and growth. These concepts have lead to job enrichment programs and Quality of Work Life (QWL). Job enrichment should not be confused with job enlargement. Enrichment provides an opportunity for psychological growth, while enlargement merely adds more tasks to the burden. Herzberg refers to job enlargement as "horizontal job loading." It is possible to enlarge a person's job to the point that even the best performer cannot handle the work load. Job enrichment means vertical loading: higher priority tasks are given to the employee. These tasks give the employee more responsibility, stimulate personal growth, and improve employee morale and productivity. Job enrichment may include any of the following.

1. Removing controls on the individual
2. Increasing individual accountability

3. Giving a person control of an entire project or subsystem
4. Delegating authority or job freedom to the employee
5. Introducing new, more difficult tasks
6. Assigning specialized tasks.

Each of these assignments shows an increasing trust of the employee and expectations of performance capabilities.

The steps to job enrichment are simple. First, years of tradition have convinced managers that jobs cannot change; approach job enrichment with a free, open mind. Second, formulate a list of changes you would like to try and prioritize them. Then, eliminate all changes having to do with hygiene factors. Eliminate generalities. Eliminate changes that expand the job rather than enhance it. Experiment with the changes that remain. Not all may work. Use a trial and a control group. Try these changes with technical and managerial groups. Once you have exhausted your first list of enrichments, draw up another. You will have learned many things from the first trial, so continue to cycle your jobs through enrichment programs. It will take a long time to cycle your programmers and analysts through an enrichment program. Productivity and quality will improve slowly, so expect it and flow with it; do not try to force the change.

2.3. Needs and Computer Systems

The evolution of humans has taken millions of years. But, as the astronaut Scott Crossfield put it, "Where else would you get a nonlinear computer weighing only 160 pounds, having a billion binary decision elements, that can be mass-produced by unskilled labor?"

When the going gets tough, everyone leaves.

In spite of our incredible anatomical computer, called the brain, humans do not respond quickly to change and tend to revert to their basic security needs when threatened. Computers, on the other hand, have evolved in less than 30 years. The rapidity of this change has caused a dramatic shift in the status quo, creating a dynamic environment that humans are generally not prepared for. This change, forced by the economics of automation, has served to alienate workers. They see it as something done *to* them, rather than *for* them.

The wider the gap between human response and technological advance, the greater the future shock that affects employees and businesses, causing rippling social problems. The system must be designed to deal effectively with the needs of the people who will use it. Whether they are clerks, programmers, or managers, the principle of human engineering remains the same. Every new system brings changes that strike deep into the foundations of each person's need. Coming to grips with these changes requires dedication and involvement.

2.4. How to Deal with Change

Why leap into the future, when you can wade into it?
A Xerox Advertisement

Although employees may not notice it, they change constantly. As they become better educated and informed, they will expect more from their work. Workers will become increasingly mobile and continue to shift from agricultural and blue collar jobs into professional, technical, and service-oriented jobs. They will lose their organizational loyalties while increasing dedication to their professions. Workers who are unable to cope with change will suffer from mental and physical stress and the associated illnesses. Employees will also require more leisure time. These changes will ripple through the organization. What should you expect?

Change will cause many of the following reactions in your personnel unless you compensate well in advance.

1. People will fear losing their jobs, positions, or their ability to cope with new work. Properly prepared for, change should not invoke the stressful situations that would otherwise affect employees.

2. People may lose interest in their work if new challenges aren't provided to replace tasks taken over by the computer.

3. Your employees will suspect management's motives for proposing change. Management always seems to want staff cuts and reduced costs. Informing employees of the reasons for change and involving them in the decision-making process will help reduce their resistance.

4. They will resent change because it implies personal criticism: if they were doing their jobs well, you would not want to computerize them. Let them know that you want to upgrade their jobs and that automation will allow you that freedom.

5.   The computer system will disrupt existing social relationships at work. Information currently shared by two co-workers will be shared by a person and a computer. Some activity will have to be found to fill the social gap. Coffee breaks and lunches become more important. Anyone locked away with a computer all day develops a further sense of isolation that is harmful to the employee and the corporation.

Installing a computer system traverses unknown ground. For example, faced with having a terminal on the desk—a possibility that I consider the dream of every programmer—a programmer might see it as a chain that reduces freedom of movement. It might imply that management wants to keep watch over them by keeping them in their work area. Electronic mail might be viewed as a method to keep them from talking to their friends except through a terminal that can be monitored for gossip and nonbusiness conversations. Electronic mail might also be seen as another chain to the desk, rather than a fast, efficient means of disseminating information. Employees may not realize that electronic mail gives them the option of working at home: spouses could trade child-rearing responsibilities while continuing to work full-time with home terminals, and people could work in the off hours, when the kids are in bed and computer response is extraordinary.

To overcome resistance to change requires education. Inform people, well in advance, of technological change. Training insures that employees are prepared to cope with renovations in their jobs. Plan for change. Will it be sudden or gradual? Gradual changes are more in line with human abilities to handle transition. Schedule work changes to coincide with slack periods. Your people will have more time to deal with them than if they're pushing against deadlines. And your commitment to job enrichment and resistance to job loading will be emphasized.

Form the habit of change. Get people accustomed to change as a natural part of an evolving, competitive business. Involve people in the decision-making process. They may have better ideas about implementing changes or see solutions that would otherwise be overlooked. Reward people for participating in change. The reward need not be monetary but might include better responsibilities, their own special project, or whatever satisfies their personal needs. Humans are infinitely different, so the rewards should be different. Management will have to take on the burden of understanding each person's psyche, but it will be worth it.

When the computer must displace people's jobs, try to retrain those people for new positions. Rely on natural attrition to reduce head count. Provide counseling and job relocation services to those people who must be dismissed. Consider the human element in system conversions and see how much easier change becomes.

3. PROGRAMMERS AREN'T MACHINES

Logic is like a sword—those who appeal to it shall perish by it.
Samuel Butler

What do we value above all else in a programmer? Logic. The programmer becomes a knight in shining armor whose logic "sword" conquers the binary consciousness of the computer. How can we fail to draw comparisons between them? But humans err. Emotions rule them. They have needs a computer doesn't have. These logical warriors are the focus of all systems developed. They cost much more than the hardware they dominate. They are the key resource, without which computers would be worthless.

The optimist believes we live in the best of all possible worlds.
The pessimist fears this is true.

As programs have automated other jobs, they will also mechanize much of the programming task. Programmers know this and fear it, just as other workers have always feared computers. They must be motivated to change with the needs of the company and the environment surrounding them. Without proper planning and anticipation of their needs, productivity and quality improvements are impossible. How do you insure human factors engineering?

4. SOLUTIONS

There are some obvious deficiencies in how we build systems for humans. As technicians, we perform wonderfully, creating the black box, but we fail to engineer the human–machine interface, which forces employees to perform work in an unnatural way, reducing their productivity. So what can you do about it?

1. If you are building a system for non-DP users, either employ a human factors or industrial engineer, or properly train your employees in human factors. Build user friendliness into your systems.

2.   Have end users participate in the design. Their contributions can quickly correct many deficient or erroneous designs.

3.   Educate end users about what a system can do. These people have little chance to investigate the possibilities on their own, so inform them. Fewer cries of "But we don't know what we want!" will be heard.

4.   The first goal of a computer system is to help people in their jobs, thereby reducing costs or improving productivity and quality. With this in mind, examine each task assigned to the computer and analyze who the computer will help or hinder by performing the task. Reject solutions that put up roadblocks or dehumanize the job.

5.   Human-engineered systems will create a demand for more systems. An example of a well-engineered system might be automatic bank tellers, from which you can get cash at any time of the day or night, including weekends. Before automation, people had to get to the bank during inconvenient office hours; now they just go to a banking machine. Because of this radical change, the bank needs fewer new tellers; customers can serve themeselves. Over 50 years ago, the dial telephone made each telephone customer an operator, simplifying efficient communication for everyone. Both of these examples represent excellent human engineering.

6.   You should build systems from components or languages that are flexible. Perhaps the black box will never change, but the input and output processing will need to bend with user's needs and new technology. Nonprocedural languages will create an environment in which end users will become their own programming staffs. Managers will be able to play "what if" games from a terminal on their desks. Screen design tools will allow easy update of input facilities. Report generators will allow quick programming of trial and one-shot programs.

5.   HUMAN IMPACTS—METHODOLOGY

5.1.   *Phased Development Methodology*

Phased methodology separates the development process into distinct activities, but it often requires more work than just diving into the project. From this standpoint, programmers and analysts will abhor the delay. Managers of the business, however, will gain renewed control of the process, improving their ability to manage system development and resulting in a positive overall impact. One group is affected favorably and one negatively.

To overcome resistance to phased methodology and project management, educate your personnel using examples from systems that provided a poor or negative cost benefit. After they become accustomed to phased methodology they should appreciate its benefits. You have to promote the best solution for the company.

5.2. End User Involvement

Active involvement of the end user serves both the user and DP. The programming staff benefits from gaining direct understanding of what is needed, so the system is built correctly the first time, eliminating the need for extensive system enhancement after conversion. Nothing is more frustrating than discovering that the project you have devoted your time to has failed to meet the user's needs. End users also benefit from participating in the definition and design process. It gives them a sense of ownership not otherwise possible, which will ease the introduction of the system into the user community. Furthermore, they get the system they want, not one designed, often poorly, for them.

5.3. Standards

Standards should not restrict the job unnecessarily. They should, however, standardize what is done. If there are two equally good ways to perform a programming or design task, standards should indicate which to use.

Standards benefit the programmer or analyst by limiting the options. If an analyst can represent logic only with an IPO, pseudocode, or program design language (PDL), then the programmer can focus on knowing one kind of design tool, not several. Training costs are reduced and programmer productivity is improved because what a programmer might expect to receive for documentation is standardized. Standard documentation is easier to read simply because the programmer becomes more familiar with it. Errors due to misunderstandings will decrease substantially.

Once again, the programmers and analysts are the end users of standards. Involve them in their development and they will readily accept and use them.

5.4. Generic Designs

The use of generic program designs does not make the analyst's job boring or less creative, but elevates the task to a new level. Rather than concerning themselves with logic details, analysts can focus on combining functions into representations of user needs.

Who is better qualified to develop generic designs than the pro-grammers and analysts who will use them? Participation increases their ownership in new methodology and technology. Generic de-signs might be generated as an offshoot of a development project. Or you might start a contest, the best designs to be selected by an independent review team. The contributors should be rewarded in a manner of your choosing. Combining designs to create the opti-mum generic design might also provide a rewarding task. You might also form design teams to work on varied solutions. Once again, the analysts are the end users, so involve them in this major job change.

Once these designs are in place, job enrichment can evolve from training an analyst to use increasingly difficult designs. Some sit-uations may require enhancements to existing generic designs. An analyst can be given this work in recognition of good performance. The day will come when a design that does not exist or cannot be formed from a combination of the existing designs is needed. Now, backed with all the knowledge of existing generic designs, analysts can create a new design for the generic library. Their ability as creative individuals will be recognized.

The company benefits from the improved productivity of the staff and the improved quality of the programs developed generically. These designs should decrease the size of the maintenance staff, freeing people to work on new development, which is often consid-ered more rewarding than maintenance. The new projects they de-velop will make the rest of the corporation more productive and improve the corporation's ability to compete.

5.5. Common Code

Common code is a specialized version of generic code, so all benefits derived from generic code apply to common code. Common code further reduces the amount of programming a development group must perform. System maintainers also find common code easier to maintain and enhance. The company saves additional resources and gains productivity by the use of common subroutines and pro-grams. The savings from common code exceed those obtained from generic programs. Much of the common code may have to be developed uniquely for each application, providing an opportunity to reward good performers—give them the creative assignments.

There is typically some resistance to common code philosophies. Proper training will encourage understanding of the benefits derived by both the company and the personnel. Working with common code in a maintenance environment and developing it for a new project will cement its usefulness to improve productivity and quality.

5.6. *Structured Testing*

Structured testing reduces the complexity of each test. It makes testing easier and therefore more productive for the programmer. It will require more tests than the old way, but each test will be simpler and take less time to complete. Since this method of testing will reduce the total time spent testing a module, programmers will adopt it with little difficulty.

The company benefits from reduced testing costs and improved quality in the released system. Having a separate system test organization will pay for itself by improving the quality of the test. System test groups, unfortunately, grow weary of testing. Rotating employees through testing assignments will help relieve the boredom and improve the quality of each test. Each employee benefits from learning how to test systems. This experience carries back into the development job, where employees will try to beat the testing organization by finding their own errors.

5.7. *Quality Assurance*

Having a QA team in the wings makes programmers and analysts defensive about their products because documents, code, and tests are all subject to review. An organization strictly oriented toward finding fault with the way things are done offends even the least egotistical programmers. A wholesale introduction of a QA in any organization will cause chaos, confusion, and resentment, resulting in lower productivity and quality. Introduced gently, however, and expanded where needed, it can improve your development and maintenance process. Better quality will manifest itself in fewer overtime hours, easier maintenance, and a controlled, productive process.

Programmers benefit from QA because reduced overtime and easier maintenance result from better documentation and programming. Programmers and analysts can also serve as their own QA group. Walk-throughs of designs and code will not only improve quality but also serve as a forum for the exchange of techniques and methodologies. This communication medium would not otherwise exist. Better quality products, provided by QA, benefit the company. Quality, however, is hard to quantify. Direct comparisons between cost reduction and the cost of the QA function may be impossible; management may be reluctant to budget and staff such a function.

5.8. Change Control

Although it is an imposition on their time, change control will be accepted by programmers because it establishes work priorities and makes tracking old problems easier. With specific work priorities, programmers and analysts know what is expected of them. Priorities also restrict work to what can be done in the allotted time, preventing over-burdening the maintenance staff.

Knowledge of previous errors may point to ways of avoiding those simple errors that often plague program development. The company benefits from improved productivity and control of the maintenance process and also because change control allows for planning and scheduling system releases.

5.9. Release Scheduling

Scheduling maintenance work into releases benefits both the user and the DP department. The user sets priorities for enhancements and fixes; DP plans releases to reduce waste of resources. The user knows ahead of time what changes to expect and when, allowing user training and revision of manuals prior to installation. The DP department gains client respect for meeting schedules and work loads in each release. If the client requires more work than can be accomplished, the client has to fight for more programmers, which means the DP manager's burden for justifying incremental growth is eased.

The computer operations staff also benefits from planning their work in advance. System releases are handled easily with preplanned backout procedures in place. All JCL or execution procedures can be updated at the same time, reducing errors. Compare this to the helter-skelter mode of operation where programs are received and implemented daily, and where expensive reruns, overtime, and poor communications between the development and operation organizations are common.

6. HUMAN NEEDS—TECHNOLOGY

6.1. On-Line Systems

Programmers prefer on-line systems over batch processing systems because they are in direct communication with the machine. Real time systems improve their ability to perform by reducing the delay between executing a job and receiving the output. Response times are critical to human performance and system acceptance. It helps if response times are fairly equal, not one second now and 15 seconds a few minutes later. Human work habits adapt easily to consistent response times. Response times should be kept under two seconds, but a significant investment of capital to substitute for the addition of more programmers is required. The reason for excellent response time requirements focuses on the operator.

The human brain is incredibly fast. If it is left without a response for more than two seconds it typically shifts to some other train of thought. When the computer finally responds, the brain registers the response through visual impulses but usually finishes its current thought before returning to the computer's answer. To be able to respond to the computer, the programmer must remember what he or she was doing and start again from that point. This is like paging in a computer: it takes "think time" to bring pages into memory and get ready to execute them again. Think time increases as response time increases. The longer a programmer has to wait for a response, the longer it will take to return to the dialogue carried on with the computer. Over the course of a terminal session, these lost seconds of think time can add up to 25-50% of the time spent— time spent more productively elsewhere. Considering that programmers spend 20-50% of their day at a terminal, improved response time can save 5-25% of their day—a significant increase in productivity.

Improved response time also affects the programmers' attitude. They are measured on production, so they become upset if the machine delays their progress significantly. Do you have programmers working in the off hours? If you do, response time may be one of your major roadblocks.

6.2. Office Automation

Programmers and analysts love having word processors. No more typing pools to fight. No more typing delays. No more days or weeks to make a change in a document. There are a few problems, however.

Older analysts, without the necessary keying skills, will tend to reject word processors. Managers will reject the idea of turning their analysts into typists; it just doesn't fall into the job description. This resistance results from traditions that have been established for years. Interestingly enough, any person can learn enough keying skills to be productive in a few weeks. Pen-and-paper analysts competing with word-processing analysts will quickly fall behind. When your paycheck is on the line, you are forced to change, quit, or retire. Most managers resist office automation, but the ones who automate their jobs now will be in the executive offices in 10 years. Office automation will free them to explore new goals and expand their productivity.

Electronic mail is also well received. No more time spent searching for people—you just leave mail for them. No more writing little notes that get lost on desks. No more leaving messages with secretaries. No more delays caused by repeated communication failures. No more time wasted in typing and distributing simple memos. The Booz and Allen study has shown that electronic mail can eliminate up to 30 minutes a day spent in unsuccessful communication attempts. Programmers and analysts like electronic mail because it allows them to answer questions when it is convenient. This situation is analogous to the response time problems previously described: the mind must leave what it is currently doing to answer questions when interrupted, then remember what it was doing and restart. Constant interruptions can significantly decrease productivity and quality. Electronic mail helps eliminate these problems. Managers will dislike electronic mail because employees will use it to send personal mail as well, which seems a misuse of company equipment. The alternative is to force employees to use telephones or to walk over and interrupt their friends, actions that are more wasteful than the use of the electronic mail. Management must recognize that the social climate at work is imperative to productivity. Electronic mail helps meet those needs without interrupting work or being costly to the company.

6.3. *Other Tools*

Compiling and testing tools will be accepted, given adequate training and time to learn to use them. Programmers need additional tools to support testing. It is the hardest process they have to deal with. Programmers will respond well to anything that makes testing less difficult and allows them to be more productive.

6.4. *Nonprocedural Languages*

These languages will be more easily accepted by younger employees. Just as diehard assembler language coders rejected COBOL and PL/1 whenever possible, diehard COBOL and PL/1 programmers will tend to avoid nonprocedural languages. The resistance to learn never ceases.

Training always takes people away from the job, thereby reducing their productivity. It takes time to become proficient in any new tool or language. Programmers and analysts will not knowingly take steps to decrease their production: that is one of the reasons they resist change. To paraphrase Woody Allen, "Employees are like sharks; they have to keep moving forward or they die. What we have here is a dead shark." Managers must make it clear that learning is an expected part of employee growth. Any employee who stops growing to meet business's changing needs is a dead shark. The business expects more from an individual because the business has to survive, not because it wants to hurt or harass an employee.

7. SUMMARY

People—the heart of any system development or maintenance project—can have a significant effect on productivity and quality. Their perception of changing methodology and technology can enhance or impede renovations in the software factory. Careful planning can include their needs while meeting the requirements of the corporation. Without a significant investment in human factors engineering, you can expect serious headaches in implementing information systems in user communities and especially in DP environments. Numerous solutions, costing only human understanding and a little extra work, provide the lubrication for a successful installation of work improvements. With proper human engineering, your employees will move into the future without reservation. Their productivity will increase measurably. Think of them when it's time for a change; they are the company.

CHAPTER FIVE

Management and Organization

The success or failure of any software project often depends on who is managing the project. This has been demonstrated so many times that it seems redundant even to mention it. Schedule slippages and cost overruns are the domain of the manager, not the programmers and analysts. Managing resources, motivating people, planning the project, and implementing the organization are all functions of the manager. Who could possibly have more impact on the productivity and quality of the system than management? No one.

To a lesser degree, the organization of the project team affects development productivity and system quality. This chapter examines ways to organize and manage system development and maintenance projects to maximize productivity and quality. The rest is up to you.

1. MANAGEMENT

The first myth of management is that it exists.

It is hard to believe that the productivity and quality of a software product hinges on just a few managers. You can add all the productivity tools and methodology imaginable, but without some proper planning, resource allocation, and personnel skills, the project will fail or overrun its budget and schedule.

1.1. Phased Development Methodology

In either development or maintenance, a phased life cycle brings control to the software process. Phased development specifies tasks to finish and their completion dates. Staffing is simplified, since relatively few people are needed until implementation. Phasing the work flow allows time to plan each phase. The completion of each phase allows you to measure progress towards the system's release and the latitude to cancel the project if it becomes infeasible.

1.2. Planning

A carelessly planned project takes three times longer to complete than expected; a carefully planned project takes only twice as long.

The first plan you need covers the *phases of development*. This plan should cover the estimates for all phases and the specific estimate for evaluating the feasibility of the project. The estimates for later phases should change as new information comes to light. This plan should identify the products of each phase and the approvals required to proceed with development.

Another of the initial plans you should develop is a *productivity and quality improvement* plan. It should detail what you require in the way of productivity and quality improvements and how you intend to get there. This plan should recommend the development tools, programming language(s), methodologies, productivity and quality measurements, and controls to be used.

Next, you'll need an *organization and staffing* plan, which details and expands the development group's organization. Are there programming teams? Who has responsibility for system design, subsystem design, program design, coding, unit testing, system testing, and so on? Few things have more impact on productivity than a poor organization and poorly defined responsibilities. Knowing the organization, staffing becomes simple.

Managers should plan for staff growth. The managers and system architects are the only people needed on the development team until the end of the definition phase. Properly executed, the first three phases of development will take 25-30% of the development process. Having the systems analysts and programmers sitting around for this period is nonproductive and creates a situation in which upper management starts demanding designs and code before the groundwork is laid. This is analogous to constructing a building before the foundation has set or even been poured. It merely results in a lot of rework to correct the problems caused.

Next, you'll need a *testing* plan. How will the system be tested? Will there be incremental releases to system test, or one giant release? Who will be responsible for module, program, and system testing? Who will perform integration and conversion testing? Should you allocate a separate group to perform system testing in the organization plan? What methodologies and technologies will system testers use to enhance testing? This plan will begin as a rough sketch, but revision at the end of each phase will expand the plan to reflect all new information. The final plan should facilitate the actions of the testing organization, improving productivity and quality at a time when many systems falter.

Finally, you will need a *conversion* plan. When will the user acceptance test begin? When should the user start training for conversion? What documents, programs, and user manuals represent a finished system? If hardware, terminals, and networks are needed to support the system, when should they be ordered to support the conversion?

Your productivity improvement plan should address methodology. One of the most beneficial methodologies is structured programming.

1.3. Structured Programming

On the surface, managing structured programming would seem easy, but implementing it can cause a rash of human factors problems. Programming has been such an egocentric job that changes are perceived as some sort of negative commentary about the programmer's work. For every structured way of doing things, there is at least one exception that your programmers will thrust in your face.

There will be arguments about GO TO statements. There are cases where a GO TO solves coding problems better than GO TO-less code. GO TO-less code may not equate to good code either. Programmers who have no idea how to write GO TO-less code will perform all kinds of coding feats to meet your expectations. They may even sabotage the program to show you that structured programming doesn't work. Programmers will bemoan the inefficiency of structured programming, and analysts will raise a hue and cry over the extent of documentation required.

All of these problems stem from people's resistance to change. You should anticipate it, provide new training, and inform the staff of the benefits the business expects to derive from its use. You should expect a variety of arguments against using structured code. What are they?

1.3.1. GO TOs. Dijkstra first suggested that any program could be developed using the three basic logic structures:

Sequential
    MOVE A TO B
    ADD B TO C GIVING D.
IF-THEN-ELSE
    IF MASTER-KEY < TRANSACTION-KEY
        PERFORM WRITE-MASTER-RECORD
        PERFORM READ-NEW-MASTER-RECORD
    ELSE
        PERFORM UPDATE-MASTER-RECORD.
DOWHILE
    PERFORM UPDATE-MASTER-FILE
        UNTIL MASTER-FILE-AT-END-OF-FILE AND
        TRANSACTION-FILE-AT-END-OF-FILE.

Each of these structures has only one entry point and one exit point, making it simple to follow the data flow. Similarly, a structured program has only one entry and one exit. Since it is made up of single-entry, single-exit logic structures, it should require only one of entry or exit. The GO TO violates these structures by unconditionally branching to God knows where in the program.

Having programmed in COBOL, before the days of structured programming, I grudgingly gave up the GO TO. It becomes so thoroughly ingrained in programmers that it may take a priest to exorcise it. So, unless you happen to be a member of the Holy Family, don't try to eliminate the GO TO; just minimize its use.

1.3.2. Inefficiency. Structured code is not inefficient. By reducing the complexity of the program, it will execute more straightforwardly. It takes 100 million executions of a statement to equal the time it takes a programmer to write the statement, so the programmer's concern with micro efficiencies must be eliminated. Optimizing compilers and faster machines will soon eliminate all efficiency questions, but they are so inbred that you may have to shoot us old-timers and let the younger set take over.

1.3.3. Creativity. My group of silver-haired colleagues will protest the use of structured programming. "You're limiting our creativity. Our old programs work just fine. What do you mean, we've been writing bad programs all these years? What do you mean, our programs are costing the company too much to maintain?" You'll have to convince us that the new methodologies are better. Well, seeing is believing. Structured programming increases programmer productivity and program quality and improves system maintenance. What other reasons do you need for implementing it?

1.3.4. Measurement. Once you begin to apply structured programming, it becomes apparent that you cannot necessarily enforce its use. You should implement the software metrics described in Chapter 6. They provide a mechanized way of tracking violations, most of which are caused by the vast complexity of the programs built today. Don't be hard on the programmers, but seek only to upgrade the program before its release. Programmers learn from their mistakes and will develop better coding habits.

1.3.5. Maintenance. Structured programming applies only to maintenance programming to the extent that all new modules or rewrites of existing modules follow the methodology. Old programs are just that—old. They were unstructured when written and will probably remain so until they are retired. Trying to patch them up and turn them into structured programs will be more time-consuming than rewriting them.

In spite of programmer resistance, the productivity and quality improvements wrought by structured programming will slowly erode the old methodology. Structured programming will become a way of life.

1.4. Resource Management

Adding manpower to a late software project makes it later.
                                                        Brooks

Anyone can make a decision given enough facts. A good man-
ager can make a decision without enough facts. A perfect man-
ager can operate in perfect ignorance.

What are your resources? Money, machines, people, and time. Let's examine how to use them.

1.4.1. Budget. First, you will need to budget the project, normally at least a year in advance of the project. What hardware will you need? How many people will be on the project and for how long? Budget for furniture, floor space, lighting, all those little things like pens and paper, and everything else that makes a project run. Without money, the project will never begin.

Upper management may try to control the Information System department by strictly controlling their budget. In doing so, they can harm the competitive position of the company. Budget crunches typically reduce new development, not maintenance, because the systems in place have to keep running. But you need new systems to provide the information that maintains the competitive position of the company.

Management may further assume that budget increases are earmarked for new development, which may not be true. Development systems entering the maintenance phase can account for the yearly growth all by themselves. Systems in maintenance may require extensive enhancements. Little of the additional budget may find its way to the coffers for new programs. Or management may assume that the purchase of new hardware indicates the continued growth of information systems, when this hardware simply replaces existing, outdated machines. These misconceptions, based on budgetary figures, lead to many of your existing problems: too much maintenance and too little development.

Management will also be skeptical of rewriting old software to improve it. The software metrics in Chapter 6 should help document problems with specific portions of the system that create the majority of your maintenance costs. These programs become increasingly hard to maintain. They tend to fail more frequently. They belong in the 20% of programs that produce 80% of the costs. Old software can give your competition an edge. For example, what happens when TWA can confirm your return seat and issue a boarding card? You don't have to stand in line for your return flight. For the same price they provide a convenience not provided elsewhere. What if your competition has a better inventory system that keeps inventory levels down and can immediately find an item in stock without the usual clerical search? You'll have to play catch-up, and in the systems game, that may be difficult.

Old software and technology also generate personnel problems. Data processing people tend to follow technology, so your old systems won't hold them on the job unless they like the security.

Delaying investments in new software and hardware can affect the corporation competitively and financially. Current management bonus programs tend to make managers focus on short-term solutions that adversely affect the long-term survival of the company. Since managers move around a lot, they are unprepared to risk their resources on long-term projects with bigger payoffs since their successors will reap the rewards. If you employ these bonus plans, consider changing them to require at least one long-term project that will follow managers wherever they move in the corporation.

How can you tell if you might be heading for trouble? Have your data processing costs been increasing with inflation and the business's growth? Has your data processing budget been growing in line with that of other companies in your business? Has your mix of development and maintenance work changed significantly over the last five years? If you can answer yes to any of these questions, you may be underinvesting. One of the first places to look for underinvestment is your computer site; do you have enough hardware?

1.4.2. Hardware. If you need a new machine for development, you should order from 6 to 18 months in advance to insure that it will be operational when you need it. If you plan to use an existing machine, make sure there are adequate facilities to support your development activities. Otherwise, you could be short of the resources you need and you will degrade the response time of others on the system. Aside from creating many bad feelings, these conditions have a negative impact on the business; needed information systems will be delayed.

If you have enough hardware, maybe you aren't managing your personnel resource as well as possible.

1.4.3. People.   Through the first three phases of development—proposal, feasibility, and definition—you will need a select development team. In the following phases, your staff may increase several times. It may not be possible to acquire these people from within the organization. Hiring programmers from a consulting firm may provide the head count you need. This approach has several advantages. These people are already trained. They are accustomed to differing assignments, so they are flexible and can pick up the project easily. They also bring good ideas and methods from the outside. If they don't work out, it's easier to dismiss them. When the project is over, you aren't stuck with a large staff to maintain. On the negative side, these people can appear as a threat to your in-house programmers, but explaining their presence as a financial consideration should help salve any wounds.

1.4.4. Time.   Time is another manageable resource. If you take too long to develop a system, it may no longer solve the problems at hand. Some development tasks can't be divided. They determine the minimum duration for system development.

Things get worse under pressure.

Once you open a can of worms, the only way to recan them is to use a larger can.

You can't build a system in less time by adding staff; adding people to a late software project only saddles the already harried development staff with new people to train and interact with. On paper, it looks like a big infusion of expertise, when, in fact, it's just another weight to bear.

Any technical problem can be overcome with enough time and money. You are never given enough time or money.

Resource management combines the available resources with some creative planning and organizing to produce a system in a limited amount of time. Resource management is easier if everyone on the project has the same goals.

1.5. MBO

Management by objectives works if you know the objectives.
Ninety percent of the time you don't.

Peter Drucker

Management by objectives continues to lead the day as a form of structured management, but applying it to programmers and analysts requires a lot of subjective evaluation. How can you judge the quality of a design or program? How can you quantify improvements? How can you measure productivity? Chapter 6, on software metrics, provides many potential tools for taking the measure of productivity and quality improvement. The methodology and technology chapters provide insights into tracking design and programming errors. Error rates should decline as analysts and programmers become more experienced.

One of the problems with MBO is that it focuses on individuals. System development is a group effort. There should be separate, group-oriented objectives for productivity and quality improvements. The programmers and analysts should meet and agree on these objectives and work toward measuring and meeting the objectives set. These meetings may even serve as think-tank sessions to identify improved methods or technology that might serve to help reach their goals. Without some sort of group goals, individual goals have no importance. An individual whose personal goals don't coincide with the team goals can upset the effectiveness of the group.

For example, a programmer whose personal goal includes improving program efficiency by 20% may not have time to enhance and modify programs properly. An analyst fascinated with a new design technology may use it instead of the standard, making it harder for the programmer and subsequent maintainers of the program to enhance or fix it. Individuals on a career path can conflict with team goals in some situations. The desire to advance their technical skills can run counter to the development and maintenance of systems. They may employ technology that is difficult to maintain or enhance. Their excellence works a hardship on the company and their fellow programmers. As structured programming can benefit the corporation and its personnel, it can also be detrimental. Group goals serve to clarify each person's contribution to the project and how their goals should intertwine with the group's.

1.6. Zen and the Art of Project Management

The media speak both highly and skeptically of Japanese management and the resulting productivity. Some forms of Japanese management will work in certain environments, but not in others. There are exceptions to every type of management style and tool. A good manager looks for new methods to improve his or her management style; to shut out the Japanese style is to overlook many potentially beneficial management philosophies. Japanese success with management styles stems from bottom-up communication, lateral communication, and participative decision making. The theory that two heads are better than one, especially when one person actually does the work, provides many productivity and quality benefits. This theory also works well because the manager knows more about the overall view of the company and its needs.

Often, the manager must lead the employee to the best decision. Presented with all of the facts and the goals of the corporation, the employee will often make the same decision that the manager would have made. Allowing their participation gives them ownership in the decision-making process. These people are not stupid. By beginning with questions to open up the lines of communication, the manager can draw out more information and perhaps modify his or her own stance on impending decisions. In a sense, this implies manipulation of the employee, but it shouldn't be viewed as such. It leaves room for the unknown aspects of a problem or opportunity to surface. In a typical American business decision, this kind of communication is rarely used. The alternative form appears as mandates or dictatorial messages to the employees. Being told what to do smacks of paternalistic control, void of free will and creates an unproductive, unhappy environment for program development.

Another form of Japanese management involves incremental decision making. Many times, especially in an information system project, a clear-cut decision to implement a system cannot be made. The manager can, however, decide to proceed based on the knowledge at hand. This is why the phased methodology is so useful; it allows the manager to continue development without forcing a total commitment to the remaining phases of development. The project can be canceled at the end of any phase. Rather than ramming the system down the user's throat, the project manager can verify the system incrementally. Why, you might ask, don't we use participative and incremental decision making more often?

Push something hard enough and it will fall over.

America is relatively young. In just 200 years, we have forged a nation. We have gotten used to making things happen, rather than letting them seek their own level, like water. Oriental culture relies on gradual change.

"Persist like water. Back it comes, again and again, wearing down the rigid strength which cannot yield to withstand it."
A Tao Saying

It is possible to circumvent an obstacle, rather than trying to knock it down. This theory can be applied to virtually every facet of a project: people, technology, and so on.

A combination of American and Japanese management styles is Theory Z management (Ouchi 1981). Theory Z is an ongoing process that has few basic principles.

1.   People need goals and objectives; otherwise they will work against progress as easily as they will for it. Goals create movement in a positive direction. They eliminate unproductive "wheel spinning" and backwards movement.

2.   People need motivation to perform tasks. Managers must supply both positive and negative reinforcements. To a small extent these include promotion and reward, but optimal motivation comes from peer and management recognition.

3.   People need to have their errors corrected. Goals and motivation are not sufficient because people will still make mistakes. Managers must step in to correct their movement along paths that are not in the best interests of the company.

4.   People must have a standard way of working such that they can all achieve corporate goals in a similar way. Imagine a football team with no standard defense or offense; when they lose, as they surely will, they have no way to suggest improvements.

5.   Goals must be revised as conditions in the work environment or the needs of the corporation change. By anticipating change, Theory Z provides a mechanism to allow a gradual metamorphosis.

Setting goals sounds like MBO, so you already know how to perform this task. The secret lies in expecting the worker to excel: workers will live up to your expectations. Every goal they set should be somewhat challenging or they will become disenchanted with their jobs. Setting three levels of goals—pessimistic, reasonable, and optimistic—should place the programmer or analyst in the position to know the different levels of expectation and how to achieve them. Goal setting, combined with proper motivation, encourages productivity, quality, and high morale.

Chapter 4 covered motivation in detail. Motivation covers many topics. It is important to note that Theory Z relies on recognition as a reward, not money or promotion, just as was suggested in Chapter 4. Recognition also includes corrective feedback. One of the hardest things a manager has to do is to correct an employee. We have that driving need, even as managers, to be accepted by our fellow workers. Constructive feedback is the only method that enables a person to modify behavior that is counterproductive. This feedback can be couched in such terms that it is perceived as constructive, not demeaning. If a programmer misses a due date, do you overlook the problem until the merit review? Tell the person he or she failed to meet the date and that you expect better performance in the future? Ask why he or she failed to meet the date and what can be done about eliminating the probability of its happening in the future? The last choice involves a participative goal-setting and decision-making process that improves worker–manager communications. Let's examine the other alternatives. Once-a-year feedback is obviously insufficient. Telling programmers they have failed merely reiterates what they already know. Asking the whys and hows of that failure shows a personal interest in their future and is apt to lead to more positive results. For optimal results, errors should be corrected as early as possible. Otherwise, the employee is likely to become defensive, and correcting the error will become increasingly difficult.

Managers must evaluate performance, looking for improvement and progress. Goals and objectives must be redefined as needed to address the changing needs of the people, the project, and the company. Theory Z is a management philosophy that develops a productive management climate.

1.7. Quality Control

Either an independent quality assurance group or local groups can work to insure quality. Using both will measurably improve the quality of your system, but because of budget or personnel resource constraints, it may be impossible to have an external group. Internal groups will achieve similar benefits.

The function of a quality assurance group is described in Chapter 9; walk-throughs, as a part of quality control, are described in Chapter 2. This section describes and evaluates Japanese quality circles—quality control groups that can grow directly from the existing project team.

Quality circles originated in American management philosophy, but are well implemented only in Japan. From their continuous dedication to improvement, the Japanese have emerged as experts in mass production, design, and operations. But that's in manufacturing, you say. True, but you are trying to establish a software factory that mass produces programs. Quality circles have employees meet for two hours weekly or monthly in small groups to develop suggestions for quality and productivity improvements. By involving both management and workers, vertical communication is vastly improved. Their purpose is to find ways to work more intelligently and make up for the cost of the meetings by improving productivity and quality. Quality circles allow the employee to contribute their experience, creativity, and personal interests to the business.

While working at Bell Labs, I enjoyed the pleasure of participating in a quality circle, although we didn't call it that. My project team and I shared ideas and convinced management to let us develop common code and prototypes of the programs we expected to build. Our productivity the first year was twice as high as any of us had expected. Ideas like these, coming from the bottom up, can often substantially improve productivity and quality.

Since the organization of your system already has a project manager, project leaders, and their project teams, you are already set up to implement quality circles. Just follow these steps.

1. Create a favorable management environment. It may take a manager's quality circle to sell the concept to the project manager and other project leaders. Train the managers to understand the participative concept of quality circles. Teach them to organize meetings with agendas, worksheets, and checklists.

2. Have the teams meet on company time, in company facilities, to indicate company commitment to the use of quality circles and their success.

3. Have employees attend voluntarily. Forcing attendance makes the quality circle into a problem rather than an opportunity.

4. Follow up suggestions and organize people to work on the most beneficial of the ideas presented. Meetings for the sake of meetings are a waste of everyone's time.

Don't expect immediate returns from quality circles. They require a change in both the workers' and the managers' thinking, and it won't take place overnight. Remember to be like the ocean and wear down the resistance gradually. The benefits that will accrue from this shift will include improved productivity and quality and reduced defects, absenteeism, and turnover. Since the organization already exists and people are used to participating in walk-throughs, quality circles will be inexpensive to implement. The return on investment can exceed 8 to 1, with an average of 3 to 1 (Ouchi 1981). Since quality circles serve as a forum for sharing work habits and knowledge, they also provide a long-term investment in employee growth.

Quality circles will threaten employees who are not used to the team concept of system development. If they are too firmly entrenched in the egocentric side of programming, they will rebel. Again, be like the ocean; peer pressure will eventually force them to modify their behavior. Managers may also rebel. The quality circle forces them to act as facilitators, not directors. This change may be difficult to swallow. But time is on your side; gradual change will rectify the situation. People who cannot adapt to the changes will probably leave the company, and perhaps that is for the best.

Most goods manufactured in Japan before 1960 were of poor quality. The expression "made in Japan" connoted poor quality. With the advent of quality circles, Japan has risen to set quality standards for electronics, photographic equipment, and automobiles. An American automobile is twice as likely to have a problem as a Japanese one; American electronic chips are four times as likely to have defects. Japan estimates that quality circles have saved over $25 billion since they were set up. You should investigate their uses in the software factory.

1.8. Ego-less Management

Perhaps the phrase that is central to the entire structured programming revolution was "ego-less programming." It implied an environment where each person's contribution was not judged, but taken as part of the team's effort toward a single goal. In football, a running back can't gain 100 yards per game without excellent offensive linemen. In politics, progress can't be made without a network of supporters. Even in love, it takes two to make it work.

The only person who seems to be a loner in the whole system development process is the manager. Because of the difference in their jobs, the technician sees the manager as someone apart. Managers, by virtue of their rank and status, may delude themselves into thinking that they are different. In truth, an ego-less manager can have a beneficial effect on the entire organization. By participating in quality circles, the manager can become part of the team, rather than its leader. By using more Zen-like management styles, the manager can improve information flow in the group. An ego-less manager seeks criticism and acts to improve his or her management style.

If you are willing to undergo the shocks that programmers and analysts go through when they first encounter a walk-through, try the following experiment. Have your subordinates evaluate you with your existing performance review mechanism. Have the reviews typed and submitted anonymously. Subordinates have typically worked for enough managers to know good from bad styles. They may point out areas in which you are weak. If all of the reviews turn out to be terribly negative, you are the major problem affecting productivity in your project. If not, then you still have some ideas about how to improve your management style. What should you do?

Group the problems that occur most frequently in the reviews according to priority. Hold a group meeting to discuss them and ways in which you intend to improve. Write yourself an MBO to improve measurably in each of the areas mentioned. Ask your people to help you improve in those areas. Ask them to correct you when you exhibit negative traits. This will be one of the most soul-searching experiences of your life and one of the best.

As managers we can get caught up in the rigmarole of budgets and politics and miss the humanistic side of our jobs. Becoming a member of the team is one of the major steps you can take to improve productivity.

1.9. Technology

America's work force first shifted from agricultural to manufacturing jobs, then from manufacturing to service-related jobs. Women began entering the job market in large numbers in 1960 and currently make up over 45% of the work force. There has also been a shift from blue collar to white collar jobs as the result of the development of a service economy.

Data processing, to date, has focused on mechanizing repetitive clerical jobs. As these jobs phase out, people are retrained to handle more technical white collar jobs. White collar workers include not only management, but also technical and professional people. These jobs have fewer repetitive tasks and more variable or decision-oriented tasks. Unfortunately, these are predominantly unmechanized.

Today, software vendors are turning their sights on the white collar market. Improvements of 15% are possible with a minimal investment. What are some of the systems they propose? They include office automation, decision support systems, on-line inquiry, and reporting systems designed to help answer those "what if" questions in a timely manner.

1.9.1. Office Automation.   Office automation includes the domain of electronic mail to improve communications, word processing to improve written communications, graphics to improve visual communication, teleconferencing to reduce the need for meetings, and inquiry reporting systems to simplify information retrieval. These are described in Chapter 3.

1.9.2. Decision Support Systems (DSS).   The new nonprocedural languages will begin to fill the void for "what if" software development. Management will find that they can extract decision-making data and then summarize or recombine it into information to answer their varied questions. Nonprocedural languages provide this capability for rapid change and analysis. As more becomes known about mechanizing management tasks, more off-the-shelf software will rise up to fill the void that currently exists. Decision support systems will transform corporate data into varied media, including reports and graphics. Subjective decisions will be reinforced by collected data. Management will finally have tools to speed up the decision-making process.

Selecting and implementing these products to advance your management into the office of the future will require dedication and a substantial investment, but think of the returns from improved productivity and the quality of decision making: your company may be able to run away from your competition, capturing larger market shares. The opportunities outweigh all of the risks.

2. ORGANIZATION

Organization can either improve productivity or impede it. There are two major types of organizations, hierarchical and matrix. Each has major advantages and often subtle disadvantages. The organizational hierarchy, shown in Figure 5.1, represents a typical way of organizing a development or maintenance group. Every employee has only one superior, simplifying work priorities and lines of responsibility. It also reduces the lines of communication among personnel, so communication failures become easy to trace. On the other hand, intergroup communication becomes more difficult. Information must travel the length of the hierarchy to be conveyed; rather than traversing just two people, it may take four or more. Less obvious problems deal with leveling the work throughout the entire project. If programmer A has no work, it is doubtful that some other project leader can obtain his or her services to fill a resource gap. Idle employees waste the company's time and do little to improve productivity.

The matrix organization shown in Figure 5.2 provides an environment where every person works either directly or indirectly with everyone else in the project. This organization mimics Japanese management philosophies that provide for enhanced lateral and vertical communication. A programmer may work with many systems analysts, providing avenues for sharing design and development philosophies. Given a broader view, even a programmer may spot deficiencies in the system design that would cause significant redevelopment. Similarly, systems analysts may work with several project managers, and so on. The idea of a matrix organization is to maximize the productivity of its personnel by allowing flexible resource management. Programmer A can work for two or more systems analysts. Working with only one analyst, the programmer may encounter slack periods, waiting for the analyst to finish a design. Working with several, no such delays should be encountered. Also, having several projects going at once gives the programmer an opportunity to balance one's own work load. Projects can be alternated while waiting for a test or just to relieve the boredom of a single task.

The matrix organization, however, does increase the lines of communication among employees. It becomes difficult to identify roadblocks or information failures. The proper combination of a matrix and hierarchy organization holds these negative factors in check.

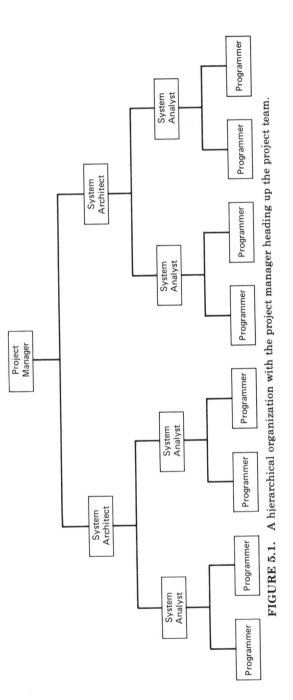

FIGURE 5.1. A hierarchical organization with the project manager heading up the project team.

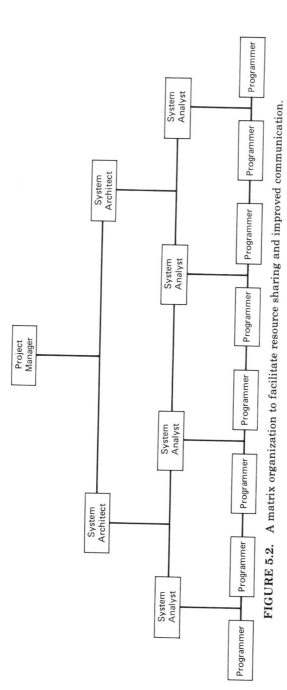

FIGURE 5.2. A matrix organization to facilitate resource sharing and improved communication.

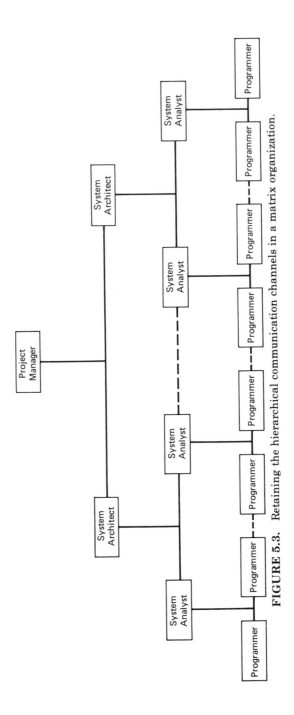

FIGURE 5.3. Retaining the hierarchical communication channels in a matrix organization.

The solid lines in Figure 5.3 show how the hierarchy can be maintained in the matrix organization, but requires a few additional lines for information transfer. Composed in this way, a programmer or analyst may belong to several project teams and work with several superiors. This structure may seem chaotic, but the improvement in dialogue, employee skills, and employee productivity will override the problems experienced.

2.1. Project Managers

The hierarchy and the matrix organization both need some central figure guiding its progress—the project manager. Typically a member of the client department, this person directs system development from both sides of the fence, setting up project teams that cross departmental boundaries—pulling together project leaders, analysts, and programmers from both the client and Data Processing departments to form specialized work groups.

2.2. Architects

The personnel directly under the project manager are the system architects. They have the overall responsibility for high-level system design. Architects should later become project leaders for subsystem development. The architectural team should consist of only one or two people to minimize definition and design problems that occur in larger teams. In a maintenance group, architects typically know the system from one end to the other and are often the best equipped to identify programs that will be affected by proposed changes. These people are also the hardest to release for new projects because they are so invaluable.

2.3. Project Teams

Project teams are people placed into work groups that tackle specific portions of the system. In either development or maintenance, these people have responsibility for a subsystem or program. A project team is typically a hierarchy, with the project leader at the top, then the analysts and programmers. In a matrix organization, these hierarchies may overlap other similar organizations that have responsibilities for other programs or subsystems. A typical system development effort should include a project team to develop standards and work procedures.

Project teams help satisfy the programmer's need for socializing and recognition at work. Working in several teams, which is possible in the matrix organization, expands their social interaction and provides a sense of unity. Project teams also improve quality through the use of walk-throughs and a common responsibility to produce an optimal system.

2.4. System Testing

A project team of special interest is the system testing team. In a typical development project, with a matrix organization, the testing group can be formed from members of the development staff. Without the typical hierarchical barriers, people can rotate through this team to support better testing and career development.

2.5. Quality Assurance

Quality Assurance teams can consist of existing project members of autonomous external groups. As an external group, QA may encounter problems in being accepted. As an internal team, however, they become a part of the team and are less likely to encounter resistance. Personnel can also rotate through this group, providing a better understanding of quality and how to achieve it.

3. SUMMARY

Management and organization constitute two important means of improving productivity and quality at a nominal cost to the company. Theory Z management styles, matrix organization, and management tools can enhance the productivity of data processing personnel by making managers more effective, providing a better work environment with fewer roadblocks, and by organizing to allow creative resource management. Emphasizing long-term rather than short-term profitability can keep a DP department competitive with other firms. Emphasis on short-term profits can hinder a DP department and adversely affect a company's long-term economic survival and ability to compete, by forcing the use of archaic computer systems and hardware.

As a manager, you owe it to your company and personnel to innovate continually, improve your management style, and upgrade departmental organization. The company benefits from improved information systems; you benefit from your people's improved performance; and your people benefit from working in a climate more to their liking. Best of all, these productivity improvements come from a low-cost solution that involves merely changing your attitudes and style of management. What could be better than that?

CHAPTER SIX

Software Metrics

One of the keys to improving productivity and quality is the ability to measure them. Software metrics provide a yardstick of system quality and project productivity. Without quantitative and qualitative measurements, you can't tell if your developing system is a lemon or a well-oiled machine. Furthermore, when it is operational you won't be able to tell what makes it a lemon or such an engineering marvel. You won't know where or what to fix, or how to recreate the excellence of a previous system. You'll be no better off than blind men trying to describe an elephant.

The reliability of systems and their maintainability are the two most important indicators of software quality. Automated measurement of software provides the only means to quantify and describe these important metrics. Without the ability to measure software quality, you cannot improve it to reduce costs and increase productivity.

Without tools to measure software quality, quality assurance and auditing functions will be hindered in examining all of the software developed. Clerical analysis of the source code is virtually impossible.

1. WHY MEASURE PRODUCTIVITY AND QUALITY?

How does a system get to be a year late? One day at a time.
                                        Frederick P. Brooks

Measuring programming productivity is not a way to evaluate programmers, but it is a means of quantifying the project's progress and the quality of the resulting designs and code. Once you can measure analyst and programmer productivity, it is easier to identify and correct roadblocks and bottlenecks that impede progress. Correcting problems early in the development process prevents schedule slippages and reduces costs.

In the past, measuring program quality was highly subjective: you could only hope that your people would design and build high-quality programs. But how could you expect a programmer to write a good program if you couldn't even describe one? By evaluating source code, you can determine the future reliability of the program and its ability to be maintained. You can also tell how easily you can enhance it, you will be able to define the code and coding techniques that provide quality in software. With the information metrics provide, you can identify maintenance-prone programs before they are even tested, then decide whether to rewrite the module or to proceed. Since coding is only 10–20% of the development cost, rewriting will be cheaper in the long run.

Metrics can also anticipate overall program quality based on documentation, maintainability, and reliability. When working with an outside vendor, metrics can provide quantifiable contract objectives. Without measurable objectives, you will never know what kind of a system the vendor is delivering.

2. HOW TO MEASURE PROGRAMMER/ANALYST PRODUCTIVITY AND QUALITY

Criticism comes easier than craftsmanship.
Zeuxis (ca. 400 BC)

Programmers and analysts keep saying that programming is an act of creation. If programming is art, how can you measure it? How do you tell a Picasso from a kindergarten original, a Ferrari from an Edsel, a Matisse from a lump of clay? With art, you evaluate its form, color, and design, from which you make value judgments. You can do the same with programs. Fortunately, software quality is more easily defined than art.

Since the arrival of structured programming, the industry has begun to quantify the "art" of programming: modularity is good; the absence of GO TOs is good. What was once considered art is now considered a science, and science must be measurable. Only the design task retains traces of artistic ability, but the generic program designs identified in Chapter 2 point out the fallacy of considering system analysis as art. General Motors would not completely redesign a six-passenger car; they would use existing, tested designs and components, changing only body styles and options. That is what you should be doing with programs, designs, and code. Instead, most programmers and analysts redesign the wheels, engine, frame, and suspension. Now you have a Ferrari, but it's always in the shop for repairs.

Programming is approaching the "software factory" concept, where program modules are the engines, tires, and transmissions produced; design documents are the blueprints; and operational documents are the shop repair manuals. In the software factory, analysts design while programmers manufacture and repair software systems. Analysts no longer create—they manufacture, and quality control is an important part of that process. Software metrics help provide that quality assurance.

There are three types of software metrics: those that predict software quality, those that actually test the quality, and those that indicate the productivity of the development and maintenance process. These metrics can be obtained from static analysis of documentation or source code, or from testing and maintenance histories of the program or system. Some of these metrics can be easily mechanized and some can't. Because of the enormous amount of source code in the corporation, manual analysis won't work; you should automate wherever possible. The question is how.

The key to any measurement process is the capture of data when they are readily available. Predictive quality metrics can be obtained during the definition, design, and programming phases of the development cycle by tracking errors and automating document and source code analysis.

The testing, conversion, and production phases of the project supply metrics of realized quality—actual quality measurements—for validation of the predictive metrics. The comparison of actual to expected quality gives you data to validate and revise your predictive metrics.

Those who speak most of progress measure it by quantity and not quality.

                                                    George Santayana

The hardest thing to measure is software production. At least when Detroit produces cars, they know how many were produced, what kinds, and so on. Comparatively, you know nothing. System development productivity equates to some function of the amount of documentation, the number of executable lines of code, and the design complexity, divided by the actual resources used. Understanding what these productivity measures mean is often difficult and may even be harmful. Productivity is the least important measurement you can derive; take care of software quality and the productivity problems will take care of themselves.

2.1. Applying Software Metrics to Documentation

If you mechanize documentation, as described in Chapter 3, it is possible to estimate the quality of the system and program designs. Creation of a unique design from a generic program design implies that the program's logic structure is sound and well tested, leaving only the application code suspect. Using design prototypes improves the resulting system's maintenance.

From a productivity standpoint, design walk-throughs should not be concerned with generic logic, only with the data transformations. Half of the time usually spent in walk-throughs is saved. Before the design walk-through, the analyst completes the skeletal design. Mechanized documentation makes it possible for the machine to examine the size and readability of the resulting document. To perform this function, the machine must be able to count the number of words, sentences, and pages in the document. The UNIX™ system can do this by means of the "wc" command or "lex," the lexical analyzer. Word, sentence, and page counts provide information about the size of the design and should correlate with the effort required to develop the program. For example, a two-page design for a 1000-line program is obviously insufficient, while 60 pages for a 50-line module is also counterproductive. Figure 6.1 shows the relationship of the amount of documentation to implementation productivity. Too little documentation leads to redesign and program rework; too much documentation confuses the programmer. The more paperwork programmers wade through, the more muck they stir up, until the design becomes totally obscured.

2.1.1. English: The Least Understood Programming Language. Once you know the size of the document, you will want to

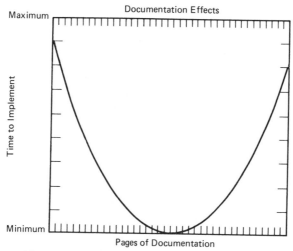

FIGURE 6.1. The effects of too little or too much documentation on program development time.

know how easy it is to read. How often have you started to read something and stopped because you had problems understanding it, or just got bored? Poorly written documents hinder productivity and cause errors during system implementation. If you want to improve productivity and quality, start measuring your definition, design, and run documents. But how do you measure a document? Using facilities such as spelling checkers, fog index calculations, differential comparison programs, and grammatical analyzers, your computer can examine the document for errors and readability, improving your productivity and document quality.

2.1.2. Spelling.

Important letters that contain no errors will develop errors in the mail.

Spelling programs check the document for spelling errors. This command improves the writer's productivity 5% by decreasing the time required for proofreading. If your programmers are as unconcerned about spelling as most are, this tool is an invaluable aid for them. Spelling also affects readers' productivity; misspelled words cause readers to reread, mentally correct the word in error, and start reading again. In the process, they can lose the meaning of a sentence or paragraph. This communication breakdown causes errors.

2.1.3. Fog Index. To discern how easily a document can be read, you can use the fog index (Gunning 1963). You will have to create this command yourself. It not only improves the writing skills of current designers, but also improves the productivity of the poor souls who have to read the maintenance and design documents. The fog index examines written text to predict the educational level required to understand the document, using the following equation:

$$\left(\frac{\text{number of words}}{\text{number of sentences}} + \frac{\text{number of words} > 3 \text{ syllables}}{\text{number of words}} \right) \times 0.4$$

Typically, the lower the reading level, the more straightforward and understandable the design. Most classical literature rates between a seventh and eighth grade reading level. The Bible tests out at six to seven. Unfortunately, technicians will write at level 12 or above. This kind of primal chest-beating is meant to convey one's technical ability rather than understandable information. Bad writing spells disaster for system implementation and maintenance.

Your fog index command should identify all three-syllable (or greater) words that might be replaced with less confusing words. It should also indicate sentences that are too long (more than 20 words per sentence). With proper feedback, analysts can hone their writing skills, eliminating counterproductive "fog."

2.1.4. English Grammar Analysis.

Some errors will go unnoticed until the book is in print.

Grammatical tools that will eventually help every child learn to write and every adult to write well are currently being developed. These tools examine each sentence syntactically for grammatical correctness and they identify errors. Since the computer does all of the proofreading, the writer's task is simplified. More importantly, the writer improves the document before it is released, simplifying the reader's job. Since they do not have to stop to reread and mentally correct bad grammar, readers will grasp the content quickly and without error. Grammatical analysis helps prevent misinterpretations, the enemy of the correct translation of the designs into code.

2.1.5. Identifying Changed Information. During system development, definition and design documents change daily. Finding these changes is often a monumental task, since there is no clear indication of what was revised. To solve this problem, comparison commands exist to mark each modified line in the document. Since the computer identifies the changed lines, the reader has only to read the marked sentences, not the entire document, thereby improving his or her productivity. The programmer is also less likely to overlook embedded changes, preventing incorrect coding of the design. Commands such as these minimize the amount of information a programmer reads or misreads, dramatically affecting the overall project productivity and quality.

2.1.6. Document Change Control.

Those who cannot remember the past are condemned to repeat it.

George Santayana

If you keep documents under change control, you can track errors that can be prevented in future designs. If a user adds a two-line change that causes two months of rework, you can nail him with it when he wants to know why you're late. If a design error causes rework, you can prevent it from happening in future systems. Definition and design documents make or break a system; errors in either stay with the system indefinitely. Control them, and you gain control of the 40% of the development process normally occupied by definition and design. Chapter 2 describes change control in detail. Only by mechanizing your documentation and storing a copy of each revision can you hope to begin to measure it. Otherwise, you're stuck with an impossible clerical task and excessive costs. Mechanized control of documents provides a base for measurements, and metrics will lead to productivity and quality improvements.

2.1.7. Quality Assurance.
If you empower a QA group, these automated tools can improve their productivity measurably. They insure that poor designs and definitions are not allowed into the development arena.

2.1.8. Management.
These writing tools can help even managers. You can identify people with writing weaknesses and improve their skills with proper training. The whole project will benefit from clear and concise documentation.

2.2. *Applying Software Metrics to Source Code*

Program quality measurement is an extremely beneficial tool for management. Measurements indicate potentially high-cost, maintenance-prone programs during their development, allowing recoding at a fraction of the cost of testing and implementing the original.

Metrics will also identify maintenance-prone programs that are already in production. These metrics, combined with the program's maintenance history, can build a case for rewriting the program to improve its ability to be maintained, thereby reducing costs. Since maintenance consumes 50–80% of your budget, software metrics provide significant productivity improvements at the minor expense of a program rewrite.

2.2.1. Automated Measurement.   Much has been said about measuring code, but little has been done about it. It is easy to measure programs and predict their behavior and cost by analyzing source code. For this purpose, we will only look at COBOL, although the measurement theory crosses all language barriers.

First of all, you must look at the language's procedural statements. In all programming languages, there are the following kinds of statement:

Decision: IF-THEN-ELSE, CASE, DOWHILE, and DOUNTIL
Functions: SORT, MERGE, CALL, PERFORM, SEARCH, and
COMPUTE . . .
Data Transformation: MOVE, ADD, DIVIDE . . .
Input/Output: READ, WRITE, OPEN, CLOSE . . .
Entry/Exit: ENTRY, GOBACK, STOP RUN

To analyze programs, the computer must count these statements as they occur in your program. This counting may be done with any string-oriented language. On IBM, the COBOL INSPECT verb will count occurrences of character strings such as "IF," "PERFORM," and "SORT." On UNIX™, the lexical analyzer provides more efficient and maintainable metrics.

2.2.2. Lines of Code.   Your first task is to write a program that counts all occurrences of COBOL's reserved words. You will find an initial version of this program in Appendix C. With this program in hand, you can derive low-level quality metrics that can be combined to provide management with information never before dreamed possible.

There are two basic lines of code (LOC) measurements: total and executable lines of code. Total lines of code includes every line in the module—comments, data declarations, you name it. Executable lines of code (ELOC) counts only COBOL's verbs—statements that *do* something. Total lines of code varies so radically that it is virtually worthless as a measurement. Figure 6.2 shows two versions of the same "IF" statement. The structured version has four times as many lines of code as the unstructured version, but provides no more work than the single line. It is more readable, however. Executable lines of code, on the other hand, counts only the action verbs. Figure 6.2 shows three COBOL verbs in each example; whether structured or unstructured, each version gives the same measurement. ELOC provides the only valid measure of coding productivity currently available.

Taking a measurement changes the system being measured.

Programmers will tend to maximize whatever is being measured.

Measuring programmers on the production of ELOC has a few drawbacks. Programmers will tend to meet whatever standard you set—not more, not less. If you want more lines of code, you'll get them. With any kind of on-line editor, they can reproduce hundreds of executable statements that execute the same instruction redundantly. Their productivity looks good and the program runs twice as long.

So unless you want to use up every ounce of computer resource you own, don't measure programmers, only their programs. Use productivity measures to identify and eliminate bottlenecks and roadblocks in the development process. Besides primitive productivity measurements, ELOC helps determine program's quality.

```
IF A > B THEN MOVE A TO B ELSE MOVE B TO A.

IF A > B THEN

    MOVE A TO B

ELSE

    MOVE B TO A.
```

FIGURE 6.2. A comparison of total lines of code measurements to executable lines of code measurements. The executable lines of code are more reliable.

A total of all executable statements (IF, MOVE, etc.) gives a good indication of the program's actual size and the potential "modularity." Don't include comments or unexecutable lines in the identification, environment, data, or procedure divisions in this count. See Figure 6.2.

People will complain that ELOC is not a good productivity measure because it penalizes high-level languages. Assembler language programmers produce five statements to a COBOL programmer's one. But you should not compare COBOL to assembler language; they are as different as night and day or apples and oranges. If you compare COBOL programs only to other COBOL programs, and PL/1 to PL/1, then ELOC will provide a stable comparison tool.

To compare programs based on their metrics, you must first normalize the numbers with respect to a common base. Total lines of code and ELOC provide this base. ELOC, divided by either 100 or 50, gives a ruler by which other metric totals are judged. Fifty and 100 are proposed limits for a program module's size. Fifty is Yourdon's magic number, while I have found 100 to be reasonable. These numbers are only proposed, not required limits; exceptions will be noted as they are uncovered. This metric is referred to as "C-LOC," the hundreds of ELOC in the program.

2.2.3. Decision Counts. The sum of the IF, PERFORM UNTIL, PERFORM TIMES, and SEARCH WHEN counts gives the total number of decisions in the module, a basic measure of program complexity and testability. This count, when divided by C-LOC, gives a metric known as decision density—that is, the number of decisions in each 100 lines of code. Decision density is a highly representative measure of complexity, the cruel task master of maintenance programming.

To understand why decision density is a measure of complexity, it is necessary to refer to a technique called "vector analysis." Vector analysis, as described in Chapter 2, indicates the number of unique paths through the code graphically. The number of paths is based on the number of decisions in a module. There is a minimum of two paths for each decision. Therefore, the more decisions a program contains, the more paths there are to test. These additional paths through the code make it harder for a programmer to follow the logic, so maintenance costs increase in proportion to the decision density.

A rule of thumb is that if the decision density exceeds 10, the program is probably too complex. Programs with a low decision density are more reliable and easier to maintain. Programs under 100 ELOC, with a high decision density, however, are still easily maintained, since the code is contained on one or two pages. For programs larger than 100 ELOC, however, repair times increase exponentially with the ELOC and decision density, as shown in Figure 2.7.

Using ELOC and decision density, a manager can predict the expected testing and maintenance costs for a program and choose objectively among rewriting the code to make maintenance easier or continuing. It is less expensive to break a module into smaller, more maintainable pieces. Since maintainability is inherent in delivered systems, and maintenance costs are 50-80% of the typical DP budget, you have an opportunity to identify and correct these problems before releasing a system. Coding takes only 10-20% of the system's development time. Since the rewrite takes less time than the original effort, significant testing and maintenance costs can be saved for a minor expenditure. From a humanistic viewpoint, the programmer's ego is battered when confronted with these stylistic problems, but the same errors will never be repeated. That's what egoless programming is all about.

2.2.4. Functions. The sum of all of the CALL, PERFORM, SORT, MERGE, COMPUTE, INSPECT, and GENERATE statements gives the total number of functions in a program. A single function can describe several hundred lines of tested code. Many functions are implemented by the compiler so they are typically reliable. The concision of function statements aids the maintenance programmer's productivity by making code simple and easy to understand. For example, it is easier to understand one CALL or PERFORM than several hundred lines of code. Functions also imply modularity, which in turn implies reliability and ease of maintenance. Modularity also indicates how easily a program can be enhanced—its flexibility.

The total number of functions divided by C-LOC gives a metric called "program level" or "function density," the number of functions per 100 lines of code. The higher the program level, the more functional and modular the program. For example, a driver module calls modules that do the actual work and should therefore have a high program level. Because the submodules perform unique functions, they should have lower ones. If, for some reason, a high-level module doesn't score well, you can identify and correct it before testing. Once again, coding comprises only 20% of the development cost, while testing accounts for 40%. A great deal of time may be saved by recoding.

2.2.5. Data Transformations. Data transformations include statements such as MOVE, ADD, and COMPUTE. They do not tell much about the program when considered by themselves, but in concert with other measures, they indicate potentially error-prone code and efficiency problems. Identifying and eliminating these problems will save you overtime and computer costs. For example, if a program has a low decision density, a low program level, and 350 MOVE statements, it may still be highly reliable, maintainable, and flexible. MOVE statements are fairly easy to maintain. On the other hand, if a program has 10 DIVIDE statements and no IF statements, then the program has no checks for zero divide errors—a common problem. If the program has many arithmetic statements but few packed decimal or binary data definition clauses (COMP, COMP-3), some efficiency questions have been overlooked. "SEARCH" versus "SEARCH ALL" efficiencies may also be noted.

2.2.6. Input/Output Count. Counts of input and output statements may show inefficiencies, such as multiple OPEN and CLOSE statements. They may also show multiple READ or WRITE statements for the same file, a common source of errors. READ INTO and WRITE FROM statements indicate the use of working storage, rather than buffer manipulation. Manipulating data in buffers is another source of error.

The total number of files in a program gives an additional complexity measure. As the number of files exceeds two (one input and one output), the program's complexity also increases.

2.2.7. Comment Count. The number of comment lines divided by the total lines of code in the program gives an idea of the program's self-documentation. Too many comments tend to obscure the code, but too few do not necessarily imply poor readability. Some programs need no comments; they are perfectly understandable. Others, with extensive comments, are sometimes incomprehensible.

2.2.8. Entry and Exit Count. Counts of the ENTRY, GOBACK, and STOP RUN clauses tell whether the program is single-entry and single-exit. If not, it is probably not well structured and should be examined. Only "informational strength" modules should have more than one entry and exit.

2.2.9. SKIP and EJECT Counts. SKIP and EJECT statements are the sentences and paragraphs of programming. They separate activities and make the program more readable. Using SKIPs before each decision helps make the decision stand out. EJECTs help separate performed paragraphs. If programs are easy to read, they will be easier to maintain.

2.3. Software Quality Criteria

Software criteria represent measurements taken during the development process. Some of these come from manual measurements, others from automated code measurement. These combine to produce software quality metrics. The criteria derived from the basic software measurements are as follows.

Auditability	Software attributes that provide for easy auditing of the software, data and results—integrity. The existence of SECURITY statements and your own auditing code will provide this criterion (manual and mechanized measurement).
Accuracy	Software attributes that provide precision in calculations and outputs—reliability. The presence of OVERFLOW and REMAINDER reserved words measures accuracy (mechanized measurement).
Communication Commonality	Software attributes that use standard protocols and interface routines—interoperability. Use of standard interfaces to your real-time system will provide commonality (mechanized measurement).
Completeness	Software attributes that provide full implementation of the functions required—correctness (manual and mechanized measurement).
Concision	Software attributes that implement a function in the minimum amount of code—maintainability (mechanized measurement). The presence of vendor-supported functions and subroutines indicates concision. The use of the CALL, PERFORM, COMPUTE, SORT, MERGE, GENERATE, and

other functional statements also provides concise implementations of the code.

Consistency
Software attributes that provide uniform design and implementation techniques and documentation—correctness, maintainability, reliability (manual and mechanized measurement). The use of standard design and coding techniques provides consistency. The use of generic program designs and programs also increases consistency.

Data Commonality
Software attributes that provide standard data representations—interoperability. Use of the COBOL COPY statement provides commonality (mechanized measurement).

Error Tolerance
Software attributes that provide continuity of operation under adverse conditions—reliability. Use of the OVERFLOW statement and data edits on numeric fields provides some error tolerance (manual and mechanized measurement).

Execution Efficiency
Software attributes that minimize processing time—efficiency. The use of packed decimal and binary data items provides some efficiencies. The use of binary searches also indicates efficiency. There are many more coding efficiencies that are machine- and installation-dependent (mechanized measurement).

Expandability
Software attributes that provide for expansion of the data or program functions—flexibility. The use of modularity, structured coding techniques, single-entry/single-exit, and local standard subroutines indicates expandability. The use of functions and subroutines also provides for program expansion (mechanized measurement).

Generality
Software attributes that expand the usefulness of the function beyond the existing module—flexibility, reusability, generality and expandability use the same basic measurements to predict whether a module can be reused. Generality also includes common code usage via COPY statements (manual and mechanized measurement).

Instrumentation	Software attributes that provide for measurements of usage or identification of errors—testability. Some compilers allow the addition of testing statements that are "turned on" as a function of the compiler parameters. The presence of these facilities in the code speaks to the code's instrumentation (mechanized measurement).
Machine Independendence	Software attributes that determine its dependence on the hardware—portability, reusability. The use of IBM's Report Writer feature of COBOL would indicate machine dependence. The use of ANSII standard language constructs would indicate machine independence (mechanized measurement).
Modularity	Software attributes that provide a structure of highly independent modules—flexibility, interoperability, maintainability, portability, reusability, testability. Single-entry and single-exit statements, 50–100 ELOC, use of CALL functions, and use of elementary variables as parameters in CALL statements indicate modularity (mechanized measurement).
Operability	Software attributes that determine the ease or difficulty of operation of the software—usability. The use of installation standard subroutines to insure adequate operational flexibility provides operability (manual and mechanized measurement).
Security	Software attributes that provide for control of the accessibility of the software and its data—integrity (manual and mechanized measurement).
Self-Documentation	Software attributes that explain the function of the software—flexibility, maintainability, portability, reusability, testability. The presence and density of comments in the program provide self-documentation (mechanized measurement).
Simplicity	Software attributes that provide implementation of the functions in the most understandable manner—maintainability, reliability, testabili-

ty. The presence of compiler functions and the use of CALL or perform statements indicate simplicity. A low number of decisions also indicates simplicity (mechanized measurement).

Software System Independence
: Software attributes that determine its dependence on the software environment (extensions of the language, operating system, data base management system, etc.)—portability, reusability. Systems written in assembler language depend heavily on the operating system to implement their functions. Higher level languages have no such restrictions. All languages are dependent on the operating system for input and output routines. The presence or absence of I/O can indicate software independence (mechanized measurement).

Traceability
: Software attributes that provide a link from the requirements to the implementation—correctness (mechanized measurement).

Training
: Software attributes that provide transition from the current environment to the new environment—usability (manual measurement).

2.4. Software Quality Metrics

One man's error is another man's data.

The following terms describe software quality.

Correctness
: The degree to which a program satisfies the user's specifications. (Does it do what you want?)

Efficiency
: The amount of computing resources required to perform a user-defined function. (Does it run on your hardware as well as it can?)

Flexibility
: Effort required to enhance the program. (Can you change it?) Flexibility is a function of modularity and generality.

Integrity
: How well the software and data are protected from security breaches. (Is it controlled or secure?)

Interoperability	Effort necessary to couple this program or system to another. (Will it interface well with other systems?)
Maintainability	Effort required to locate and repair errors in the program. (Can you fix it?) Maintainability is a function of the decision density, program level, modularity, ELOC, comments, and documentation.
Portability	Effort required to transfer the program from one machine environment to another. (Will it run on either your minis or mainframes?)
Reliability	The degree to which the program can be expected to perform its function without failure. (Does it work accurately all of the time without failure?) Reliability depends on accuracy, consistency, error tolerance, modularity, and simplicity.
Reusability	The extent to which the module or program can be used in other applications. (Can it be partially or completely reused in other programs or systems to save development costs?) Reusability is a function of generality, modularity, software independence, and self-documentation of the program.
Testability	Effort required to test structurally and insure correctness. (Can you test it?) Testability depends on decision density, program level, modularity, and comments.
Usability	Effort required to learn, operate, and use system input and output. (Can the computer center run it? Can the user operate it easily?)

Some of these metrics are interrelated, such as flexibility and maintainability. Others, such as reliability and efficiency, are independent. The interrelation or independence of these metrics results from the criteria used to produce them.

As you gain experience with the use of your basic metrics, you will learn how to apply them to the creation of metric criteria and quality metrics. The mathematics to correlate each basic measure to observed is complex, requiring regression analysis. This analysis provides weighting values for each measurement you take. Find the statistician in your company and apply these weights to build your management metrics.

Software measurement is evolving. It can help you quantify what qualities you want in a developing system and how to measure them. The first point you need to consider in assessing the quality of the ultimate program is the design.

2.5. *Design Analysis*

A program should be coded toward a specific goal. On-line data entry programs for hundreds of users should be efficient, reliable, and maintainable. Big data crunchers may need to be efficient but not necessarily highly maintainable. By quantifying program quality, your programmers will know what is expected of them. Knowing what qualities are required makes programming towards those goals easier. Knowing they will be measured invokes the Hawthorne effect: people always perform better when they know they are being observed.

When building a new system, the first problem is to identify the important software qualities. The next problem is how to specify them in the requirements. As the developing system evolves, the need to determine how well it satisfies those requirements arises.

Each software system will be unique in its quality requirements. Several basic system characteristics affect the quality requirements and must be evaluated before specifying the requirements.

1. The system will affect human lives (automatic pilot software). Reliability, correctness, and testability are the most important quality factors. Would you fly in an aircraft having software tested to the same degree as your application program's?

2. The system must be flexible, maintainable, and portable. A system that will live more than two years must change and evolve with the organization or it will cause more harm than benefit.

3. Real-time systems must be efficient, reliable, correct, and usable. If you have 400 users on-line, response time is critical, as is down time. For every minute the system is down, you lose 400 people-minutes, nearly seven hours. Furthermore, what if those 400 people are managers, inquiring about information to make critical decisions? The opportunities lost cannot be recovered.

4. Classified information or financial data must be protected and auditable. System integrity is the quality factor needed.

After initial evaluation of the relative importance of the quality factors, the manager must then evaluate the trade-offs between costs and quality. Maintainability and efficiency trade-offs are based on system requirements. Similarly, the cost to implement a system can be traded for lifetime cost savings. A more flexible, maintainable system may take longer to build, but the lifetime maintenance costs will be reduced.

It is the project manager's responsibility to make these evaluations and trade-offs. Software metrics serve as immediate feedback to allow pretest and prerelease adjustments to the system, thereby saving time and money.

Once you have established goals and programmers know how to meet them, automated measurement is the only way to insure the quality of the product. Then, as experience indicates how measures may be weighted and combined into more complex measures, software metrics will evolve into an even more significant management tool.

2.6. Maintenance Analysis

Software metrics help decrease maintenance costs. Evaluation of your existing programs will indicate specific programs that may be maintenance-prone, because of their decision density, lines of code, and program level. If historical trouble reports bear out these predictions, a program rewrite is called for. This rewrite should decrease the maintenance load for a reasonable initial cost.

Pareto's Rule states that 20% of all programs usually incur 80% of the maintenance costs. Finding and correcting this 20% means a substantial savings. If you were to reduce your maintenance costs by 50%, you would have all the people you need to start working on backlogged projects—projects that will help keep you ahead of your competition.

3. APPLYING SOFTWARE METRICS TO TESTING

One of the most important things you can do during testing is to track your errors. What kind were they? What caused them? Some of this error tracking can be completely automated, some must be performed manually. You can extract program failures from the system run messages. Some programs never fail; others seem to do so constantly. Program faults found in testing indicate the probability of failures in operation.

What kind of program faults are these? Failures occur from nonnumerical mathematical operations, subscripts getting out of range, dividing by zero, and so on. Tracking these types of flaws, you can develop walk-through checklists that will decrease these problems. You can develop standard error prevention code to check for nonnumerical fields and to check upper bounds on subscripts. You should also track errors that do not result in failures, such as rounding errors, misaligned data parameters, and improperly calculated results. This measurement quantifies the correctness of the program. Does it do what the user wants? These errors also indicate what kind of errors to expect in production.

You should also track how many times a module is tested. The number of tests should correlate with the number of errors found; otherwise your staff is failing to record errors properly. The number of tests should correlate with the time required to test the module. Track how long it takes to test a given module, program, and system. Correlate these figures with the predictive metrics previously discussed. Did the decision density correlate with how long it took to test? It should have. If the decision density was greater than 10 and only two tests were run on the module, the programmer may have overlooked some of test cases.

The vector analysis mentioned previously is a good method for developing structural test cases. But how do you insure that you got everything? It's easy with the help of some compilers and program observation software. COBOL compilers, such as the CAPEX™ compiler, provide analyzer features that will track how the program runs. They count every time a line is executed. If a line was never executed, you don't have all the test cases you need. If a leg of the program is tested 50,000 times, you have more of that test case than needed; you can cut it down.

4. APPLYING SOFTWARE METRICS TO PROGRAM/ SOFTWARE RELEASES

Track errors found in production in the same way as you track testing errors. Does this tracking turn up different errors? It should, because processing volumes are so much greater. How do the errors found in production correlate with the errors found during testing? Errors found in production should occur in roughly the same density as the ones found during testing. If such is not the case, you have new errors to add to your checklists. If the same errors are found, you will know without exhaustive testing which programs are fairly error-free during testing. You'll also identify programs that should be inspected with a fine-toothed comb. The expenses of incurring a production error are far greater than the cost of correcting a program in testing.

Also track the number of times a program is transmitted into production between releases. If the program is transmitted several times for error corrections, it indicates either a poor maintenance staff or a bad program, either of which may be identified and corrected. It is the goal of all metrics to tune the process, providing cost benefits to the corporation and uninterrupted leisure time for the employee. I always hated 3 A.M. wake-up calls from the computer center. The Saturdays and Sundays I've spent working would add up to one hell of a vacation. Overtime is a financial drain on the company and an emotional drain on the employee; cut it down. Just by tracking what happens in testing and production, you will begin to indicate when and where to reduce these errors.

Tracking the errors that occur during testing provides the necessary measures of the program's quality. This process can be automated by summarizing the number of times a program is tested and the number of times it fails.

Never test for an error condition you don't know how to handle.

The number of times a programmer submits a job should correlate with the decision density previously calculated. Decision-dense programs should take longer to test exhaustively or should require more tests. Of course, if the programmer tests such a program only once and proclaims its correctness, I would have someone else look over the test cases and try it again.

The hidden flaw never remains hidden.

Programs that fail frequently during testing are likely to fail in production. Tom Gilb, in his book, *Software Metrics*, suggests that most errors will be found before release, but that the ones not found will be like others that were.

You can further automate the tracking of errors to keep up with such errors as incorrect calculations and invalid output. Gaining an in-depth knowledge of typical errors will help prevent future errors of the same kind. Develop walk-through checklists to find those punctuation errors or computational rounding errors. Better yet, develop a mechanized analysis program to ferret out these potential hazards. Remember, it costs you 10 times more to correct an error in testing than it would have cost during coding.

Keep track of how problems are solved and identify them as definition, design, or coding errors. If definition errors are creeping into your testing, something in the definition phase is rotten. The same holds true for the design phase. If the error is in definition, you might want to halt all activities and identify potentially related problems.

5. SUMMARY

The only lesson history has taught us is that man has not yet learned from history.

Software metrics are a tool to predict a program's performance and cost to the organization. They identify potential problem programs for correction. They cannot be used as a strict good-versus-bad measure since the objectives of each program may vary, but metrics can be used to see if a program has met its objectives. Knowing that their program will be measured tends to make programmers more conscientious. Knowing that their product will be measured, software houses will also be precise in meeting a system's criteria. Metrics can also be a productivity tool in the hands of a Quality Assurance group. Since metrics can only "predict" the quality of a product, they are not valid without actual inspection of the code, but they do automate the selection of programs to evaluate. Therein lies their worth.

An "art" cannot emerge as a science until there is a way to measure it. With the emergence of software metrics and their validation, the age of software engineering is upon us.

CHAPTER SEVEN

Reliability— What a Concept

If builders built buildings the way programmers wrote programs, the first woodpecker that came along would destroy civilization.

Computers are unreliable, but humans are even more unreliable; any system that depends on human reliability is unreliable.

What is reliability? To the programmer, reliability means getting a good night's sleep. To the manager, it means reduced overtime expenditures, less time spent fixing bugs, and more time spent productively enhancing the system or developing new systems. To the operations manager, it means fewer reruns and lower overtime. To the user, it means getting correct data, timely delivery, and lower costs for reruns. It improves business opportunities by providing timely information. Reliability is one of the cornerstones of an information system, a cornerstone we often try to add to the system after it has been built.

Reliability problems are responsible for much of the high cost of software, so improving programmer productivity can only partially reduce costs. Reliability will reduce your maintenance and testing costs. If your shop has the typical 75% maintenance, 25% development work mix, reliability may decrease your programming costs substantially. You must enhance productivity and find ways to produce a more precise product.

There are four ways to approach reliability.

1.   Plan for and install the cornerstone before the system is constructed.
2.   Have each program detect errors in the system's construction or operation, and report them.
3.   Have the system correct the errors it discovers.
4.   Allow certain errors to occur, but isolate them so that they cause little harm.

1.   BUILT-IN RELIABILITY

There's never time to do it right, but there's always time to do it over.

The best way to insure reliability is to plan for it and build it into every phase of development. Reliability begins not with coding, but with the first harsh cries of the user who needs some way to handle a task that has grown too complex. They start an enormous communication process among humans and machines that culminates in a software system. In these interactions lie the seeds of unreliability. The most onerous villains in the development process are these human connections.

The most immutable barrier in nature is between one man's thoughts and another's.

William James

At each exchange, a person must interpret what another is saying and translate that information into other products, such as designs and code. Because of the scope and ambiguity of the English language, the translation process often fails to discern the subtle nuances of the speaker's meaning. An error creeps in and reliability declines ever so slightly. Each error is so small as to go unnoticed, often for years. But multiply these small errors times the thousands, perhaps millions, of communications that occur in any development project and reliability flies out the window.

Although somewhat better, because of the restricted languages used, programmer and computer interfaces create another problem. The computer can only think logically, and since it is a software system, it is also somewhat unreliable. The programmer must translate the design into some foreign language called "code." As usual, when speaking a second language that is practiced infrequently, the translation leaves something to be desired. The best programmers think and speak in code when they converse with the machine.

A computer program does what you tell it to do, not what you want it to do.

Let's examine what happens when an average programmer begins a dialogue with the machine. The computer's operating system has been programmed in code to understand English-speaking people talking in ALC, FORTRAN, COBOL, PL/1, or whatever. It expects everything to be spelled out explicitly. Spoken English allows us to leave out words, phrases, and sentences because the listener will fill in the blanks. If the programmer leaves out a word, the computer edits with its binary pen and writes cryptic computer-speak messages at the end of the document, just as your freshman English teacher did. If the programmer leaves out a sentence, the computer thinks nothing of it, since it knows of no relationships among sentences. The programmer can leave out entire paragraphs and so long as they are not referred to elsewhere, the computer will not miss them. You can even tell a computer program to abort and it will unthinkingly commit suicide over the most trivial problem. How stupid can a thing be?

The programmer is faced with interpreting the errors produced and doing something about them. Like two people who speak on different planes, each explaining what they think the other said, the programmer tries to overcome a language barrier and work with the computer. Like some lovesick sailor in a foreign port, the programmer doggedly continues trying to get the computer to understand. At least the sailor can depend on sign language; the programmer has no such luck.

The programmer deals with compilers and testing aids, all of which have their own languages. No wonder testing is such a difficult process. Armed with several English–compiler, English–JCL, English–operating system language manuals, the programmer voyages into the world of the computer. It is like a five-day tour of eight countries.

Finally, when the program runs, it produces English-like reports. The language of the reports is often in that limbo between English and code that gives the programmer, analyst, user, auditors, and operations staff a new language to understand. New language cross-references spring up in the form of user guides, operations manuals, and so on.

You can probably appreciate now the problems that each human-human, human–machine, and machine–machine interaction can cause. Let's examine each interface point for ways to correct these problems.

1.1. User-Data Processing Interface

Complex problems have simple, easy-to-understand wrong answers.

The purpose of Newspeak . . . is to make all other modes of thought impossible.

George Orwell

The first major interface problem occurs when the user and the Data Processing group first meet. The user speaks in the tongue of his or her job, complete with acronyms and pat phrases that often mean a great deal more than they seem to. The DP types speak some cross between English and computer-speak, similar to George Orwell's Newspeak. The user often feels alienated, as if he or she has just stepped through the Twilight Zone into *1984*. The analyst, smug in his or her knowledge of the computer, assumes the position of superiority. The system architect may fail to understand all of the user's problem. Users may not adequately express their needs. Omissions affect the analyst's understanding, since the DP person cannot divine what is needed. The result is an error-ridden system. The question of how to get these two forces cooperating and understanding each other remains.

1.1.1. Methodology. Since both participants are human, let's fall back on English. Establishing a standard development process, as was recommended in Chapter 2, specifies the information the DP person needs at each phase to proceed in the interests of the user. Similarly, the user structures the information returned to the analysts at each phase. In this way, clear guidelines can evolve to eliminate errors in understanding, improving reliability.

1.1.2. Technology. Using a common office automation system for development and communication as described in Chapter 3 will improve the quality of written documentation and the quantity and quality of communications by means of electronic mail. The communication of information from the user to the DP staff will also be more timely. The users and analysts can ask and answer questions in hours instead of days. But how does this improve reliability?

Rather than impede their development, programmers and analysts will often make an assumption and continue development. Sometimes the question gets referred to the user, sometimes not. Each assumption provides an opportunity for error to creep in. Second-guessing the user's needs is a risky business. Providing a convenient method of requesting information and sending answers helps eliminate assumptions and improve reliability. Office automation also improves productivity, as was described in Chapter 3.

Mechanized systems can structure the evaluation of project feasibility, requirement specification, and testing validation. Requirement specification systems, such as PSL/PSA, are perhaps the most important systems to improve reliability. These mechanized systems insure that all facets of definition have been covered, thereby improving system reliability. Such systems further provide a common language to enable the user and DP to understand requirements. Since it is a structured language, and not English, incorrect interpretations are less likely—and fewer errors result.

Nonprocedural languages, in the hands of the user, further improve reliability and productivity. Users become the development staff: they know what they want and communicate only with the computer, not through a programmer or analyst. Since users are their own analysts, programmers, and testers, there are fewer possibilities for human–human translation errors. The DP department need only set up the user's data base.

1.1.3. Organization. Users should manage the project team. Their full-time dedication to the system through a project manager will give them better control of the project and serve to improve communications. The project manager, schooled in both user-oriented tasks and data processing, should act as an interpreter and solve many translation problems. This person also keeps track of development progress on both sides and can insure consistent development.

1.2. Project Team Interface

The project manager, system architects, system analysts, programmers, and system testing team must all interact. Each interface provides another avenue for unreliability to walk in and infect the system. Systems always change while under development. Failure to communicate changes introduces new design errors. Analysts have trouble interpreting the system architecture. Programmers have trouble interpreting program designs. In spite of these problems, there are ways to reduce the probability of error.

1.2.1. Methodology.

The phased development process structures the work in manageable pieces. The architects, analysts, programmers, and testers are responsible for specific products at each phase. Each of these products must adhere to specified standards that define the interface between each person in the development group. Without standards, analysts would have a hard time understanding what architects wanted. Similarly, programmers could not understand analysts, and so on. Walk-throughs, to inspect designs and code, would not be possible, since everyone would be doing his or her own thing. Standards also allow consistent communication between the group's members, eliminating misunderstandings caused by the form of the information presented. Once these problems of form are out of the way, development personnel can focus on the content of the information.

Generic program designs provide an avenue to both programmer productivity and reliability. First, system architects can view the application as groups of functions. Rather than getting into detail, the architect may anticipate the available generic designs and formulate the system as a combination of existing generic designs. The analyst will have less trouble understanding this generic architecture. The analyst should design only the transformation of the data passing through the system, thereby simplifying the design process and improving reliability. Generic designs should also be easily understood by programmers. Since they do not have several different analysts' writing styles to deal with, their comprehension increases. The programmers should also have generic, error-free code to match the designs. Even if generic errors are discovered later, it is easier to pinpoint and fix only the programs that contain the errant code than it is to analyze and fix perhaps 100 different implementations of the same design

Walk-throughs help detect translation errors in each of the implementation steps. System architecture can be reviewed by the systems analysts, provoking a dialogue between the system architects and the analysts that will reduce misunderstanding. Similarly, program and module designs can be reviewed by the programmers and analysts. The goal of these sessions is to reduce design complexity, thereby improving program reliability.

The generic concept can be extended to common subroutines that are needed for the system, and the analyst can reduce the coding necessary to complete the project. These common routines also tend to be better designed and tested than several unique versions, and they have only one specific interface, which is usually simple and easier to understand than several different ones. This simplification reduces complexity and improves reliability.

1.2.1.1. Structured Methodology. Structured design will reduce complexity by implementing smaller modules that are easier to comprehend. Modules designed in this fashion should be more functional and independent and should not have bizarre interfaces to other modules, so coding and testing will be easier because of their simplicity. Structured code is also more readable. Since the programmers have smaller modules to comprehend, maintenance will be easier and less costly.

1.2.1.2. Program Language Selection. Selecting a programming language can either improve or degrade reliability. Assembler language should not be used. COBOL, PL/1, and Pascal provide more suitable vehicles to implement structured coding. They are also supported with a wide variety of available compilers and diagnostic facilities. Because they are widely used, you will not have trouble finding programmers who know and understand the language.

High-level languages are also more portable than assembler language; if you ever decide to change hardware vendors, your coding effort will not be completely lost. High-level procedural and nonprocedural languages, especially the latter, provide more reliable human interfaces.

If you want to let users develop their own software, they will perform better and more reliably with nonprocedural languages. They are designed to cushion the user from the intricacies of the machine, keeping them from worrying about data types and all those little problems that plague the COBOL programmer.

Not until the program has been in production for at least six months will the most harmful error be discovered.

1.2.1.3. Software Metrics.   As was described in Chapter 6, static analyzers can scan the code, looking for potential reliability problems. To be programmed to look for them, the metric programs must anticipate possible errors. They can provide information only about known problems. From a quality standpoint, however, they overlook fewer errors than a human reading the same code. In the course of investigating other program metrics, you may also stumble over potentially unreliable code, so metrics will also produce benefits by focusing your attention on the code. Static measurement tools may continually expand as you find other common reliability problems; the final goal is zero-fail software.

1.2.1.4. Error Tracking.   Tracking each error that occurs in the design and development process can provide a useful history of the most common errors. Static analyzers can be constructed to look for these errors, or checklists can be developed to aid in walk-throughs of designs and code. Either way, typical errors can be caught easily and removed, leaving more time for in-depth analysis of the design or code for more complex errors. Tracking errors not only improves reliability but significantly improves productivity by reducing testing time and costs.

1.2.1.5. Change Management

The more innocuous the modification appears to be, the further its influence will extend and the more plans will have to be redrawn.

Systems change dramatically between their inception and death, and each change provides an opportunity for error to creep into the system. A change that is not well managed and implemented can seriously affect the reliability of the system. For these reasons, managing change is imperative to keep the system running smoothly. As described in Chapter 2, change management controls the when, where, why, and how of changing the system.

Often the simplest change has ripple effects throughout the system. Adequate change control covers system modifications and the impacts of each proposed change. Changes made at random or under pressure usually introduce more errors into the system than they remove. Change control should be invoked for definition and design documents, so that the design can be frozen on a certain date. The project team then has a solid document to work from, reducing the chance of misinterpretations or information loss caused by the constant change. The definition and designs can change, but the modifications to the entire system should be undertaken in a controlled fashion after the original has been completed. If the system is built from the top down, each incremental release into system testing can reflect the design changes.

One of the major reasons for project cost overruns is improper handling of system changes. The system's reliability suffers from the constant uncontrolled changes inflicted on its parts. By controlling maintenance and enhancements, you gain the ability to look at the overall picture of what needs to change. You can arrange work according to priority and fit it into the schedule. if the schedule needs to change to encompass the changes, an adequate case for schedule slippage can be built, using change tracking.

1.2.2. Technology. Programmers and analysts spend much of their time communicating. They spend time in meetings and walkthroughs and in discussing project problems informally. They ask for and receive information from others about the project. This information exchange can take upwards of 25% of their time. Electronic mail facilities can improve this communication, improving productivity, information flow, and reliability. Word processing systems make document changes easier, promoting an atmosphere conducive to change. Up-to-date documentation properly reflects the current system, allowing people to be brought on board quickly and correctly. Word processors also insure excellent documentation for the system maintainers. Better documentation means easier maintenance, fewer errors, and higher reliability. Word processing systems provide many other useful facilities. Spelling dictionaries take the worry out of proofreading documents, finding spelling errors that confuse the reader. Once you confuse the reader, you dilute the meaning of the document and cause translation errors to occur. Forthcoming software products will edit your document for English syntax errors, improving productivity and reducing information transfer errors. Metrics, such as the Fog index described in Chapter 6, indicate how easily the document can be read. You can revise the document to reduce its complexity and reduce the chance of translation errors.

1.2.2.1.   Program Generators.   The program generators described in Chapter 3 provide many reliability benefits. First, they are based on generic designs that have been carefully implemented to observe all of the structured methodologies. They should be the most reliable designs and code in your program library because of their extensive use and testing. Using a program generator to create the skeleton of the program enforces modularity and prevents typing or translation errors. It also encourages self-documentation of the program by including descriptive comment sections. Since each module has been coded and reviewed carefully to prevent standards violations and eliminate common reliability errors, program generators will help enforce standards while reducing program failure rates. Having the generator provide the logic allows the programmer to concentrate on the transformation of the data, reducing the complexity of the progamming task, thereby improving reliability.

Use of program generators also improves the transfer of information from the developers to the maintainers. The maintenance staff will need to know only a few generic designs and the few unique ones, not an entire selection of unique designs and code, making generic designs easily understood and easy to maintain.

1.2.3.   Management/Organization.

1.2.3.1.   Project Manager.   Having one person, preferably a user, managing the project provides an interpreter between the user department and Data Processing. This person's knowledge of DP and the application system places him or her in the appropriate position to improve communications throughout the project. The project manager should be receiving all system documentation, which can be routed to each team that might find it informative. The project manager may also spot major design or definition shifts well in advance, providing a better opportunity to control the change. Better control of the project, improved communication, and project management will significantly enhance the reliability of the system.

1.2.3.2.   Project Teams.   The word "team" implies working together. Programming was an egocentric process until project teams and walk-throughs forced a change in philosophy. Project teams form a tight-knit organization for sharing information, techniques, and work habits. Project teams contribute to the vertical and horizontal communication that affects the reliability of the system. Project teams may have problems, however. If the team becomes too egocentric, with little or no communication with the rest of the development staff, it may inflict greater damage on the system than a single programmer. Project teams must integrate to share information or they can affect the reliability of the system negatively through communication failures.

1.2.3.3. System Testing. Having a separate system testing organization will improve reliability. Its goal is to find software errors. The programmer's objective, on the other hand, is to develop programs that run. System testing will find more errors because of its objectives. A system testing group can also help police the user's involvement. Tests are more likely to be performed to the letter of the system definition, rather than the intent of the user, which forces the user to keep the definition up-to-date and to state objectives and requirements clearly. The better the definition, the better the system will operate.

1.2.3.4. Quality Assurance. Having a separate QA organization invokes the Hawthorne effect: people perform better when they know they are being measured. When they know they are being observed, the development team is more likely to do it right the first time, rather than take shortcuts. Quality assurance can provide the user with status reports that were not previously available. The user can step in and provide the impetus to change the development schedule to allow better quality. QA tools can track the development team's quality, allowing them to make corrections before QA review and preventing them from pursuing objectives of poor quality until the infrequent QA intervention makes quality problems apparent.

QA enforces a common way of working and adherence to standards that might otherwise be avoided. This standardization and the resulting quality will ultimately improve the reliability of the system.

1.3. Programmer-Machine Interface

1.3.1. Time Sharing.
Giving the programmer an on-line terminal improves the dialogue between the person and the machine. In the old days, programmers got their hands directly on the console; this was perhaps the optimal form of communication. Then someone invented card readers and the programmer and the machine became like two good friends who have moved to different states:

they continue to communicate, but the quality and content declines. They lose that familiarity that brought them so close to begin with.

Time sharing systems re-establish that link. Talking to the computer over a telecommunications network is like talking long distance: the communication is direct; the two can interact and carry on an active dialogue. Each can stop to ask the other questions about the conversation. They exchange information more freely, with little or no delay. This enhanced dialogue improves programmers' ability to do their jobs, so it will also improve reliability.

1.3.2. Compilers. Many compilers provide diagnostics of code that cannot be executed, data that are invalid or unreferenced, or logic that may result in incorrect program execution. Some compilers provide run-time diagnostics. They indicate untested program paths, loops executed 101 times instead of 100, and statements that use more resources than the others. All of this information can be used to tune the program, removing errors and inefficiencies.

1.3.3. Interactive Testing Tools. Using structured methodologies, the programmer builds small, easily tested modules, which can be compiled and tested in one terminal session, using interactive tools. On-line compilers and testing tools provide a continuous information exchange between human and machine as they run a program. This real-time, rather than after-the-fact, diagnosis provides the programmer with current information about program errors and failures. Again, rather than communicate by means of a printed document, the programmer and computer interact directly, improving information flow and reliability.

1.4. System Testing—Machine Interface

The system testing group must deal with all of the tools the programmer sees and a few more besides. The testing organization may use test data generators to build the data bases required. It may also deal with data dictionaries. To improve its ability to digest the computer's output, the group may have to build its own testing system to automate each rerun and output verification.

1.4.1. Test Verification. One of the simplest but most often overlooked testing tools is the differential comparison program. Comparison programs can identify the differences between two runs of the same program, which can reduce the amount of data that must be analyzed by 90%. The computer reduces the complexity of the verification task by reducing the data presented. This not only makes the expected changes visible, but also illuminates unexpected differences. Inspecting system output is often difficult and humans often overlook similar yet different results; unexpected errors are missed and reliability declines. Differential comparison programs never overlook changes.

The programmer can also use this tool to examine changes between program versions. If you have mechanized documentation, you can examine definitions, designs, and operation manuals for changes. Reducing the amount of data for analysis improves system testing's productivity and quality.

1.5. User–Machine Interface

System developers often forget that the user is not a highly educated DP technician, so they forget to build the user–machine interface to cope with the user's skills. In the typically clerical jobs that have been automated, entry level skills might include a high school education and some typing. System developers have become hardened to the computer's unfriendliness, but they continue to build the same problems into their own systems. Confronted with an unfriendly system, the user may try various random inputs to break the system actively. A user who becomes frustrated with the computer or loses trust in it may revert to manual procedures. It is then a difficult job to rebuild that person's faith. The user's perception of the system's reliability may be far below its actual reliability. Interfaces that are friendly to the user, combined with reliable system software, will aid the user–machine interface significantly.

A specialized project team of industrial or human factors engineers can help improve the dialogue between the user and the machine. Industrial engineers examine how work is done, how it could be done to improve productivity, and how it could be done to improve reliability of the output, and they can design the resulting inputs and outputs to reflect those needs. This team examines the system's human factors, and incorporates them into the design. Human factors engineering began with the aviation industry, making aircraft instruments easy to read, even in combat. It has expanded to all fields relating to humans; it should also encompass software design. As the reliability of an aircraft is the result of many people's efforts, so is the reliability of a software system. Human factors are involved in designing, building, testing, and using the software system. Industrial engineers provide a means to improve the system's human engineering and thereby improve its reliability.

A variety of screen design and report writer tools exist to support better design of the human–machine interface. Working in concert with the user, system analysts can validate input procedures and output formats in real time. Communication with the user and the usefulness of the inputs and outputs are increased. Creating input records or screens makes users think about how they currently work and how they want to work with the new computer system. Using report writers to get an idea of the best report formats, users have complete control over what they receive. Interactive system design not only helps improve user acceptance, but also places the responsibility for system definition in user's hands, where it should be. Creating the human interface before designing the system helps solidify the requirements, reducing in-progress development and maintenance changes to the system. Minimizing change not only reduces the chance of a schedule slippage, but also improves the reliability of the system.

2. DETECTING ERRORS TO IMPROVE RELIABILITY

Every solution breeds new problems.

In any series of calculations, errors tend to occur at the end opposite to the end at which you begin checking for them.

Having the computer check itself and catch errors helps minimize the damage the error can propagate throughout the system. It also makes it easier to find and repair the source of the error. The major problem with this philosophy is that the designers must think up all the possible errors that can occur and plan for them. Error detection code adds complexity to the system, so it is possible to introduce more errors into the system than the code will correct. But let's examine ways to improve reliability by using error detection.

2.1. Methodology

The phrase that comes to mind is "defensive programming." Defensive programming includes many ways to detect errors. Here are some examples.

1. In an update program, counting the records read, added, and deleted, and comparing this sum to the records written should produce a balanced total. If not, the program has created or deleted records it should not have. Programs that process data can compare the total records processed to the total number of input records. When processing millions of records, it becomes impossible to track the loss or creation of a single record without the aid of the program.

2. Division by zero is another prime source of error. Your program can check each division statement with a preceding IF or catch the error after the fact with an overflow check.

3. Blanks in numerical fields cause further data-related errors. Your program can catch these errors by editing the field or handling the overflow check. Data passed from other programs may be edited before use. Interface errors are one of the most common problems.

4. Table subscripts exceed their limits and write over other parts of the program. Your program controls these errors by checking the subscript after incrementing or decrementing it. Negative subscripts are also a potential problem. Some compilers start their table subscripts at zero and others at one, adding further confusion. When testing of subscript ranges is being done, one of the most common errors checks the table maximum as follows:

IF (TABLE-SUBSCRIPT = TABLE-MAXIMUM)

Invariably, the subscript exceeds the TABLE-MAXIMUM and eats everything in the program's data storage. A better implementation is

IF (TABLE-SUBSCRIPT > TABLE-MAXIMUM

OR < TABLE-MINIMUM)

Since many programs use tables as a means to minimize program maintenance—changing tables instead of programs—proper table handling should be paramount in the minds of developers.

5. Programs designed to analyze the data base can uncover data corruption. In a significantly large data base system, these programs are imperative to the reliability of the system.

These are just a few of the many errors that can occur. Knowledge of your common errors should provide further insight into the kinds of defensive programming to build into your systems.

2.1.1.   Quality Assurance.   After the system has been in operation for a year, and perhaps every year thereafter, Quality Assurance should conduct a system performance review. The results of this study should suggest ways to improve its reliability as part of the system's quality.

2.2. Technology

Knowing what errors to check for, how can you insure that they are checked? Static analysis of the program provides one solution. Analyzers examine your source code and produce information about potential sources of program errors. Checking for your own local standards may require the development of your own analyzer. You can modify the software metrics program, found in Appendix C, to look for your own specific defensive programming techniques. Running an analyzer against your programs provides a specific list of potential problems to check. You can find these problems easily when you know what you're looking for. Correcting the code is also easy.

A few efficiency nuts around your shop may complain about the few extra milliseconds that defensive programming techniques add to the program's run time. But just one program failure will destroy those efficiency savings. Write your programs to prevent program failure.

2.3. People

Programmers, being the egomaniacs that they are, may protest all of this defensive programming: "How dare you insinuate that my program has errors in it? How can I produce the program on schedule if I have to build all of this other stuff into it?" A bit of careful explaining about the company's requirements and the costs of poor reliability should answer most of those gripes. Educate your programmers about the cost of a failure. What does it cost in machine time, operator time, wasted forms, and information delay? What does it cost for an on-line system to fail, causing data base destruction and putting hundreds of users into an unproductive mode? The answer can run into thousands of dollars a minute. Your company can't afford those system failures. Prevent them.

2.4. Management

Management concerned with reliability should understand the worth of longer development times to save maintenance costs. The investment is nominal, the rewards are great. It will be a hard nut to crack, but the benefits of building it right the first time should not be underrated.

3. CORRECTING ERRORS TO IMPROVE RELIABILITY

Once a program is fouled up, anything done to correct it only makes things worse.

Error correction assumes that you know what errors will occur and how. Further, it assumes that you know how to correct them. Considering the infinite possibilities for error, the possibility of handling even the most damaging errors correctly is slim. If you can predict potential errors, they should be designed out of the system, not anticipated with lots of error-handling code that may be unreliable as well.

4. ALLOWING ERRORS TO IMPROVE RELIABILITY

It is possible to identify input data errors and write them selectively to an error file for reprocessing, allowing the good data to pass through, raising a flag to signal that something went wrong in the program, and allowing simpler correction of the error at a later time. Some sort of error report should also be produced. Again, this process assumes that errors can be predicted and handled uniformly, an unlikely assumption.

5. SUMMARY

You must build reliability into the system from the beginning; it is difficult and costly to try to add it later. You can try to detect or correct errors as they occur, but the development effort required only adds to your costs and burdens the code with complex error-handling routines that are probably error-ridden as well. You have the methodology, technology, and personnel at your disposal to insure reliability; use them.

CHAPTER EIGHT

Maintenance

If a program is useful, it will have to be changed.

Expansion means complexity, and complexity, decay.

Maintenance—50-80% of your budget—consumes resources vital to developing new projects and keeping ahead of competition. Maintenance adds enhancements that require further support of the system. Every new system you build adds to this burden, further reducing your available resources. How can you reduce this nightmare? It won't be easy, but it can be done. First, examine your existing maintenance programs. Some were written before structured programming and are hard to understand and maintain. Some were written after structured programming; their maintenance costs vary.

Beauty is only skin deep, but ugly goes clean to the bone.

Each system has programs that have been enhanced to the point that they are no longer maintainable. They were once simple programs that grew and grew and finally devoured Cleveland. Intuitively, everyone knows which programs cause all of the problems, but no one seems to know how to fix them. You may not be able to quantify how much time you spend on them, and you probably can't tell what's wrong with them. So you continue to build the same problems into other programs, compounding your maintenance burden. The only solution requires identifying those problem modules and rewriting them.

1. IDENTIFYING MAINTENANCE-PRONE SOFTWARE

Chapter 6 describes the implementation of a software evaluation program. You will need this program to uncover your maintenance-prone programs. Additionally, if you have a history of the maintenance performed on each program, it will help pinpoint your problem programs. Having developed the measurement program described in Chapter 6, you will be able to automate the examination of your source code. There are several measurements of source code that indicate the inherent maintainability of the program.

1. The number of executable lines of code (ELOC)
2. The total number of decisions
3. Decision density
4. The total number of preprogrammed functions
5. Program level (function density)
6. The number of GO TOs
7. GO TO density
8. The number of entries and exits
9. The number of NOT conditional clauses
10. The number of comments
11. The number of EJECT and SKIP statements
12. The use of structured code

Let's examine how each of these indicates software maintainability.

1.1. Executable Lines of Code

The executable lines of code (ELOC) measurement includes each statement that does anything, like MOVE, PERFORM, ADD, and so on. It does not include comments, data definitions, or key words like FROM, TO, VARYING, and UNTIL. When examining each of your source modules, look for ELOC that exceed 100. Figure 2.7 shows the relationship between a module's size, in ELOC, and the time required to repair it. Maintenance costs can be cut dramatically by keeping module size under 100 ELOC.

Yourdon recommends modules of a maximum of 50 statements. This number refers to the maximum ELOC that will fit on one page. Once a program exceeds two pages, a programmer has to flip from one page to the next to trace program flow and can easily lose track of exactly what the program is doing from page to page. You may find that programs in older systems have 1000 ELOC or more. These are potentially impossible to maintain; if not impossible, they may take weeks or months to enhance or fix, a situation that is intolerable with the rising costs of DP maintenance.

The best way to fix these obese programs is to identify the unique functions in the program and move them into a module of their own. Most of these programs perform multiple functions, so rather than having all of them in-line, the functions can be called from the original module using only the required data, thereby restricting the interface between this singular function and the main module. This selective "data coupling" keeps the maintenance programmer from using data in common working storage by accident.

Modifying the program to call each function improves the module strength and coupling. Moving functions into separate modules changes the module coupling from common to data coupling, and changes the module strength from procedural to functional strength. Data coupling and functional strength are the best possible module attributes.

The most important point you should consider when reducing a module's size is insuring that programmers do not just move unrelated groups of code into a separate module with no emphasis on proper separation of functions. If they just break the code into 100-ELOC chunks and put them in separate modules, you will have a problem even worse than your original one.

1.2. Decisions

Each decision—represented by an IF, UNTIL, or WHEN—adds an additional path through the code, each of which must be remembered by the programmer when trying to maintain or enhance a module. Humans typically cannot remember more than seven things at one time, which is why phone numbers have seven digits and human factors engineers try to minimize the complexity of any human system to seven levels. For these reasons, you should try to restrict the complexity of any module to seven decision levels. Fifteen should be your maximum. As you examine your programs, you will find that most will exceed these limits, and some, which are probably incomprehensible and unmaintainable, will have hundreds of decisions.

There are some exceptions to this rule. If you use an IF-ELSEIF-ELSEIF form of case statement, the case statement counts as only one decision. In a large case statement, these decisions could include hundreds of comparisons, but the case statement is typically as understandable as a simple IF statement. An example of a COBOL case statement is shown in Figure 8.1. The same is true of the SELECT statement. Each WHEN statement is based on one decision point—the SELECT. So the decisions you have to worry about are the straight IF-THEN-ELSE and PERFORM-UNTIL.

Another exception to the decision—maintainability rule involves an edit program. It may take many decisions to validate each field in the input. The program will have hundreds of decision points but will be easy to maintain. Edit modules have functional strength since they perform only one function—editing fields. Cross-field validations should be performed in a separate module, however; they are considered a different function.

1.3. Decision Density

Decision density depicts the number of decisions in each 100 ELOC. Figure 8.2 shows the driver module for a simple update program. The decision density in modules under 100 ELOC can be high with-

```
IF A = 1 THEN

    FIRST CASE

ELSE IF A = 2 THEN

    SECOND CASE

ELSE IF A = 3 THEN

    THIRD CASE

ELSE

LAST CASE.
```

FIGURE 8.1. A sample CASE statement, indicating its relative simplicity compared to a nested IF statement.

```
PERFORM READ-TRANSACTION-FILE.

PERFORM READ-MASTER-FILE.

PERFORM UPDATE-MASTER-FILE

    UNTIL EOF-ON-MASTER-FILE AND

        EOF-ON-TRANSACTION-FILE.


    GOBACK.


UPDATE-MASTER-FILE.


    IF MASTER-SEQUENCE < TRANSACTION-SEQUENCE THEN

        PERFORM WRITE-MASTER-FILE

        PERFORM READ-MASTER-FILE

    ELSE IF MASTER-SEQUENCE = TRANSACTION-SEQUENCE

        PERFORM UPDATE-MASTER-RECORD

    ELSE IF MASTER-SEQUENCE > TRANSACTION-SEQUENCE

        PERFORM ADD-MASTER-RECORD.

        Executable Lines of Code = 11

        Decisions                =  4

        Decision Density         = 37%

        Functions                =  7

        Function Density         = 63%
```

FIGURE 8.2. A sample update program, showing how the decision and function densities affect a program's maintainability.

out affecting the maintenance of the program. In modules larger than 100 ELOC, decision density should be under 15; otherwise, you have a candidate for maintenance problems. Decision density focuses on keeping the complexity of each 100 ELOC under the "seven" bogey previously described. You will find that modules with a low decision density are probably easier to maintain. Again, I say "probably" because metrics can only predict maintainability; you have to inspect the code to verify the existence of problems. Other programs will have a decision density of 20–25. These may be hard to understand and modify, consuming inordinately more maintenance resources than other programs.

Correcting these decision-dense programs will require an investment to identify functions and remove some of the decision-dense functions into smaller, more comprehensible modules. It will also improve functional strength and data coupling; your programs will become easier to maintain and enhance.

1.4. Functions

In COBOL, functions include CALL, COMPUTE, GENERATE, SEARCH, and PERFORM statements. In PL/1, functions also include any of the preprogrammed subroutines and built-in functions.

Function statements have a special impact on maintainability: they represent a function concisely. They represent a pretested, error-free module that has a concise function. Used in place of in-line code, they can be considered a simple statement, simple and easy to debug.

When working toward the solution to a problem, it always helps if you know the answer.

Consider Figure 8.2 again. Each perform represents hundreds of lines of code, but understanding the logic is easy. Functions provide major signposts to direct the flow of the program. A programmer trying to discern where to make a change or find an error should know precisely how to continue the search for the errant function. This is why functions directly affect maintainability; they predict the module's functional strength. The more functions you have in a module, the easier it will be to enhance or repair.

1.5. Program Level

The density of functions in the code indicates the module's functional strength. Any density over 20% means highly functional, maintainable, and flexible modules. Consider the metrics program itself. It has almost 500 ELOC, two decisions, and 49% functions. Although it is greater than 100 ELOC, its decision count means that there are only two paths through the code, so it will be simple to test. The program level shows that there are 49 functions for every 100 lines of code. The program uses functions, rather than many lines of code. These functions can be easily rearranged to provide a different implementation of the program; if the programmer had to move multiple statements instead of a single function, more errors would occur. The programmer would also have a harder time locating the code to move; it is easier to grasp one statement than many.

Programs that score under 10 for program level can be modified to use PERFORMs and CALLs to improve functional strength and maintainability. Preprogrammed subroutines and functions should be substituted wherever possible. Increased functional strength will improve the program's maintenance.

1.6. GO TOs

GO TOs are an unconditional branch to somewhere in the program. They violate every law of structure ever written and make testing the module more difficult. In older systems, one of the most common violations involves using the GO TO instead of a simple IF-THEN-ELSE. Figure 8.3 shows a common GO TO version of an IF-THEN-ELSE, a common error of FORTRAN programmers. FORTRAN does not provide the IF-THEN-ELSE statement, so the programmer must use a GO TO. The same is true of assembler language programmers, who use "branch on condition" statements because of the absence of an IF-THEN-ELSE construct.

```
IF A = B THEN

    GO TO NEXT-LABEL.


MOVE '95' TO ERROR-CODE.

CALL 'ABEND' USING ERROR-CODE.


NEXT-LABEL.


    IF A = B THEN

        NEXT SENTENCE

    ELSE

        MOVE '95' TO ERROR-CODE

        CALL 'ABEND' USING ERROR-CODE.
```

FIGURE 8.3. A comparison of two ways to implement an IF-THEN-ELSE statement. The first example uses a GO TO in a manner common to assembler language programmers.

Figure 8.4 shows another common error—using GO TOs instead of PERFORM VARYING. This holdover from FORTRAN and assembler language uses a GO TO instead of the functional PERFORM or CALL statement, decreasing the module's functional strength.

GO TOs are easily perverted into a structural violation. In the process of enhancing a module, programmers often insert GO TO branches in paragraphs that have no sequential relationship to the processing. These changes can twist the program into an untestable, unmaintainable ogre. Mechanized analysis can identify programs that show an increase in GO TOs; check them before you release them.

There are two valid uses of GO TOs: to GO TO the end of a PERFORMed paragraph and to implement a CASE statement. Figures 8.5 and 8.6 show these two implementations. They can be implemented as an IF-THEN-ELSE, however.

```
GOTO Loop


    SUBSCRIPT = 1.

BEGIN-LOOP.

    SEQUENTIAL STATEMENTS

    ADD 1 TO SUBSCRIPT

    IF SUBSCRIPT > TABLE-MAXIMUM THEN

        NEXT SENTENCE

    ELSE

        GO TO BEGIN-LOOP.


PERFORM Loop


    PERFORM BEGIN-LOOP

        VARYING SUBSCRIPT FROM 1 BY 1

            UNTIL SUBSCRIPT > TABLE-MAXIMUM.
```

FIGURE 8.4. A comparison of the GO TO and PERFORM VARYING versions of a DOWHILE statement. The GO TO version mimics an assembler language programmer, as in Figure 8.3.

```
PERFORM LOOP-PARAGRAPH THRU LOOP-PARAGRAPH-EXIT.


LOOP-PARAGRAPH.


    SEQUENTIAL STATEMENTS


    IF A = B THEN


        GO TO LOOP-PARAGRAPH-EXIT.


    SEQUENTIAL STATEMENTS


LOOP-PARAGRAPH-EXIT.


        EXIT.
```

FIGURE 8.5. The possible use of a GO TO to exit a performed paragraph. This may not be considered a structure violation.

1.7. GO TO Density

You might expect an older program to have two or three GO TOs in every 100 ELOC. You will find others with up to 10 GO TOs in every 100 ELOC. These programs probably violate structure in ways that you've never dreamed. The kludge they produce is probably unmaintainable, so the only way to improve them is to rewrite them, using structured techniques. Mechanized analysis will automate the discovery of this maintenance-prone code.

1.8. Entry and Exit Counts

A module should have one entry and one exit (except modules that have informational strength, which should have more than one), and your programs should have one entry for every exit. Multiple exists with only a single entry or multiple entries with only a single exit can cause major problems. If you have a program with an entry/exit imbalance, you probably have a severe structural violation that should be corrected.

1.9. NOT Conditions

The NOT condition in IF and UNTIL decisions has caused a multitude of maintenance problems. Often the NOT clause is used as

```
                          GO TO PARAGRAPH-1,

                              PARAGRAPH-2,

                              PARAGRAPH-3

                              DEPENDING ON VARIABLE-NAME.


                          MOVE '96' TO ERROR-CODE.

                          CALL 'ABEND' USING ERROR-CODE.

                      PARAGRAPH-1.

                          CASE 1.

                          GO TO EXIT-PARAGRAPH.

                      PARAGRAPH-2.

                          CASE 2.

                          GO TO EXIT-PARAGRAPH.

                      PARAGRAPH-3.

                          CASE 3.

                          GO TO EXIT-PARAGRAPH.


                      EXIT-PARAGRAPH.
```

FIGURE 8.6. The use of the GO TO DEPENDING ON statement to implement a CASE statement.

shown in Figure 8.7. Unfortunately, the NOT condition does not say what something is—only what it is not. If something is not equal to zero, it may be less or greater than zero. Programmers often miss one or the other side of the implied conditions. The simple solution involves the use of the NEXT SENTENCE statement, as shown in Figure 8.8. If there are more NOT conditions than AND and OR conditions, the program might be considered more maintainable with the NOT conditions rewritten as NEXT SENTENCEs.

```
                                  IF A = B THEN

                                      NEXT SENTENCE

IF A NOT = B THEN                 ELSE

    MOVE '97' TO ERROR-CODE           MOVE '97' TO ERROR-CODE

    CALL 'ABEND' USING ERROR-CODE.        CALL ' ABEND' USING ERROR-CODE.
```

FIGURE 8.7. Use of the NOT condition to eliminate the use of the NEXT SENTENCE statement.

FIGURE 8.8. Use of the NEXT SENTENCE statement to eliminate the use of confusing NOT conditions.

1.10. Comments

Every program requires a certain level of in-line comments—the only kind of documentation that seems to be maintained—to document the code. Comments can either help or hinder the maintenance of a program. The density of comments gives an indication of the program's self-documenting properties. The comment density represents the number of comments divided by the total number of lines in the program, not the ELOC. A density of 10% may be considered reasonable; less than that and the program would have to be easily readable from the code alone. Programs of less than 100 ELOC should be easily readable without many comments; programs containing more lines of executable code or more comments should be considered less maintainable. More comments tend to obscure the code, making it harder to understand, enhance, or repair.

Some programmers use comments to nullify executable lines of code. Unfortunately, maintenance programmers do not notice these comments and follow the logic through nonexistent code. Figure 8.9 shows an example. Deleted lines should be deleted, not commented out. Deleted source code should be maintained by the library system as backup.

Find your preferred level of comments, then use standards and measurements to enforce good commenting. Your maintenance load will decrease.

```
        IF A = B THEN

            MOVE C TO D

*           MOVE E TO F

            PERFORM SOME-PARAGRAPH

        ELSE

            MOVE D TO E

*           MOVE F TO G

        PERFORM SOME-PARAGRAPH.
```

FIGURE 8.9. Use of comments to save changed lines of code should be forbidden. Most source maintenance libraries can store these changes.

1.11. EJECTs and SKIPs

EJECTs and SKIPs enhance readability by separating code into meaningful chunks. EJECTs should separate paragraphs that perform different functions. SKIPs should precede CALLs, PERFORMs, and IF statements. SKIPs can also separate in-line functions from one another.

1.12. Structured Code

The code itself should be indented to make reading easier. Figure 8.10 shows some suggested ways of indenting code. Only one executable statement should exist on each line of the program. Otherwise, a programmer may overlook the additional statements. ELSEs should always align with the IF statements they compliment, but they can still cause problems, as is shown in Figure 8.11; the maintenance programmer can more easily understand how the IFs and ELSEs relate if this style is used. Without this indentation, the maintenance programmer might assume that the nested IF and the subsequent ELSE belong together.

1.13. Efficiency

Efficiency analysis can find other problems. In COBOL, internal numerical variables should be PIC S9(4) COMP SYNC or PIC S9(?)

COMP-3. Variables used as subscripts should also be PIC S9(4) COMP SYNC. Simple examination of programs that have a high number of PIC 9 clauses without either COMP or COMP-3 may clear up many efficiency problems. It may also find indexes or subscripts that are also PIC 9; they should also be COMP SYNC. You may also find that the indexes were originally set as PIC 99 and now the maximum table size is 150. Occasionally, the program will have problems but you will not know why; your subscript goes out of range.

You may also find variables that are PIC 9(3) that are moved to variables of PIC 99, truncating the high-order digit. All kinds of problems turn up. You may also find the SEARCH verb used on tables that have grown too large to search sequentially; a binary search will work much more efficiently. In the process of checking your search statements, you should also check to see if they have an AT END clause. Otherwise, the program may use invalid data when it finds no match in the table. These problems are difficult to find.

```
IF condition THEN

    sequential statements

ELSE

    sequential statements.

IF case-1 THEN

    sequential statements

ELSE IF case-2 THEN

    sequential statements

ELSE IF case-3 then

    sequential statements

ELSE

    error processing.

PERFORM paragraph-name

    VARYING index-name

    UNTIL condition.
```

FIGURE 8.10. Suggested statement indentation to improve code readability.

```
IF A = B THEN

     SEQUENTIAL STATEMENTS

     IF C = D

          SEQUENTIAL STATEMENTS

ELSE

     SEQUENTIAL STATEMENTS.
```

FIGURE 8.11. This example shows one of the hazards of indented IF–THEN–ELSE statements. The indentation may not reflect the true code path. The ELSE path is taken only if C $\neq$ D.

1.14. Rewriting Modules and Programs

If it would be cheaper to buy a new unit, the company will insist upon repairing the old one. If it would be cheaper to repair the old one, the company will insist on the latest model.

This section has identified many coding techniques that provide maintainable code. Getting in and rewriting errant modules will take time and increase the number of modules you maintain, but it will reduce the complexity of each submodule. You should not initiate wholesale rewrites of entire systems. Remember Pareto's rule: perhaps only 10–20% of your programs cause 80% of the costs. Concentrate on the top 20% indicated by the metric evaluation. You should not leap in and start upgrading your modules in some random fashion, but concentrate on the programs you are always enhancing and fixing. One way to identify them requires tracking every change to the system.

2.   ERROR TRACKING

Now that you know from the metrics analysis which programs are most maintenance-prone, you can begin to modify them. To know which programs to start on, you will need to know the maintenance history of all of your modules. Error tracking, by means of change requests or whatever you use, provides you with information about the frequency of change or repair. Repair work is probably an insignificant amount of your costs, however. Enhancements take all of your resources and then some.

Examine your error history. If certain programs have a high enhancement rate and metrics have predicted that they are maintenance-prone, begin working to improve their metrics. Improving all of your programs may take a long time, but you have no other choice.

3. SOFTWARE DEVELOPMENT

While developing programs, you have the opportunity to insure that no maintenance-prone programs escape detection and enter production. Using the methodology described for identifying poor quality programs that are already in maintenance, you can identify similar newly developed modules and correct them before they are ever compiled, tested, or put into production. Correcting developing programs will reduce testing costs. Reducing these modules to smaller, less complex modules will simplify testing each submodule. The reduction of these programs will improve their functionality, module coupling, and module strength. The combination of these three improvements will bring about quality and maintenance improvements.

4. SUMMARY

This chapter has identified ways of lightening your maintenance work load by rewriting maintenance-prone programs. Identifying maintenance-prone programs and repairing or rewriting them is the only way to reduce maintenance costs. Combining the software metrics described in Chapter 6 with actual maintenance histories on all of the programs in your shop will allow you to identify and correct those programs. Using similar techniques on your newly developed programs will prevent programs from entering testing or conversion until they meet your minimum quality specifications. Identifying these programs before they enter the maintenance phase will cut the costs of maintaining these programs, freeing vital resources for development of additional systems to support your information needs in this decade and the next.

CHAPTER NINE

Quality Assurance

Why would anyone want to establish a quality assurance function? Why do you need to audit the development of systems and the products produced? Your personnel are producing the best possible code, aren't they? May I suggest that you don't really know.

Quality assurance will improve the programming product, improve productivity, cut costs, and ultimately reflect on the financial bottom line. As the Industrial Revolution brought about the need for manufacturing standards and quality inspections, software engineering will demand the same control of the products produced. As software evolves toward the software factory concept, quality assurance must evolve to hold the line on development and maintenance costs. It provides a means to insure that software products are developed on schedule, within cost, and in compliance with performance requirements. Japan's management regards quality control as a cost-saving measure; American business views it as an unpleasant intrusion on the profit side of the financial statement.

Software quality must be built in; it cannot be added later. Auditing the development process therefore becomes the only way to catch deviations early and correct them.

1. WHAT IS QUALITY ASSURANCE?

Quality Assurance involves many functions.

Standards development
Requirements certification
Phase document review
Design walk-throughs
Code inspection
Software measurement
Test planning
Audit planning
Data collection and analysis
Error tracking
Defect prevention
Corrective action
Certifying new programming tools
Configuration management

Each of these activities adds layers of control to the development process; the goal is to improve the quality of your software.

1.1. Standards Development

Before a quality assurance team can function effectively, the process of developing and maintaining code must be standardized. Otherwise, quality control deteriorates into opinionated battles over what quality is and what it is not. Standards eliminate this squabbling and simplify the task.

Proper standards do not restrict the programmer or analyst; they enhance their interaction with others. Standards select the best way of coding or designing, and encourage its use. The best way may be debatable, but one way should be selected and adhered to. Without this common way of working, it becomes difficult to hold meaningful walk-throughs, code inspections, or quality audits.

Lack of programming standards often "marries" the programmer to the program, since no one else can understand it. The current maintenance nightmare is a direct result of working differently. Documentation is not maintained because it varies widely. Programmers have a hard time understanding three or four different implementations of the same structured coding construct or general routine. They also have a hard time understanding several different kinds of structured design technique—IPOs, data flow diagrams, and so on.

Standards benefit programmers by releasing them from bondage to their own code. They improve productivity in walk-throughs of designs and code. They improve maintenance productivity by restricting the varied set of information a programmer or analyst must know to enhance or modify the program. It takes time to learn several different design methodologies, time spent more productively elsewhere.

What kind of standards do you need? Since errors are most easily fixed in the early stages of development, it is natural to develop standards by phase of development. First, you'll need some standard means of proposing a project. This proposal should examine what problems the system will solve, what opportunities will be gained, the costs and benefits of the system, and the preliminary schedule for implementation. Next, a feasibility standard should describe how to document the system's cost effectiveness and viability in relation to resource availability and technology. Further revisions to the problems, opportunities, benefits, costs, and schedules should be delineated.

Now, here are a few key standards. Requirement and definition standards establish a meaningful way of communicating the user's needs to the development staff. Traditionally, this path has caused most communication failures. Clarifying the means of specifying requirements will reduce many of the errors that normally occur because of misunderstandings. This standard should not abnormally affect users, however. Why should they have to learn some software engineering dialect when they already know English? Information should, however, be grouped in meaningful ways to facilitate the transition into design.

Next, you'll need a system architecture and detailed design standard to form a bridge among the system architect, the systems analysts, and the programmers. Providing a programmer with IPOs one day and Nassi–Schneiderman diagrams the next is not the way to improve productivity. Select a set of design tools that have little overlap and make them standard. Overlap refers to the redundant presentation of data in varied formats. For example, consider the redundancy in IPOs and pseudocode or among data flow diagrams and structure charts.

Next, a standard way of testing becomes imperative. Without it, how will Quality Assurance possibly audit the results for validity? How will structural tests be verified? Top-down testing folds in here to provide specific unit and integration tests. The volume of each test should not be overwhelming.

Standards for conversion, maintenance, and self-auditing software will enhance the quality control function as well as the products produced. Quality control's maximum impact occurs during definition, design, and code. During these stages, the project's future quality is built into its components.

Analysts and programmers should develop the standards they use. This activity increases their acceptance of and adherence to a common working philosophy. Standards should not be viewed as unalterable commandments, but rather as a mechanism to control the work flow and quality of the end product. Standards should be dynamic; they should change with technology, methodology, and the needs of the corporation.

1.2. Requirements Certification

Requirements represent the first chance for error to creep into the system. Some aspects of the system are missed or forgotten; others are described incorrectly. The cost of correcting an error in this phase of development is 1% of the cost to correct it in implementation. The chance to certify the requirements gives the company an opportunity to reduce future costs substantially while providing a more reliable system. Quality assurance should perform this function.

Having a standard requirements definition gives QA the basis to examine the document for oversights and errors; its function is to spot errors, not correct them. The clean-up function belongs to the development group.

Requirement statement languages (RSL) or problem statement languages (PSL) have automated much of this analysis. If you are developing a system over 250,000 lines you might invest in one of these systems. No quality assurance team, no matter how good, can handle too large a definition effectively.

1.3. Phase Document Review

After the completion of each phase, the project manager must develop a phase document. This document covers costs, schedule changes, productivity, and quality of the development effort. QA gets involved to review the measures taken to insure that the project is meeting corporate quality objectives. Based on QA's review, the management body in charge of system development should either approve or disapprove the continuation of work. It may cost some damaged egos to rework parts of the previous phase. It may cost some productivity losses for the first few projects that encounter a quality assurance function, but once management's commitment to higher quality becomes apparent, programmers and analysts will strive to meet that objective.

1.4. Design Walk-throughs

Walk-throughs of system architecture and program designs were an early stab at quality control. They constitute, in effect, a quality control circle of peers that get together to improve quality. They can degenerate into fierce battles about the definition of quality, but design standards will help reduce the bickering. These meetings also serve as a forum for exchanging techniques and information that would not otherwise occur in a development project. The errors found during this phase reduce the errors that must be corrected in coding, testing, or production.

The QA team should assist in holding these walk-throughs until everyone has learned the positive ways of presenting constructive criticism. QA should instruct the development team in proper walk-through procedure because it cannot possibly review all designs. The QA group should, however, attend occasional walk-throughs to insure that quality standards are being met.

1.5. Code Inspection

Code inspections, just like design walk-throughs, improve programmer productivity and system quality. Quality assurance can automate standards compliance checkers to reduce the work in this job. Software metrics give further indications of the quality of the code and point out programs that should potentially be reworked. Code inspections can significantly reduce testing and implementation costs.

1.6. Software Measurement

The static measurement tools described in Chapter 6 provide input to software quality assurance. The software metric programs can examine the code for structured programming, efficiency, GO TO-less code, audit trails, and so on. Compiler cross-reference and error listings provide further input. Compiler error messages point to potential program problems. Cross-reference listings indicate unreferenced data items that could be misused accidentally by future maintenance programmers.

Run-time program analyzers exist to examine run-time program efficiencies. They also point to coding paths that have not been executed. Compilers, such as the CAPEX Optimizer III, have analyzer and detector features that indicate each statement executed, how many times it was executed, and the percentage of CPU time each one used. This analysis can point to programs with efficiency or execution problems.

1.7. Test Planning

Test planning involves defining all of the tests that a module, program, or system will undergo. Will modules be unit-tested along each of their structural paths and for all possible combinations of input and output? Will these modules then be integration-tested for each linkage between modules? Will programmers test the entire program, using test cases established in unit testing? Will a separate system testing organization validate the system with its own separate test cases?

Quality assurance can provide input into the development of these plans. Better methods of testing will evolve. The QA group can monitor the use of methods, then, based on results, define the "best" testing environment. Development groups do not have the time to keep all of these statistics and evaluate them. Let your QA group track, document, and review methodology to improve all phases of development and maintenance.

1.8. Audit Planning

All new systems require audit trails, which provide means of tracking the program's performance and detecting security violations. Financial systems require extensive audit trails. Other systems may require only tracks of the number of records processed and assurance that the proper version of the program was run. In these cases, the program performs its own quality assurance. A human cannot be expected to catch the fact that the program processed all but one record out of 20 million. Quality assurance can provide background on the most common errors to be caught by such a function. QA may identify programs that have insufficient audit trails and provide basic and advanced designs for self-auditing systems. Since the computer can audit its performance much more easily than a staff of humans, planning and building these controls into a new system is essential. They cannot be added later except at considerable expense.

1.9. Data Collection and Analysis

Quality control must collect statistics on error types and their frequency. The data they collect on virtually every step of the development and maintenance process help identify ways to improve. This improvement affects not only productivity, but quality as well. This data collection must be automated as much as possible, because it is not possible to assimilate the data in any manual way. You will have to design and build systems for Quality Assurance.

1.10. Defect Prevention

Having collected all of this information about where errors occur, Quality Assurance must propose and implement ways to prevent those defects from recurring. The group should develop quality checklists for walk-throughs and static analyzers to locate as many program defects as possible. It may also develop programs to insert bugs into the code. This methodology, known as bebugging (Gilb 1977), will modify the code prior to the walk-through. By examining the number of inserted and existing bugs found during the walk-through, the QA group can predict the number of undiscovered bugs in the program. For example, if 20 bugs were inserted and the walk-through found 15 inserted and 15 existing bugs, the group could conclude that five bugs, other than the inserted ones, still remain in the code.

1.11. Corrective Action

Having identified the errors, Quality Assurance must have a means of insuring that corrective action is taken. The old axiom "We don't have time to do it right, but we do have time to build it over" still seems to apply. If the development or maintenance group takes no action, the quality assurance function has no value to the corporation. Only by correcting problems can people be freed up to participate in other work, thereby improving productivity and enhancing the quality of the code.

1.12. Certifying New Programming Tools

Since quality assurance already collects data about data processing, it can quantitatively judge the value of new programming tools. Does installing a new tool improve productivity and quality, reduce them, or leave them unchanged? By installing new technology and methodology selectively in special test groups, Quality Assurance can monitor the changes in productivity and quality. Once the trial has run for six months or more, QA can quantify the benefits or costs of the new technology. Perhaps QA will find that the benefits do not exceed the costs, or that the tools provide intangible benefits, such as better quality documents, programs, or opportunities. Quality Assurance has the best data to evaluate, propose, and certify new program tools.

1.13. Configuration Management

Programs are constantly changing. Many different people work on the same program: some are fixing it, some enhancing, and some building anew. There may be several different versions of a program running in the field. Program documentation is revised along with each of these code changes. Configuration management seeks to control how all of these people, documents, and programs interact. Without control, programmers will overwrite others' changes. Programs that should not be released will be. Chaos will rule. QA can specify the means of controlling documentation revisions by means of document release libraries. Similarly, source code and programs can be controlled. Configuration management tools include source code libraries such as LIBRARIAN™ and PANVALET™, program control through PANEXEC™, and others.

Data processing and word processing are rapidly converging. The time when they will both contribute to the total information system is approaching. Using UNIX™, source code and documents are all managed under one source library—SCCS (Source Code Control System).

Configuration management improves quality by reducing errors caused by overlapping development and maintenance activities. It also improves productivity by reducing the confusion that occurs when several hundred documents and thousands of source modules undergo constant change and revision. Quality Assurance should implement the procedures and technology to support configuration management to provide you with the maximum quality improvements possible.

2. IMPLEMENTING THE QUALITY ASSURANCE FUNCTION

Phased in with the development of your productivity program, Quality Assurance dovetails naturally with the evolution of the software factory.

There always seems to be a hue and cry for top management support for new methodology. The formation of a quality assurance function obviously requires resources to staff the function. But many of QA's functions can be performed by the developers themselves. For example, design walk-throughs and code inspections must be done by the programmers and analysts. Groups often develop their own internal standards for requirements, definition, design, code, and test. Formalizing these for the whole department can be done by committees of programmers and analysts. Your technicians will readily accept quality control when they are a party to the function's development.

Currently, your analysts develop the test plans. Consolidating the mass of test plans into a coherent corporate testing philosophy can be done by committee. Audit planning can also be performed by the analysts.

If you implement a phased development process with the specific products recommended in Chapter 2, quality analysis of those products will be easier. In effect, phased development implements a standard way of developing projects, with standards that Quality Assurance can enforce.

Most installations have some form of configuration management in place. Identifying weaknesses can be done by committee. New software or methodology should be installed to give Quality Assurance a starting point to control the process.

The most important functions of Quality Assurance—data collection and analysis, error tracking, defect prevention, and taking corrective action—need staffing and resources. These functions seek to prevent repetition of errors in later systems. If you know the major sources of error and can identify the most frequent errors, Quality Assurance can actively find ways to reduce them, and certify definitions, designs, code, and tests.

When entering into a new development project of some magnitude, you can staff the quality assurance function moderately for that project. The QA group becomes part of the development team and works to develop all required quality control procedures. At the conclusion of the project, the Quality Assurance group can spin off to implement the function for the entire department.

3.   QUALITY ASSURANCE TOOLS

Tools allow inspection of programs, designs, and tests in a way not possible manually. These tools effectively reduce the number of data provided by the varied sources into an amount that can be interpreted, so that the quality engineer can "see" the product in a way not previously possible. Most of these tools improve the quality person's productivity and, as a minor sideline, improve quality.

Compilers
Basic program diagnostics
Change tracking system
Differential comparison of programs
Requirements processor
Run-Time analysis
Simulators
Source code control
Preprocessors
Test data generators
Static document and code analyzers
Standards analyzers
Regression testing tools

3.1.   Compilers

Compilers provide useful quality control information. They indicate fall-through logic, unexecutable logic (code following a GO

TO), unreferenced data names (that should not exist or be provided to the program because their existence violates structure rules), and statements that were not executed during testing. Cross-reference listings indicate each statement that has access to a particular variable. Some even tell where a variable name is modified, used in a calculation, or used to replace another data item. Checklists provide a means for analyzing the code for quality violations. The compiler listing simplifies certification of the code. It is even possible to automate analysis programs to ferret out the quality violations.

3.2. Basic Program Diagnostics

Compilers also provide diagnostic facilities like traces and debug statements. These can often be misleading, however. Program traces and debugging statements operate only when the program has specifically turned them on. In the many experiences I've had with them, they served to bury the programmer with trace listings that were harder to follow than the program code. They can be helpful to a limited extent. Program analyzers can be used to determine runtime efficiencies. Programs to simulate networks and determine response time problems exist. Diagnostic programs, like ABEND-AID™, can analyze program abends. Each of these diagnostics provides additional information about the quality of the program.

3.3. Change Tracking Systems

An automated change tracking system allows further control of the development and maintenance processes. Tracking each reason for a change to the system provides an understanding of the process of change. For example, the question "Why is this system six months late?" is often asked. Well, the definition changed 58 times during the two-year development period, causing 340 design changes and as many program changes. The additional cost of in-flight changes amounted to six months.

A change tracking system automates much of Quality Assurance's data collection. Changes can be attributed to errors in definition, design, code, and test. Enhancement requests also cause change. Fields indicating the reason for change—logic error, coding punctuation error, and so on—give a more precise definition of the problem origin. They contribute to the reduction of future similar errors, improving programmer productivity and program quality.

3.4. *Differential Comparison of Programs*

It is often difficult to identify the changes between two versions of a program. The UNIX Source Code Control System will provide this information; most source maintenance systems do not. The upcoming PANEXEC source maintenance system will provide similar capabilities.

Maintenance often introduces new errors into a program. If an error does not exist in the old version, but does in the new, then the changes are probably at fault. Finding those changes may be difficult. Differential comparison of the two programs indicates which lines were added, changed, or deleted between versions. The programmer can focus on these lines first and then expand the search for the bug, often reducing bug-finding time by half.

The Quality Assurance team can use this program to compare two sets of test results for validity, two versions of a program for quality improvements, or two sets of documents for changes.

3.5. *Requirements Processor*

The use of such requirements processors as the Problem Statement Language/Problem Statement Analyzer provides the Quality Assurance team with an invaluable tool to certify the quality of the user's requirement specifications. By automating the description of the user's system, the tasks performed, and the data flow through the system, PSL/PSA can analyze the specification for errors. This automated analysis will substantially improve the productivity of the Quality Assurance group. It need not plow through hundreds of pages of definition because the machine correlates the data descriptions with the flow of information and its processing, identifying the major deficiencies unerringly. The Quality Assurance team should review the resulting analysis only to verify that the system has met its quality criterion.

3.6. *Run-Time Analysis*

Run-time analyzers provide data about the program's execution and efficiency. Boole and Babbage provide one such analysis tool. Network simulators can provide information about the system's response time and provide load testing. With the continued growth of on-line systems, these simulators will evolve into systems that pound the system exhaustively, cranking out varied reports of the system's activities and response. Each of these tools help QA verify that the system has met the user's performance specifications. Without them, it would be difficult to verify system performance without standing behind the user with a stopwatch and a scorecard. The more mechanized the system development and maintenance process becomes, the easier it will be to verify the quality of the resulting products.

3.7. Source Code Control

Source code maintenance systems are at the heart of any configuration management philosophy. They provide a uniform way of creating, storing, updating, and retrieving source code or text. At a bare minimum, they provide a secure base for testing the program. What should you look for in a maintenance system?

UNIX's SCCS is one of the best maintenance systems. It allows you to maintain each version of the file by storing only the changes between releases and levels, and to store source by its release number as well as the level number, thereby mechanizing many of the renaming standards now used to control the copies of programs stored in regular source maintenance systems.

SCCS also provides for key word substitutions. You can embed key words for the release and level numbers, user ID, and compile and update dates into your code or document. When you extract the source for a compile or print, these key words expand to allow automated audit trails. This system provides an optimal mechanism to fully automate the audit trails throughout your system—from the original documents to the programs released into production.

3.8. Preprocessors

Preprocessors operate on the code before it is compiled. A beneficial preprocessor changes poorly indented code into local structured format. These program beautifiers relieve the QA group of having to verify that the code adheres to standards. It also relieves programmers of worrying about standards in the heat of development: they slap the code out and the preprocessor puts it into the proper format.

Preprocessors can also turn on special Quality Assurance code in each program to provide run-time data for later analysis, providing a simple way to collect statistics for annual or biannual performance reviews without affecting the operation of the system on a daily basis.

3.9. Test Data Generators

With the advent of data bases and data dictionaries, test data generators provide an efficient means of producing the test files needed to exercise the system. They also provide a means to generate data for recursive testing. Since Quality Assurance must validate the system's test results, a tool to create test data to their own specifications improves their productivity.

3.10. Static Analyzers

Quality Assurance uses software metric tools to automate the verification of software quality. These measurements can determine the presence or absence of structured programming, GO TOs, defensive programming, efficient coding techniques, modularity, and so on. These analyzers simplify the quality assurance job by isolating specific programs as potential problems. The QA group can then analyze a vastly reduced number of programs in the system. Focusing its attention on the "worst" programs in the system can dramatically affect the benefits derived from code inspection. The problem programs are identified and corrected before they can cause further harm or costs.

The document analysis tools described in Chapter 6—spelling checkers, grammer syntax analysis, and fog index calculations—can be used to improve the quality of the documents and provide Quality Assurance with productive tools to evaluate the quality of all document products from the system. This analysis is too expensive to perform manually; static analysis provides the only productive way to measure document quality.

3.11. Standards Analyzers

Tools that analyze documents, code, and test results for adherence to standards can substantially improve Quality Assurance productivity. Like the static analyzers, automated standards analysis will select only the significant problems, reducing the volume of information that the QA group must review. These tools also focus their attention and action on the major problems, so the corporation gets the most return for its investment.

3.12. Regression Testing Tools

The ability to recreate a test of a specific problem or set of problems gives Quality Assurance a tool to validate the output of system testing. These tools consist of procedures and test files to allow recreation of previous tests. Then the differential analysis program can compare the previous results to the current results, indicating added, changed, and deleted output. The Quality Assurance group can focus its validations on just this modified data, not on the mass of unchanged output. The system's quality should improve noticeably from action taken as a result of this evaluation.

4. SUMMARY

There are many tools to help insure the quality of the products manufactured in the software factory. You can partially implement the Quality Assurance function using your analysts and programmers in the normal course of their daily work. Since Quality Assurrance groups have no measurable impact on productivity or the bottom line, you will have a hard time justifying their existence on strictly intangible benefits. But you will notice many benefits from the creation of a QA group, such as improved quality and reduced maintenance. Unfortunately, you probably have a significantly large backlog of work to consume the money you save; more work gets done for the same cost, but your bottom line doesn't change.

Implementing the software factory requires an investment in new methodology and technology to insure improved productivity and quality. Only through actively assuring quality can you verify that your systems are the most maintainable, flexible, reliable, and efficient systems possible, while finding ways to refine your software factory to produce more goods at lower cost. Quality control is a major force in any factory; plan for its inclusion in your software manufacturing plant.

CHAPTER TEN

Auditing

In any collection of data, the figure most obviously correct, beyond all need of checking, is the mistake.

As systems become increasingly complex, it becomes impossible for humans to audit the processing. The chances for theft or fraud increase with the complexity of your computer system. The possibilities for loss due to errors and omissions rises dramatically. Chances for information loss increase because of lack of controls. Companies stand to forfeit penalties because of failure to meet government auditing regulations. Computer theft, fraud, and defalcation have raised eyebrows with their impacts. With the increasing dependence upon electronic fund transfer, major thefts are possible. There were at least 400 known cases of computer crime over an eight-year period. The average heist: $500,000. Recent government legislation has made computer fraud a felony. Who is held responsible? Management.

Management does not want to be surprised with court cases or the loss of company funds, nor does it want to find that important data have been pirated and sold to the highest bidder. With the increasing dependence on real-time transaction processing systems and data bases, it becomes more difficult to prevent such surprises. The only way to help eliminate these problems is through a corporate EDP auditing plan.

The plan must include ways to provide internal controls, so that the machine can check itself. It must include ways to reproduce the actions of the system so that auditors can review the system. It must include ways to control changes to a system; no one has easier access to the system than the programmers. It must include plans to secure sensitive data and ways to track the user who modifies data; otherwise it is impossible to establish responsibility for violations. And if the person who is responsible cannot be identified, upper management will take the rap.

So you need to protect yourself from external security breaches and internal fraud or embezzlement. The obvious problem is that all of these controls add more requirements to already burdened system development projects. The other option requires adding these audit trails later, an expensive proposition.

Consider the auditor. Improving the auditability of systems improves their productivity. The more efficient they are, the less likely you are to suffer the loss of data or money. The loss of 10% of your operating revenues would equal a lot of program development.

The resources you invest in audit controls should balance with the sensitivity of the data being manipulated. Some systems will need minimal investment, others a substantial investment. Possibly the major problem with audit controls is that you cannot prove their worth until your system has been violated or one of your officers imprisoned. For this reason, auditability must be recognized at all management levels and planned into every system. You would never develop a system without user requirements; you should never build one without examining its audit requirements as well.

1. SYSTEM DEVELOPMENT CONTROLS

One of the ways to enhance the auditability of a system is to control its development and continuing maintenance. These controls include the realms of methodology and technology.

1.1. Project Management

Project management provides a control mechanism for gauging the growth of a system. The project manager audits the development process for delay and incompleteness. Project management also includes the auditing staff, who analyze the developing system's internal controls.

1.2. Structured Programming

The philosophies of structured programming encourage the development of high-quality, easily auditable systems. Walk-throughs serve as audits of designs and code. System testing acts as an auditing group to insure that your results are correct.

1.3. Program Change Control

One of the first places that you are most vulnerable is from within the information system department itself. Programmers can pirate and sell internal software for personal benefit. They can modify systems to produce extra paychecks or nullify bills. They can pirate internal data and sell them to competitors. To audit the development and maintenance process adequately, there must be an audit trail from the change request to the production program that actually runs in the field. First, you must have a change request. This document spells out what must be changed, who initiated the change, who approved the change, and who is assigned to implement it. It should have a unique number associated with it that can be tracked through the entire system.

The programmer or analyst should make the necessary design changes and indicate the change request number on the revised documents, along with the date accomplished. The programmer should then retrieve the source module to be changed. This module should contain the following information in the data declaration section of the code.

1. The module name
2. The date changed
3. The release and level number of the source code being changed
4. The change request number
5. The programmer's name or user ID

These notations can be used as internal program documentation and internal audit trails, and with generic audit modules, as you will see in a moment. Now you have a link from the original change request to the design document to the program source code. When the program is compiled, the change information in the source code is compiled along with the rest of the program, propagating the version information into the object and load modules. Unfortunately, this information cannot be readily extracted. The program has to abort to allow inspection of the version information. There are a number of ways around this problem.

On IBM, the program that links compiled modules into object and load modules has a facility to place identification records (IDR) on your object and load modules. These IDR records can later be printed by an IBM utility program that scans binary modules. The process requires, however, that the programmer re-enter the information from the source module for each compile or link of the program.

Another possibility allows the company to invest in a generic module that prints the version information from each module when it is executed. Each run of the program is thus tied to specific modules. A substitute module cannot be run easily in the original's place. This generic audit module improves productivity by supplying a common interface to all programs. It supplies a common human-machine interface to the operations staff and auditors that have to review the system's output, improving productivity. The audit module should be highly reliable, not have any effect on the system or its efficiency, and tie into a run control system that insures that your programs are not run out of sequence or rerun covertly.

2. AUDITING TOOLS

The auditor often brings up the rear, identifying problems after the fact. Although auditors should contribute to the development of systems, they also have to follow up after the system is in operation. Because of enormous processing volumes, they cannot possibly do an adequate job without some tools to support their efforts. Fortunately, many of these already exist; they just need to be tapped for their information. As you have seen thus far, application programs can provide the best tool because they operate in real time, gathering information and summarizing it for the auditors. Other sources of auditing tools include the following.

1.   Operating systems
2.   Data base management systems
3.   Source control libraries
4.   Compilers
5.   Software metrics

Other systems provide generalized auditing functions and generalized system analysis. You can build your own specialized software to support the auditors' needs.

2.1. Generalized Audit Software

Generic audit software performs functions that the auditors can specify with minimum effort. These programs allow them to examine files and data bases for quality, completeness, consistency, and correctness. They provide a means to compare fields and perform calculations. They can select, report, and analyze portions of the data base. As auditing needs increase, more software will become available. The best sources of information about newly developed audit software are DATAPRO and the technical journals. Purchasing this software will provide maximum cost benefits, reducing the delay before they are implemented and retaining your development staff for income-producing projects. These tools will help your auditors become more productive and effective, and their effectiveness will affect the quality of your products.

2.2. Generalized System Software

Every system has utility programs to sort, merge, and print files. They aid the auditor in reducing the number of data to be analyzed. Each operating system keeps audit trails of each activity in the system to provide accounting of system use. Data base management systems keep logs of transactions and activity against the data base. There are programs to trace the flow of data through a program and the activity of the program. Each of these can facilitate the auditors' job when examining systems for correctness.

2.3. Specialized Audit Software

Regression testing allows the auditor to run parallel tests with old and new systems to verify output. Financial analysis programs can examine data bases, reducing the volumes of data to meaningful amount for analysis. They can provide further statistical analysis of the data, isolating those that might be out of range. Embedded audit modules can monitor run control and specific sensitive inner workings of each program as needed. These audit modules can create files for auditor examination as well. Each of these software systems aids an auditor's quest for solutions to the enormous problem of verifying systems. They should be examined and implemented as your organization requires.

2.4. Data Administration

The existence of a separate data base administration function assists the auditors by designing security into a data base rather than adding it later. This function also prohibits spurious changes in the data base. Data administration audits the design and administration of the data base, contributing to the control and security of corporate information.

3.   INTERNAL CONTROLS

A normal application system consists of six phases that must be audited and controlled: the origination of the transaction, the transaction's entry into the system, the communication of the data from the terminal to the computer, the processing of the transaction, storing and retrieving the results of the transaction processing, and the processing and creation of the output. Each phase requires its own internal controls. Some are more easily performed by the machine.

3.1. Originating the Transaction

Preparing a transaction is typically a manual task. Audit procedures should cover who can originate a transaction, who should approve it, who should enter it into the computer, and how errors should be prevented, detected, and corrected. These are manual procedures that are not easily automated.

3.2. Transaction Entry

Both batch and remote terminal data entry require auditing. Audit controls include who may enter transactions, how to validate the data, how to verify and balance transaction processing, error identification and reporting, and how to correct errors.

Batch processing may require input to be created close to the final processing point, minimizing the exposure of the data while in transfer to the processing site. It also minimizes the risk of loss or delay in receiving the data.

Batch systems should have internal controls to validate that they are run in sequence, their input is complete and on schedule, control fields and totals are in balance, and errors are properly handled and tracked. Batch systems can have a run control interface that prohibits incorrect running of its programs. Logging transactions as well as balancing the added, deleted, changed, and rejected transaction will improve the system's auditability.

The use of header and trailer records can further improve auditability by balancing the number of records entered versus those produced in a given run. The loss of a single record is difficult to track when millions of records move through the system daily.

Remote terminal entry may be controlled in a number of ways.

1. The data entry terminal can be physically secured in a remote building. The building or terminal should not be accessible except during working hours.

2. User or terminal authority levels prevent the person using the computer from executing commands that are not authorized for use. Unauthorized data base modification can be prevented in this way.

3. Similar authority levels may apply to each item in the data base, to prevent unauthorized retrieval of information from the data base.

4. Terminal sign-on procedures deter unauthorized users from tapping into the system. Usual sign-on procedures include password protection and accounting validation.

5. The entered transaction should be validated for correctness and tracked by means of auditing information concerning the date, time, and user entering the transaction. The system should report users who issue unauthorized commands.

6. The system should immediately report errors to the issuing terminal for immediate correction. It should suggest possible corrections and default values.

7. The system should summarize all activity against the data base, including add, change, delete, and rejected transactions. It should also balance all input transaction totals with the changes to the data base and report all discrepancies.

3.3. Communication Controls

These controls cover the accuracy and completeness of data transmission from remote locations to the processing site and include data protection, security, privacy, error identification, and reporting. These controls are typically built into the operating system and not the application program. In addition, many are hardware restrictions built into the network, not the actual programs.

3.4. Data Processing

Internal program controls validate the accuracy, correctness, and completeness of transaction processing. They also identify errors and report them. This control manifests itself in several ways.

1.   Transaction codes often control how the incoming data are processed. The logic to handle processing by transaction code is fairly generic and can serve as a prototype for all such systems.

2.   Control totals within the program that are passed to subsequent programs serve to verify that all data are processed and none are lost.

3.   Sequence checks, arithmetic overflow checks, exception reporting, and file control totals all serve to verify correct processing.

4.   Transaction error reporting and transaction error hold files provide error conditions that can be recreated for auditing and data processing.

3.5. Data Storage and Retrieval Controls

These controls insure data security, privacy, error handling, backup, recovery, and retention. Application data, normally stored in some kind of data base, can be protected and audited by means of the following controls.

1.   Individuals or groups that are allowed to use them may have access to data and files. Systems that provide this kind of protection in an IBM environment are RACF and ACF2, data security packages. IBM's IMS has similar protections built in to protect

data down to the field level. Files may also be protected by password security.

2. Header and trailer records provided by operating systems on tapes and disks provide a level of security against inadvertent erasure.

3. Operating system transaction logging provides tracks to terminals and users extracting or modifying data.

4. Data base verification programs examine the data base offline and report errors and out-of-range conditions.

A variety of manual controls over the distribution of the final reports helps protect the information until it reaches the end user.

4. PRODUCTIVITY ISSUES

Most of the audit controls described depend on the program to verify its own operation continuously. This means that you will have to build these audit trails into every new program. The productivity consequences put an additional load on your programmers and analysts, but by proper planning, you can minimize most of these negative impacts of audit requirements while improving the quality of the programs produced.

The internal auditing controls described are generic; they can be designed and implemented in every new system. Building them into existing programs may be prohibitively expensive, however. Designing each control in a generic fashion permits its inclusion in every prototype design and program developed for your software factory. These built-in controls will reduce the burden of supplying audit facilities. They improve the productivity not only of your auditors, but also your DP staff. Generic audit designs will eliminate the errors inherent in having many unique designs. Your generic program logic will have been extensively tested, so that only the interfaces to the generic routines may require testing. Generic control logic will provide a standard interface across all systems, which will make Operation's job easier since they will have one, and only one, type of control philosophy to understand. Their productivity will improve. The auditors will also benefit from a standard interface.

5. SUMMARY

The complexity of application systems makes automatic auditing a requirement. Neither the auditors nor the users can verify the processing and output of the system adequately. So the system must check itself.

The internal controls required will demand analyst and programmer resources to design and build them into every system, which puts an additional load on the development organization that can be reduced by use of generic audit trail designs, code, subroutines, and programs. Without a corporate approach to auditing, the productivity and quality of systems will suffer from the additional load provided by auditing and government requirements. Planning a corporate auditing philosophy in cooperation with the EDP auditing department will insure that future systems meet the minimum daily requirement for control and security. Without such controls, your corporation, its assets, and its management are all in peril from fraud, embezzlement, and government audits. Auditing can be performed with a minimum expenditure of development resources through a number of home-grown productivity tools. Developing them is up to you.

CHAPTER ELEVEN

Buying Software to Improve Productivity

Would you ever consider building your own car? Designing and manufacturing engines, tires, axles, and transmissions would be prohibitively expensive, but you'd get exactly the kind of car you wanted. On the other hand, you could go to all the different car dealers and select a car that fits your basic needs, add available options, and for a significantly lower cost have a car that meets most of your requirements. Not only that, but you could also have that car today, not two years from now when you finish building your own. If you need transportation today, building your own car is not a viable option. Besides, in two years, government safety and emissions standards will probably make your car illegal.

Software is much the same. There are hundreds of software companies nationwide producing vanilla software systems: they will not provide all the options your company needs, but they can be installed in a month or two. If your programming staff consists of one office manager, who inherited the programming job, or 1000 analysts and programmers, buying software can fill the software vacuum.

Purchased software can provide a competitive edge. Buying generic software—such as payroll, accounting, financial, and system software—can allow development of management information systems that provide your managers with data for better decision-making. Your competitor may also follow this path, but at least you are no worse off. The continuing shift of the work force into white-collar jobs indicates that software systems to support them will provide the edge for shaving the competition. To improve productivity, quality, and cost reduction, consider buying software.

1. HOW TO LOOK FOR SOFTWARE

More than 7000 software packages are available, as of this writing. These packages provide a wide diversity of function, application, cost, and benefit. There are two types of software package: systems software and application software. System software helps people use the computer. Application software helps people run the business. System software includes operating systems, compilers, query and report languages, and all manner of programs to improve the efficiency of the computer operation. Application software includes generic payroll, accounting, ledger, inventory control, scheduling, and other common business systems. Application software also extends into specific software for manufacturing, health care, insurance, banking and other industry-related systems. Trends indicate a massive growth in application software.

2. WHERE TO FIND SOFTWARE

Some software is probably available in-house: with minor modification, your existing systems may meet your needs. This is especially true in large corporations where there is little or no communication between departments about the software each uses.

Computer manufacturers provide another source of software. They often provide only system software, but they may be able to refer you to other companies running application software that can be purchased. You might also research corporations similar to your own in other parts of the country. They might have the software you need and be willing to share it since you are not in direct competition. It also reduces their cost for the system.

User groups provide another source for software. To meet their common need for software, user groups spring up and share software with similar users all over the country. The software provided, however, will have no support and could prove to be a problem instead of an opportunity.

Software houses provide varied software packages and services. These companies either have the system you need or one they can modify easily to meet your needs, or they can custom build a system to your specifications. They may have a generic system that can be easily installed on your machine, which is far more cost effective for both of you. Selling multiple generic systems allows the software company to price the product at 10–20% of development cost. As with the automobile example, generic systems provide economies of scale that in-house custom development cannot.

There is a wide variety of application software. Some of the major types available are as follows.

1. Accounting
   a. Accounts payable
   b. Accounts receivable
   c. General ledger
   d. General accounting
   e. Billing
   f. Financial information systems
   g. Tax
   h. Auditing
2. Banking and Finance
   a. Loans
   b. Trusts
   c. Savings deposits
   d. Checking account deposit and credit
   e. Vacation, Christmas, retirement, certificate deposits
   f. Stock and bond management
   g. General bank accounting
   h. Property management
   i. Financial control
   j. Business planning
   k. Funds transfer
   l. Credit card administration
   m. Check processing
   n. On-line teller functions
   o. Automatic teller systems
3. Education
   a. Research systems: modeling, statistical analysis, computer-aided design

b. Computer-aided instruction
c. Student information systems
d. Student registration
e. Personnel
f. Accounting, billing, planning, and publishing

4. Insurance
   a. Personnel
   b. Policy administration
   c. Claims handling
   d. Underwriting
   e. Investment management
   f. Financial systems

5. Manufacturing
   a. Production planning and control
   b. Marketing
   c. Distribution
   d. Computer-aided design

6. Medical and Health Care
   a. Hospital and patient care administration
   b. Personnel
   c. Finance and accounting
   d. Patient care services: laboratory systems, etc.
   e. Insurance systems
   f. Physician services: billing, diagnostic, appointment scheduling

7. Payroll and Personnel
   a. Government reporting
   b. Wage and salary administration
   c. Employment services
   d. Benefits administration
   e. Record keeping
   f. Employment and recruitment
   g. Personnel management

8. Sales and Distribution
   a. Retail automation: sales, accounting, marketing
   b. Financial
   c. Warehousing: delivery, labor, inventory control
   d. Distribution
   e. Mail-order systems
   f. Hotel management systems

There are turn-key system suppliers who assist you in selecting software and hardware and following through on the total installation. They may provide the easiest way for a company using manual procedures to computerize. A word of caution: the turn-key vendor should be reputable. You don't want to be left with an unsupported system. The hardware selected should provide means for growth. That is the function of computers—to allow company growth at a lower incremental cost.

Finally, computer stores are springing up nationwide. Once again, be cautious. These systems provide a way to computerize at a low cost. Plenty of software exists to support them. But they may be programmed in BASIC or some other language that will be difficult to transport to larger machines as you expand.

3. THE MAKE OR BUY DECISION

What are the key points to think about before making the make or buy decision? Financially, it is probably cheaper to buy your software. Many intangible benefits, however, may tip that balance.

1. Custom in-house development may take 10 to 100 times as long to develop or may be impossible with the existing staff.

2. Purchased software may meet only 30-50% of your needs.

3. Your software department may resist purchased software. There's a pleasure inherent in building your own that you can't derive from using purchased systems.

4. Purchased software may provide functions you don't want.

Don't be fooled into buying a great piece of hardware, which is what many vendors are interested in selling. What you need most is the right software. The function of a car is to provide transportation. You can purchase a Mercedes-Benz because it is the ultimate engineering marvel, but if you have nine kids, a Volkswagen bus would better meet your needs. Select your hardware not on the basis of its wonderfulness, but on how it meets your software needs.

4. HOW TO ACQUIRE SOFTWARE

As with any software development, a systematic approach to selecting software will improve the resulting quality of the system.

Consider following the same phased methodology described in Chapter 2. Should it become apparent that purchased software will not meet your needs, most of the groundwork for in-house development will have been laid.

It is assumed that the proposal and feasibility phases have been completed, pointing to purchased software as your best alternative. So now the user has to specify the requirements for the new system. These should include the basic function the system must provide to meet the minimum basic needs, as well as an "added factors" section—niceties that make the system more useful should be listed in order of priority to help decide among systems. Requirements should also include costs. What is the most the user will pay?

The computer environment may also be a question. If you already have a computer, you may want software that will run on it. That would be cheaper than buying different hardware for each application. For a new installation, you should select hardware that supports a wide variety of software packages that you will need at some point. Plan ahead. The availability of software is one of the reasons IBM dominates the mainframe market and DIGITAL dominates the minicomputer market.

Once the requirements are defined, the search for compatible software can begin. The DATAPRO Research Corporation compiles information on application software. It describes the varied systems and compiles surveys of user satisfaction. For a nominal price, DATAPRO provides you with a concise directory to all kinds of software. Technical journals such as *DATAMATION* and *Computerworld* advertise new systems as they appear on the market. Local consultants may provide a similar service. Use all the resources you can find.

Begin selecting software that meets all of your basic requirements, so that you have a small group of systems from which to select the best one. If no system meets the basic criteria, there is no other choice but to custom build the system yourself. It's as simple as that.

Assuming that you do find some viable application systems, you have to decide among them. Compare the software packages to the detailed requirements developed by the user. Which packages provide the higher priority options? Which systems can be easily modified to produce these options? Is the source code provided to allow changes? Is the system adequately documented? Can the system be installed by the date you need it? Each of these questions further reduces the number of systems to be evaluated.

Ask each vendor for a list of user contacts. Seeing a system in action is different from looking at it on paper. Ask probing questions about what the users like and dislike about the system. Now that they have the system, what options would they like to have on it? How well does the vendor support them? What kind of installation problems were encountered?

If you have an opportunity to benchmark the new system on your computer, by all means do so. Benchmark tests involve running the system in an environment that simulates your own office. Test data must be created, run, and verified. All this takes extra time and effort, but remember that you will be running this system for a long time; find out about it before you spend a lot of time and money operating it. The software vendor will tend to resist this kind of testing unless he or she has a good system. Benchmarks are essential when the package is not widely used. Stick to software that has been well received and widely used, if possible.

Now, make your decision to build or buy. If you decide to buy, you will need to negotiate a contract for support. Invest in a lawyer to analyze the contract and help resolve deficiencies. The contract should provide training, installation assistance, and maintenance.

Finally, the vendor should help install the software package and should be required contractually to provide support throughout a software verification test. Much like a benchmark test, the verification test assures that at least one cycle of processing has been completed and has provided satisfactory results.

Some time following installation, perhaps six months, you should conduct a performance review of the software. Is it being used effectively? Is it providing the benefits expected? Is it providing benefits not originally planned? What are the deficiencies and limitations of the package? From this evaluation, you will understand more about your software requirements. Next time you buy a package, you will be in a better position to evaluate and state your needs to the vendor.

5. DEVELOPING SYSTEM REQUIREMENTS

In developing requirements for purchased computer systems you must ask the following questions.

1. Does this system meet all of your minimum requirements?
2. Will it run on your computer?

3. What other software do you need to run the application system?

4. Compare your list of enhanced features to the packages available. Which one meets more of your needs?

5. Does the package perform well enough for your present and projected needs? If the system will support only eight terminals and 50 clients, what happens when you expand?

6. Is the package flexible? Can it be enhanced to meet your changing needs? Is source code provided so that you can change the system?

7. Is the package easy to install?

8. Is the package easy to use?

9. Is the system well documented?

10. What support will the vendor provide?

11. How widely used is the package?

12. What is the total cost of the system, including acquiring, installing, and maintaining the package?

13. Is the package sold or leased?

6. CONTRACT NEGOTIATIONS

Contracts can be painful or useful. Here are a few key points to cover when negotiating a contract with a vendor.

1. How long will the vendor provide installation support, correcting bugs and providing required enhancements? The vendor should not charge for installation support. How long will the vendor provide continued support? What will this support cost?

2. If benchmarks, certification, and verification tests indicate that the system is unsuitable, how long do you have to return the system for a refund?

3. What is the vendor's penalty for failure to provide timely delivery and installation of the package?

4. Vendor support should be spelled out for installation, training, and maintenance. Costs for these services should also be identified.

5. The contract should specify how the system will be delivered. Will there be source code or object modules? Will they be delivered by tape, disk, or cards? How will documentation be delivered? How many copies are provided and what is the cost of additional copies?

6. The vendor will require that the software not be copied or resold.

7. Payment, in full, should not be required until all services are performed and the software is installed, tested, and working.

It is your responsibility to get the most function per software dollar. If packaged software doesn't meet your needs and you can't get the resources to develop in-house, maybe you need to look elsewhere.

7. SOFTWARE DEVELOPMENT CONTRACTING

Suppose you were looking for a home. You would have several options: you could design and build your own; you could buy a home already designed and built; or you could contract with an architect and builder to construct your home. Constructing your own home takes time and possibly costs more than having a builder do it. Buying an existing home gives you most of what you need in a house but rarely everything you want. Contracting to build your dream house is another possibility. It takes more time than buying an existing house, but less than building your own. Custom construction may cost more than either buying an existing home or building your own. If you have time to wait but not the time to expend yourself, then contracting may be the best way to get the home of your choice. The same is true of software.

A generic package may not meet your needs. You are already two to three years behind in developing all of the software you need. Contracting to develop the software you need may be the only way to meet your current resource shortage. It also keeps staffing levels down so that when you do catch up, you will not have excessive overhead.

There are specific items to examine when contracting for software development.

1. If you were contracting for a house, you would look for a dependable builder, one who had been in the business awhile, not one about to go out of business. The same holds true for software; look for a reliable firm.

2. You would also want a builder who produces quality homes. The software firm you select must be contractually obligated to produce what you deem to be quality software. You must specify the development process, definition, design, coding, and testing standards. You may, as the Department of Defense does, specify the need for a quality control group to oversee the development. You may specify software quality as a function of the software metric programs described in Chapter 6.

You take a number of risks when contracting for software development.

1.   If a dispute arises over the development, you may forfeit all payments to that date and you may not have anything to show for them. One way around this problem is to specify deliverable products that may be exchanged for the payment at each stage of development. Deliverables include requirements, designs, code, documentation of all types, and tested programs. Specify them in the contract.

2.   Development schedule slippages are legendary. These affect the delivery of software and the ultimate use of the product. Penalties can be imposed on the vendor, but they also cause the vendor to deliver unfinished, poor quality products. Bonuses may be provided for early delivery, but they cause initial schedules to be inflated.

3.   The vendor may use your resources, people, and computers, to assist in the development. The use of these resources should be contractually stipulated and controlled.

4.   The quality of the end product may not meet your needs. As was previously stated, quality should be specified as clearly as possible. You may require review and acceptance of the products produced at each phase.

5.   The vendor, because of your development work, may build a system that gives you a competitive edge. The vendor should be prohibited from marketing your system or building similar systems for a specified period. For example, an inventory control system that reduces your your stock by 30% without affecting your sales will reduce your costs and allow you to reduce prices, providing you with a competitive edge. The vendor could supply your system to competitors for a much lower cost than originally charged, since there are no development costs. You might allow the vendor to market the product, providing royalties from the system sales.

Contracting for software development can be risky, but it provides you with an alternative to buying or building software. It provides you with a highly productive, timely means to implement software systems that would otherwise be impossible because of resource constraints. It is like adding staff that can disappear when the project is complete. It helps hold the line on costs without jeopardizing your competitive stance.

8. SUMMARY

Buying application software and contracting for software development can increase your productivity, providing timely systems to meet your information needs. These systems have some drawbacks, but if you can find an appropriate fit, they will fill your software vacuum until you can build your own system or a new package that is even better comes out. By substituting cash for people, you can have information systems in place within weeks of your perceived need. They enhance your ability to compete, increase your revenues, and help your department evolve toward the software factory.

CHAPTER TWELVE

Implementing Software Engineering

The unfortunate thing about this world is that good habits are so much easier to give up than bad ones.

Somerset Maugham

The chains of habit are too weak to be felt until they are too strong to be broken.

Samuel Johnson

The most difficult problem you will face in trying to implement software engineering and the software factory concept is people's natural resistance to change. Like those of any other department being automated, data processing personnel will respond slowly to change. They will actively resist it, spending more time trying to subvert, disprove, and prevent change than it would take them to accept it.

On the other hand, a few hardy souls will take up the standard and charge into the crusade. As they make productivity and quality gains, nonbelievers will be forced to keep up. People who cannot handle the change will move into other jobs.

Darwin's theories apply to data processing evolution as well as to the evolution of species. Every advancement will create better jobs for some employees and discard others. It is incumbent upon the corporation to retrain these fallen employees if possible or to assist them in finding other jobs. The DP evolution improves the strength of the company and improves its chances of surviving in a competitive marketplace.

Confronted with the problems facing information system development, the corporation will request direct employee involvement in initiating and implementing change. Your DP personnel should see change as a meaningful choice for their own security and survival as well.

Since the introduction of application systems has only an intangible effect on the corporation's ability to make a profit, it is difficult to stimulate management to invest in expanded software development. As the competitive potential of the computer comes fully to light, productivity and quality improvements will become essential to better marketing and increasing the bottom line.

As you implement software engineering, look for gradual change. Look for your first converts. Look for top management interest. Each of these signals success.

1. IMPLEMENTING PRODUCTIVITY AND QUALITY IMPROVEMENTS

Obviously, you want to begin improving productivity and quality where it will have the most benefit—the areas where you spend most of your DP dollars. In most companies, maintenance consumes over 50% of the budget, so it is the logical place to start.

2. MAINTENANCE

Chapter 8 described how to improve maintenance, requiring rewriting maintenance-prone programs identified by the software metrics program. Development of the software quality metrics program requires little effort. The analysis of your existing program modules and their correction will require dedication and an ongoing review and revision process. Upgrading your existing programs should begin as soon as possible, interweaving quality improvements with normal maintenance activities. Many of the corrections suggested require only an hour or two of the programmer's time.

The maintenance productivity and reliability improvements will more than compensate for the time spent.

Identifying and correcting maintenance-prone programs are the only ways to decrease your maintenance load, freeing members of your staff to work on new development. Unless you actively pursue quality measurement and improvement, your maintenance costs will continue to skyrocket, leaving you precious little resource to keep up with the rest of the industry.

3. APPLICATION CONTROL

Next, you will need to gain control of the development process. Implementing the phased methodology described in Chapter 2 will provide management with increased control. Release control and change management also improve project control. This methodology improves productivity and quality by reducing the confusion and chaos normally associated with a poorly managed project. Once your development process is sufficiently structured, you can begin developing the software factory.

4. SOFTWARE FACTORY

The software factory requires the application of manufacturing techniques to program development. The programmers and analysts must learn how to use a component approach to system development. They should no longer think in terms of logic structures, but of functional structures and how to combine them in the quickest way possible to produce a program.

The software factory requires the purchase or development of program and application generators, as described in Chapters 2 and 3. They will require an investment to retrain your employees in their use, but your productivity can improve 100—200%. The use of generic program logic will also improve the reliability, maintainability, and quality of your systems. The result: timely, low-cost application systems.

5. INFORMATION CENTER

The wave of the future is upon us. Use of the information center concept and nonprocedural languages gives you the ability to off-load some of your programming to the user. The use of nonprocedural languages gets the user off your back for the development of trivial report and one-shot "what if" programs, freeing your personnel to work on high-priority custom software.

Historically, the major productivity improvements have come through quantum leaps in programming languages. The productivity leap from assembler language to COBOL was over 500%. Nonprocedural languages provide the same sort of potential. Those of you who tap this productivity reserve will leapfrog over your competition's ability to hold the line on programming costs.

In the near future, computers will become as easy to use as your telephone or pocket calculator. Nonprocedural languages are a step in this direction. In just a few years, with the advances in hardware technology, you will have a two-megabyte minicomputer board in your terminal with all the peripheral storage you need.

The ability to distribute information and processing to this level will produce major changes in how people work. With this kind of power available at a reasonable price, it makes sense to let the user write most of his or her own software in a nonprocedural language. The user gets the information required in minutes instead of the days or months normally required if he or she were to go through a Data Processing group.

Your technicians can also benefit from nonprocedural languages; they will be able to create a prototype of a system in a few days or weeks, instead of spending months or years developing a COBOL system. The user can quickly identify design problems that are then easily corrected. Once a working system is available, you can decide if you should rewrite it in COBOL or PL/1 for efficiency reasons.

Nonprocedural languages provide productivity benefits of 100–1000%. To overlook them will restrict your corporation's evolution; you'll find yourself on a weak, if not dead, branch of the evolutionary tree.

6.   OFFICE AUTOMATION

The chance to automate your office provides the first opportunity to distribute the data in your central computer into the office, where they are so desperately needed. Many of the current office automation systems offer a variety of communication links to your central processors. Retrieving data will be simple.

The text processing and graphics capabilities of your office system will allow the manipulation of the data into a diverse spectrum of output that facilitates good management decisions. The word processing and electronic mail features of these systems will further improve white-collar productivity and quality, with their resulting impacts on the corporation. Office automation systems also offer a variety of query and nonprocedural languages. The support for these systems will continue to grow, putting a highly productive tool in the hands of each manager, professional, technical, and clerical person in the organization.

7. PEOPLE

Your major obstacle to building the software factory will be people—your management, technicians, and clerical people—everyone. Some of them are clamoring for office automation, but you can bet they'll fight measurements and new languages. Managers will question the costs and benefits of new technology. But you can't get something for nothing. You can use the methodology in Chapter 2 to improve the work flow, thereby improving productivity. But as usual, the more beneficial results come from more costly solutions.

Programmers like to progress with technology, but they don't like for it to make sudden quantum leaps. You may have to migrate from where you are to where you want to be, and it will take time.

8. YOUR SOFTWARE FACTORY

I've listed the major productivity- and quality-enhancing methodologies and technologies in the order I think most important. Make a list of those you would like to explore, in order of priority. Then, simply begin trying them out. Work on the human factors of anything you want to install. People are the major barrier to change. Plan your changes to minimize the human problems. Evaluate your progress. Are the changes working or not? Do they meet the needs of the corporation and employees? Review and revise your plans as new information comes to light.

Like some medieval surgeon, you are exploring the possibilities of performing major operations on your corporation. It has never been done before, but you have to get in and revitalize those arteries of information. You have to stimulate the movement of data throughout the corporation, providing life-giving sustenance to the organism. Without information, the company is like a blind animal: it cannot hunt for new markets; it cannot predict coming storms; it cannot find shelter; it is prey for any prowling competitor. Perhaps it is only myopic now, but without your constant and immediate attention, the corporate vision will decline until it ultimately trips and stumbles into a crevasse.

All of the productivity and quality improvements in this book will stimulate your corporate health through improved information flow and better quality information. Without them, your company cannot live through the decade; and that ultimately will affect every employee. So begin the construction of your software factory; it is the heart of your information flow. It is your first-strike capability against the competition. The use of software manufacturing techniques will plunge your corporation into the new era of software engineering. Software development and maintenance have finally come of age.

Bibliography

Amadio, M. A., "Breaking the software bottleneck," *INTERFACE*, 27-33, Summer 1980.

Anthony, R. N., J. Dearden, and R. F. Vancil, *Management Control Systems*, Irwin, Homewood, IL 1972.

Baker, F. T., "Chief programmer team management of production programming," *IBM Syst. J.*, No. 1, 56-73, 1972.

Bjork, L. A. Jr., "Generalized audit trail requirements and concepts for data base applications," *IBM Syst. J.*, **14**(3), 229-245, 1975.

Bloch, A., *Murphy's Law*, Price/Stern/Sloan, Los Angeles, 1977.

Bloch, A., *Murphy's Law, Book Two*, Price/Stern/Sloan, Los Angeles, 1980.

Boehm. B. W. et al., *Characteristics of Software Quality*, North-Holland, New York, 1978.

Booz, Allen, and Hamilton, Inc., *Booz, Allen Study of Managerial/Professional Productivity*, Booz, Allen, and Hamilton, New York, 1980.

Bowen, W., "Better prospects for our ailing productivity," *Fortune*, 68-86, December 3, 1979.

Brooks, F. P. Jr., *The Mythical Man-Mouth*, Addison-Wesley, Reading, MA, 1975.

Brown, G. D., *Advanced ANS COBOL with Structured Programming*, Wiley, New York, 1977.

Buss, M. D. J., *"Penny-wise approach to data processing," Harvard Bus. Rev.*, 111-117, July-August 1981.

Canning, R. G., "The challenge of increased productivity," *Computerworld*, 5-10, September 1, 1981.

Cerf, V. G. and A. Curran, "The future of computer communications," *DATAMATION*, 105-114, May 1977.

Chooljian, S., "The move toward auditability," *INTERFACE*, 9-12, Fall 1978.

Christensen, K., C. P. Fitsos, and C. P. Smith, "A perspective on software science," *IBM Syst. J.*, **20**(4), 372-387, 1981.

Cooper, J. D. and M. J. Fisher, *Software Quality Management*, Petrocelli, New York, 1979.

Corum, P. J., "Computer audit software," *INTERFACE*, 27-29, Spring 1980.

Couger, J. D. and R. A. Zawacki, "What motivates DP professionals," *DATAMATION*, 116-123, September 1978.

Couger, J. D., "The Project Manager: Kingpin in personnel motivation," *Computerworld*, 49-56, September 1, 1981.

Daly, E. B., "Organizing for successful software development," *DATAMATION*, 107-120, December 1979.

Dean Witter Reynolds, Inc., *Random-Access Monthly*, Industry Periodical, 1-20, December 1979.

Deutsch, C. H., "Productivity: The difficulty of even defining the problem," *Business Week*, 52-53, June 9, 1980.

Digital Equipment Corporation, *Distributed Systems Handbook*, Digital, Maynard, MA, 1978.

Dunn, R. and R. Ullman, *Quality Assurance for Computer Software*, McGraw-Hill, New York, 1982.

Fabun, D., *The Dynamics of Change*, Prentice-Hall, Englewood Cliffs, 1969.

Feuer, A. R. and F. B. Fowlkes, *Relating Computer Program Maintainability to Software Measures*, Proceedings of the 1979 National Computer Conference, June 1979.

Fox, J. (Ed.), *Proceedings of the Symposium on Computer Software Engineering*, Vol. XXIV, Polytechnic Press, New York, 1969.

Gehring, R. L., "The office as an information system," *Forbes*, 96-105, March 30, 1981.

Gilb, T., *Software Metrics*, Winthrop, Cambridge, MA, 1977.

Gildersleeve, T. R., *Data Processing Project Management*, Van Nostrand, New York, 1974.

Glass, R. L. and R. A. Noiseux, *Software Maintenance Guidebook*, Prentice-Hall, Englewood Cliffs, 1981.

Gordon, R. L. and J. C. Lamb, "A close look at Brooks' law," *DATAMATION*, 81-86, June 1977.

Gottfried, I. S., "Understanding the new breed of DPer," *Computerworld*, 11-13, September 1, 1981.

Gunning, R., *More Effective Writing in Business and Industry*, Cahners Books, Boston, 1963.

Gunther, R. C., *Management Methodology for Software Product Engineering*, Wiley, New York, 1978.

Hagamen, W. D. et al., "A program generator," *IBM Syst. J.*, **14**(2), 102-133, 1975.

Halstead, M. H., *Elements of Software Science*, North-Holland, New York, 1977.

Hamming, R. W., *One man's view of computer science*, J. *ACM*, **16**(1), 10, 1969.

Herzberg, Fredrick, "One more time, how do you motivate employees?", *Harvard Bus. Rev.*, 53-62, January-February, 1968.

Hinrichs, J. R., *Practical Management for Productivity*, Van Nostrand, New York, 1978

Jancura, E. G. and A. H. Berger, *Computers: Auditing and Control*, Auerbach, Philadelphia, 1973.

Johnson, S. C., and M. E. Lesk, "Language development tools," *Bell Syst. Tech. J.* **57**(6), 2155-2176, Part 2, 1978.

Justis, R. T., "America feasts on Japanese management delicacies—Quality Circles," *Data Management*, 30-43, October 1981.

Kapur, G., "Toward software engineering," *Computerworld*, 1-10, October 23, 1980.

Kernighan, B. and P. J. Plauger, *The Elements of Programming Style*, McGraw-Hill, New York, 1974.

Kernighan, B. and P. J. Plauger, *Software Tools*, Addison-Wesley, Reading, MA, 1976.

Kurkall, R. E., "EDP auditing and systems design," *INTERFACE*, 32-35, Spring 1980.

Leavitt, D., "Reusable code chops 60% off creation of business programs," *Computerworld*, 3-4, October 29, 1979.

Lohr, S., "Overhauling America's business management," *New York Times Magazine*, January 4, 1981.

Luke, R. A. Jr., "Matching the individual and the organization," *Harvard Bus. Rev.*, 17-34, May–June, 1975.

Main, J., "How to battle your own bureaucracy," *Fortune*, 54-58, June 29, 1981.

McClure, C. L., *Managing Software Development and Maintenance*, Van Nostrand, New York, 1981.

McCusker, T., "Examining the office of the future," *DATAMATION*, 120-121, February 1980.

McGill, A. J., "The office as an Information System," *Forbes*, 118-124, March 30, 1981.

McKee, R. B., "Computer . . . program thyself," *Data Management*, 36-37, October 1980.

MacKenzie, R. A., *The Time Trap*, AMACOM, New York, 1972.

Metzger, P. W., *Managing a Programming Project*, Prentice-Hall, Englewood Cliffs, 1973.

Milson, J. H., "Automating documentation aids in software maintenance," *Data Management*, 15-17, April 1981.

Mintzberg, H., *The Nature of Managerial Work*, Harper and Row, New York, 1973.

Murphy, E. F., "The office as an Information System," *Forbes*, 108-116, March 30, 1981.

Myers, G. J., *Reliable Software through Composite Design*, Petrocelli, New York, 1975.

Myers, G. J., *Software Reliability*, Wiley, New York, 1976.

Myers, G. J., *The Art of Software Testing*, Wiley, New York, 1979.

Noll, P., *The Structured Programming Cookbook*, Mike Murach & Associates, Inc. Fresno, CA, 1978.

Ouchi, W., *Theory Z: How American Business Can Meet the Japanese Challenge*, Addison-Wesley, Reading, MA, 1981.

Pascale, R. T., "Zen and the art of management," *Harvard Bus. Rev.*, 153-162, March-April, 1978.

Patrick, R. L., "The productivity gap," *DATAMATION*, 131-132, December 1979.

Perlis, A., F. Sayward, and M. Shaw, *Software Metrics*, MIT Press, Boston, MA, 1981.

Rathbone, R. R., *Communicating Technical Information*, Addison-Wesley, Reading, MA, 1972.

Rice, J. G., *Build Program Technique*, Wiley, New York, 1981.

Ritchie, D. M. and K. Thompson, "The UNIX time-sharing system," *Bell Sys. Tech. J.*, **57**(6), 1905-1930, Part 2, 1978.

Roman, G-C, "An argument in favor of mechanized software production," *IEEE Trans. Soft. Eng.*, **SE-3**(6), 406-415, November 1977.

Schoenblum, E., "Productivity in perspective," *Data Management*, 12-16, October 1980.

Schoenblum, E., "Productivity in perspective," *Data Management*, 47-50, November 1980.

Schultz, B., "Revolution not here yet—Turing Winner," *Computerworld*, 12, November 12, 1979.

Sherwin, D. S., "Management of objectives," *Harvard Bus. Rev.*, 149-160, May-June 1976.

Shneiderman, B., *Software Psychology*, Winthrop, Cambridge, MA, 1980.

Stanford Research Institute, *System Auditability and Control*, Institute of Internal Auditors, Altamonte Springs, FL, 1977.

Stearns, M., "ABC's of good management start with a Z," *Data Management*, 36-54, October 1981.

Stearns, M., "Japan as a mirror for American management," *Data Management*, 45-48, October 1981.

Stevens, R. T., *Operational Test and Evaluation*, Wiley, New York, 1979.

Stone, J., Professionals Will Endorse Office Systems, *Computerworld*, 37, November 12, 1979.

Tharrington, J. M., "A Manager's guide to measuring programmer productivity," *Computerworld*, 57-66, September 1, 1981.

Thayer, T. A., *Software Reliability*, North-Holland, New York, 1978.

Tomeski, E. A. and H. Lazarus, *People-Oriented Computer Systems*, Van Nostrand, New York, 1975.

Uhlig, R. P., "Human factors in computer message systems," *DATAMATION*, 120-126, May 1977.

Viens, H., "The human network," *Computerworld*, 67-74, September 1, 1981.

Vignone, A. F., "Modular developments improve program design," *Computerworld*, 28-29, February 4, 1977.

Walton, R. E., "Improving the quality of work life," *Harvard Bus. Rev.*, 15-16, May-June 1974.

Weizenbaum, J., *Computer Power and Human Reason*, W. H. Freeman, San Francisco, 1976.

Westin, A. F., "The impact of computers on privacy," *DATAMATION*, 190-194, December 1979.

Widtfeldt, J. R., "Jumping on the quality circles bandwagon," *Data Management*, 32-35, October 1981.

Weinberg, G. M., *The Psychology of Computer Programming*, Van Nostrand, New York, 1972.

Wohl, A., "A Review of office automation," *DATAMATION*, 116-119, February 1980.

Young, L. H. Ed., "Voice mail arrives in the office," *Business Week*, 52-53, June 9, 1980.

Young, L. H. Ed., "Boosting productivity at the top," *Business Week*, 74, July 14, 1980.

Young, L. H. Ed., "Missing computer software," *Business Week*, 46-54, September 1, 1980.

Young, L. H. Ed., "Stunted growth of productivity," *Business Week*, 65-124, March 30, 1981.

Yourdon, E. N., *Techniques of Program Structure and Design*, Prentice-Hall, Englewood Cliffs, 1976.

Yourdon, E. N., *Classics in Software Engineering*, Yourdon Press, New York, 1979.

Zachmann, W. F., *Keys to Enhancing System Development Productivity*, AMACOM, New York, 1981.

Zelkowitz, M. V., "Perspectives in Software Engineering," *Computing Survs.*, 10(2), 197-216, June 1978.

APPENDIX A

Generic Update Program

```
       IDENTIFICATION DIVISION.
       PROGRAM-ID. 'PGMNAME '.
       SECURITY.
      ***************************************************************
      *                                                             *
      *  SOFTWARE SECURITY STATEMENT                                *
      *                                                             *
      ***************************************************************
       AUTHOR. YOUR COMPANY.
       DATE-WRITTEN. MM/DD/YY.
       REMARKS.
      ***************************************************************
      *                                                             *
      *  MAIN PROGRAM: PGMNAME                                       *
      *                                                             *
      *  PROGRAM DESCRIPTION:                                        *
      *                                                             *
      *  SUBROUTINES CALLED OR REQUIRED:                             *
      *                                                             *
      *  REFERENCE: (JOB DEFINITION, IPO, ETC)                       *
      *                                                             *
      ***************************************************************
       EJECT
       ENVIRONMENT DIVISION.
       CONFIGURATION SECTION.
       SOURCE-COMPUTER. IBM-370.
       OBJECT-COMPUTER. IBM-370.
       INPUT-OUTPUT SECTION.
       SKIP2
       FILE-CONTROL.
       SKIP2
      ****************************************************************
      *                                                              *
      *  SELECT STATEMENTS MUST BE ORDERED AS FOLLOWS:               *
      *                                                              *
      *      INPUT, INPUT/OUTPUT, OUTPUT, SORT                       *
      *                                                              *
      ****************************************************************
       EJECT
       DATA DIVISION.
       SKIP2
       FILE SECTION.
       SKIP2
      ****************************************************************
      *                                                              *
      *  FILE DESCRIPTIONS                                           *
      *                                                              *
      *  COPY FDS FOR ALL DISK AND TAPE DATASETS                     *
      *  CREATE FD FOR ANY CARD DATASETS                             *
      *                                                              *
      *  FILE DESCRIPTIONS SHOULD BE IN THE FOLLOWING ORDER:         *
```

```
*                                                              *
*      INPUT, INPUT/OUTPUT, OUTPUT, SORT                       *
*                                                              *
****************************************************************
 SKIP2
**** NONE
 EJECT
****************************************************************
*                                                              *
*                PGID    DATA  DICTIONARY                      *
*      ABBREVIATION                 FULL DESCRIPTION           *
*                                                              *
*      C                            CONSTANT                   *
*      EOF                          END OF FILE                *
*      I                            INDEX                      *
*      PARM                         JCL PARAMETERS             *
*      S OR SW.                     SWITCH                      *
****************************************************************
 SKIP3
 WORKING-STORAGE SECTION.
 SKIP2
 01  START-WORKING-STORAGE          . PIC X(27)
         VALUE 'WORKING STORAGE BEGINS HERE'.
 SKIP3
****************************************************************
*                                                              *
*   CONSTANTS                                                  *
*                                                              *
****************************************************************
 SKIP2
 01  CONSTANTS.
         05 C-ADD                    PIC X     VALUE '1'.
         05 C-ADD-ERROR       COMP  PIC S999  VALUE +1.
         05 C-DELETE                 PIC X     VALUE '3'.
         05 C-DELETE-ERROR    COMP  PIC S999  VALUE +5.
         05 C-DUMP-OPTION            PIC X(4)  VALUE 'DUMP'.
         05 C-CHANGE                 PIC X     VALUE '2'.
         05 C-CHANGE-ERROR    COMP  PIC S999  VALUE +10.
         05 C-YES                    PIC X     VALUE 'Y'.
         05 C-1               COMP  PIC S9    VALUE +1.
 SKIP2
****************************************************************
*                                                              *
*   STANDARD 01 LEVELS                                         *
*                                                              *
****************************************************************
 SKIP2
 01  PGID-VERSION-INFORMATION.
         05  MODULE-ID               PIC X(8)  VALUE 'PGMNAME '.
         05  SOURCE-CODE-LEVEL       PIC X(6)  VALUE 'RR.LLL'.
         05  VERSION-DATE            PIC X(8)
```

```
                    VALUE 'MM/DD/YY'.
        SKIP2
        01  COUNTS SYNC.
            05  PROGRAM-CALL-COUNT COMP    PIC S9(7) VALUE ZERO.
            05  ADD-COUNT                  PIC S9(7) VALUE ZERO.
            05  DELETE-COUNT               PIC S9(7) VALUE ZERO.
            05  CHANGE-COUNT               PIC S9(7) VALUE ZERO.
            05  REJECTED-COUNT             PIC S9(7) VALUE ZERO.
        SKIP3
        ****************************************************************
        *                                                              *
        *  WORKING STORAGE -------- TABLES                             *
        *                                                              *
        ****************************************************************
        SKIP1                                            01330000
        *  NONE
        SKIP3
        ****************************************************************
        *                                                              *
        *  WORKING STORAGE --------  REPORT HEADERS AND FOOTERS        *
        *                                                              *
        ****************************************************************
        SKIP1
        *  NONE
        SKIP3
        ****************************************************************
        *                                                              *
        *  WORKING STORAGE -------- ERROR MESSAGES AND CODES           *
        *                                                              *
        ****************************************************************
        SKIP1
        *  NONE
        SKIP3
        ****************************************************************
        *                                                              *
        *  WORKING STORAGE  -----  RECORD STRUCTURES                   *
        *                                                              *
        *  THESE SHOULD BE COPIED OR CREATED FOR ALL DISK AND TAPE     *
        *  DATASETS THAT ARE INPUT OR OUTPUT FROM THIS PROGRAM.        *
        *                                                              *
        *  COPYLIB RECORD STRUCTURES MUST HAVE SAME NAME AS THE        *
        *  SELECT AND FD AND END WITH THE CHARACTER "S"                *
        *                                                              *
        ****************************************************************
        SKIP2
        01  TRANIN-KEY.
            05  KEY-FIELD1             PIC X(?).
            05  KEY-FIELD?             PIC X(?).
        01  MASTIN-KEY.
            05  KEY-FIELD1             PIC X(?).
            05  KEY-FIELD?             PIC X(?).
```

234

```
      SKIP2
      01  W-TRANIN-REC. COPY TRANINS.
      01  W-MASTIN-REC. COPY MASTINS.
      EJECT
     ****************************************************************
     *                                                              *
     *  LINKAGE SECTION IS NEEDED BECAUSE THIS MODULE IS CALLED     *
     *  BY ANOTHER MODULE.                                          *
     *                                                              *
     ****************************************************************
     *
      LINKAGE SECTION.
      SKIP2
     ****************************************************************
     *                                                              *
     *  CALLING PARAMETERS ARE ENTERED HERE IN THE ORDER THEY       *
     *  SHOULD BE USED ON THE CALL STATEMENT. FOR USE OF COPYLIBS   *
     *  PARAMETER-1 SHOULD BE THE SAME NAME AS USED IN THE CALLING  *
     *  PROGRAM.                                                    *
     *                                                              *
     ****************************************************************
     *
      SKIP2
      01  L-ADD-COUNT                    COMP PIC S9(7).
      01  L-DELETE-COUNT                 COMP PIC S9(7).
      01  L-CHANGE-COUNT                 COMP PIC S9(7).
      01  L-REJECTED-COUNT               COMP PIC S9(7).
      EJECT
      COPY COBSTAND.
      EJECT
      PROCEDURE DIVISION.
      SKIP2
     ****************************************************************
     *                                                              *
     *  CALLING PROGRAMS SHOULD USE THE FOLLOWING CALL STATEMENT    *
     *                                                              *
     *    CALL 'PGMNAME'.                                           *
     *                                                              *
     ****************************************************************
     *
          ENTRY 'PGMNAME'.
      SKIP2
          IF PROGRAM-CALL-COUNT = 0 THEN
      SKIP2
           CALL 'STDMSG' USING COPY STDMSG.
      SKIP2
          ADD C-1 TO PROGRAM-CALL-COUNT.
      SKIP2
     ****************************************************************
     *                                                              *
     *    READ SORTED TRANSACTION FILE AND MASTER FILE TO           *
```

```
*    INITIALIZE THE PROCESS. THEN DO THE UPDATE COMPARISON  *
*    UNTIL ALL TRANSACTION AND MASTER RECORDS HAVE BEEN      *
*    PROCESSED.                                              *
*                                                            *
**************************************************************
 SKIP2
     CALL 'VALIDTRN' USING
         W-TRANIN-REC.
 SKIP1
     CALL 'READMAST' USING
         W-MASTIN-REC.
 SKIP1
     PERFORM TRAN-MASTER-MATCH
         UNTIL W-TRANIN-REC = HIGH-VALUES
         AND   W-MASTIN-REC = HIGH-VALUES.
 SKIP1
* CLOSE MASTER OUT
     CALL 'WRITEMAS' USING
         W-MASTIN-REC.

 SKIP3
**************************************************
*                                                *
*                 EXIT PGID                      *
*                                                *
**************************************************
 SKIP2
     MOVE ZERO TO RETURN-CODE.
 SKIP1
     GOBACK.
 EJECT
******************************************************************
*                                                                *
*  MATCH MASTER AND TRANSACTION                                  *
*                                                                *
******************************************************************
 SKIP2
 TRAN-MASTER-MATCH.
 SKIP2
     MOVE TRANIN-FIELD1 TO KEY-FIELD1 OF TRANIN-KEY.
     MOVE TRANIN-FIELD? TO KEY-FIELD? OF TRANIN-KEY.
     MOVE MASTIN-FIELD1 TO KEY-FIELD1 OF MASTIN-KEY.
     MOVE MASTIN-FIELD? TO KEY-FIELD? OF MASTIN-KEY.
 SKIP2
******************************************************************
*                                                                *
*  ASSUME MORE MASTER RECORDS THAN TRANSACTIONS SO CHECK         *
*  FOR COPY MASTER ACTION FIRST                                  *
*                                                                *
******************************************************************
 SKIP2
```

```
      IF TRANIN-KEY > MASTIN-KEY THEN
   SKIP1
*            **************************************************
*                 *                                          *
*                 *  COPY THE MASTER RECORD TO OUTPUT AND     *
*                 *  THEN READ A NEW MASTER RECORD            *
*                 *                                          *
*            **************************************************
   SKIP1
           CALL 'WRITEMAS' USING
               W-MASTIN-REC
   SKIP1
           CALL 'READMAST' USING
               W-MASTIN-REC
   SKIP2
      ELSE IF TRANIN-KEY < MASTIN-KEY THEN
   SKIP1
*            **************************************************
*                 *                                          *
*                 *  CREATE A MASTER FROM TRANSACTION OR      *
*                 *      ERROR OUT THE INVALID TRANSACTION    *
*                 *                                          *
*            **************************************************
   SKIP1
           IF TRANIN-UPDATE-TYPE = C-ADD THEN
   SKIP1
*                  **************************************************
*                       *                                          *
*                       *  CREATE THE NEW MASTER RECORD             *
*                       *  THEN READ A NEW TRANSACTION              *
*                       *                                          *
*                  **************************************************
   SKIP1
               CALL 'ADDMAST' USING
                   W-TRANIN-REC
   SKIP1
               ADD C-1 TO ADD-COUNT
   SKIP1
               CALL 'VALIDTRN' USING
                   W-TRANIN-REC
   SKIP1
           ELSE IF TRANIN-UPDATE-TYPE = C-DELETE
   SKIP1
*                  **************************************************
*                       *                                          *
*                       *  CALL THE ERROR ROUTINE AND               *
*                       *  THEN READ A NEW TRANSACTION              *
*                       *                                          *
*                  **************************************************
   SKIP1
               CALL 'ERROR' USING
```

```
                        W-TRANIN-REC,
                        C-DELETE-ERROR
        SKIP1
                   CALL 'VALIDTRN' USING
                        W-TRANIN-REC
        SKIP1
                   ADD C-1 TO REJECTED-COUNT
        SKIP1
              ELSE IF TRANIN-UPDATE-TYPE = C-CHANGE
        SKIP1
        *         ***************************************************
        *         *                                                 *
        *         *  CALL THE ERROR ROUTINE AND                     *
        *         *  THEN READ A NEW TRANSACTION                    *
        *         *                                                 *
        *         ***************************************************
        SKIP1
                   CALL 'ERROR' USING
                        W-TRANIN-REC,
                        C-CHANGE-ERROR
        SKIP1
                   CALL 'VALIDTRN' USING
                        W-TRANIN-REC
                   ADD C-1 TO REJECTED-COUNT
              ELSE
        ************* TRANSACTION CODE ERROR ******************
        SKIP1
        *         ***************************************************
        *         *                                                 *
        *         *  CALL THE ERROR ROUTINE AND                     *
        *         *  THEN READ A NEW TRANSACTION                    *
        *         *                                                 *
        *         ***************************************************
        SKIP1
                   CALL 'ERROR' USING
                        W-TRANIN-REC,
                        C-CHANGE-ERROR
        SKIP1
                   CALL 'VALIDTRN' USING
                        W-TRANIN-REC
                   ADD C-1 TO REJECTED-COUNT
        SKIP2
           ELSE
        ************ TRANIN-KEY = MASTIN-KEY **********
        SKIP2
        *         ***************************************************
        *         *                                                 *
        *         *  CHANGE OR DELETE THE MASTER RECORD OR          *
        *         *  ERROR OUT THE INVALID TRANSACTION              *
        *         *                                                 *
        *         ***************************************************
```

238

```
      SKIP2
            IF TRANIN-UPDATE-TYPE = C-CHANGE
      SKIP1
                  CALL 'CHGMAST' USING
                        W-TRANIN-REC,
                        W-MASTIN-REC
      SKIP1
                  CALL 'VALIDTRN' USING
                        W-TRANIN-REC
      SKIP1
                  ADD C-1 TO CHANGE-COUNT
      SKIP2
            ELSE IF TRANIN-UPDATE-TYPE = C-DELETE
      SKIP1
                  CALL 'READMAST' USING
                        W-MASTIN-REC
      SKIP1
                  CALL 'VALIDTRN' USING
                        W-TRANIN-REC
      SKIP1
                  ADD C-1 TO DELETE-COUNT
      SKIP2
            ELSE IF TRANIN-UPDATE-TYPE = C-ADD
      SKIP1
                  ADD C-1 TO REJECTED-COUNT
      SKIP1
                  CALL 'ERROR' USING
                        W-TRANIN-REC,
                        C-ADD-ERROR
      SKIP1
                  CALL 'VALIDTRN' USING
                        W-TRANIN-REC
      SKIP1
            ELSE
      SKIP1
                  ADD C-1 TO REJECTED-COUNT
      SKIP1
                  CALL 'ERROR' USING
                        W-TRANIN-REC,
                        C-CODE-ERROR
      SKIP1
                  CALL 'VALIDTRN' USING
                        W-TRANIN-REC.
      EJECT
 *****************************************************************
 *                                                               *
 *   RETURN COUNTS TO SUMMARY PROGRAM                            *
 *                                                               *
 *****************************************************************
      SKIP2
      0002-RETURN-UPDATE-COUNTS.
```

239

```
SKIP2
    ENTRY 'UPDCNTS' USING
        L-ADD-COUNT,
        L-DELETE-COUNT,
        L-CHANGE-COUNT,
        L-REJECTED-COUNT.
SKIP1
    IF PROGRAM-CALL-COUNT = ZERO THEN
SKIP1
        CALL 'STDMSG' USING COPY STDMSG.
SKIP1
    ADD C-1 TO PROGRAM-CALL-COUNT.
SKIP2
    MOVE ADD-COUNT TO L-ADD-COUNT.
    MOVE DELETE-COUNT TO L-DELETE-COUNT.
    MOVE CHANGE-COUNT TO L-CHANGE-COUNT.
    MOVE REJECTED-COUNT TO L-REJECTED-COUNT.
SKIP2
    GOBACK.
```

APPENDIX B

Document Prototypes

```
WRITENR ENTER DOCUMENT TYPE (IPO, PSEUDOCODE, MEMO, LETTER, ETC)
READ &DOCTYPE

WRITENR ENTER NEW DOCUMENT NAME
READ &DOCNAME

COPY PROTOTYPE.LIBRARY(&DOCTYPE) &DOCNAME..DATA
```

February 12, 1982

person
title
location

paragraphs

your name
your title

Attachments

Copies to:

IPO CHART

Function Continued from	Project PROGRAM NAME	Function	Chart Seq 0001 01	Page 01
Chart Seq ----	Author author		Date mm-dd-yy	

INPUT	PROCESS	OUTPUT
	1. Dowhile there are lines	
input1--->	A. process1	output1
input2	B. process2	output2
input3	C. Move data until end of line or High Values or "1"	output3
input4	D. If end of line add 1 to line count go to next line	output4

Function Continued To

	chart seq ---- ---
Step No.	Extended Description	Legend
step	desc	leg

243

APPENDIX C

COBOL Software Metric Program

```
IDENTIFICATION DIVISION.
PROGRAM-ID. 'METRICS '.
AUTHOR. JAY ARTHUR.
DATE-WRITTEN. 07/09/80.
DATE-COMPILED. 07/09/80.
REMARKS.
     **********************************************************************
     *                                                                  *
     *   MAIN PROGRAM METRICS                                           *
     *                                                                  *
     *   PROGRAM DESCRIPTION:                                           *
     *                                                                  *
     *       COMPUTE METRICS OF A GIVEN PROGRAM'S QUALITY BASED        *
     *       ON COUNTS OF VARIOUS COBOL STATEMENTS IN THE PROGRAM      *
     *       REPORT THOSE CONSTANTS AND ACTUAL METRICS DERIVED.        *
     *                                                                  *
     *                                                                  *
     *   SUBROUTINES CALLED OR REQUIRED:                               *
     *                                                                  *
     *   REFERENCE: (JOB DEFINITION, IPO, ETC)                         *
     *                                                                  *
     *       METRICS FOR COBOL SOURCE PROGRAMS - JAY ARTHUR 7/80 *
     *                                                                  *
     **********************************************************************
EJECT
ENVIRONMENT DIVISION.
CONFIGURATION SECTION.
SOURCE-COMPUTER. IBM-370.
OBJECT-COMPUTER. IBM-370.
SKIP3
INPUT-OUTPUT SECTION.
SKIP2
FILE-CONTROL.
SKIP2
**********************************************************************
*                                                                  *
*    SELECT STATEMENTS                                             *
*                                                                  *
**********************************************************************
SKIP1
* INPUT
     SELECT COBOLIN               ASSIGN TO UT-S-COBOLINI.
SKIP1
* INPUT/OUTPUT
SKIP1
* OUTPUT
     SELECT REPORTO               ASSIGN TO UT-S-REPORTO.
SKIP1
* SORT
EJECT
DATA DIVISION.
```

```
      SKIP2
      FILE SECTION.
      SKIP2
      ********************************************************************
      *                                                                 *
      *    FILE DESCRIPTIONS                                            *
      *                                                                 *
      ********************************************************************
      SKIP2
      * INPUT
      SKIP2
      FD  COBOLIN
          RECORDING MODE IS F
          RECORD CONTAINS 80 CHARACTERS
          LABEL RECORDS ARE STANDARD
          BLOCK CONTAINS O RECORDS
          DATA RECORD IS COBOLIN-RECORD.
      SKIP1
      01  COBOLIN-RECORD            PIC X(80).
      SKIP2
      * INPUT/OUTPUT
      SKIP2
      * OUTPUT
      SKIP2
          COPY RPT133F.
      SKIP2
      * SORT
      EJECT
      ********************************************************************
      *                                                                 *
      *               METRICS    DATA   DICTIONARY                     *
      *       ABBREVIATION                 FULL DESCRIPTION             *
      *                                                                 *
      *       C                            CONSTANT                     *
      *       EOF                          END OF FILE                  *
      *       I                            INDEX                        *
      *       PARM                         JCL PARAMETERS               *
      *       S OR SW                      SWITCH                       *
      ********************************************************************
      SKIP3
      WORKING-STORAGE SECTION.
      SKIP2
      *****************************************************************
      *                                                             *
      *               VERSION INFORMATION                          *
      *                                                             *
      *****************************************************************
      SKIP1
      01  PROGRAM-VERSION-INFORMATION.
          05  C-PROGRAM-NAME        PIC X(8) VALUE 'METRICS '.
          05  SOURCE-CODE-LEVEL     PIC X(8) VALUE 'REL.LEV'.
```

247

```
        05  PRODUCTION-DATE         PIC X(8) VALUE 'MM/DD/YY'.
        05  COMPILE-DATE            PIC X(8) VALUE 'MM/DD/YY'.
        05  COMPILE-TIME            PIC X(8) VALUE 'HH:MM:SS'.
        05  PROGRAM-CALL-COUNT      PIC S9(7) COMP SYNC VALUE ZERO.
    SKIP2
    01  START-WORKING-STORAGE           PIC X(27)
            VALUE 'WORKING STORAGE BEGINS HERE'.
    SKIP3
    ***************************************************************
    *                                                             *
    *   CONSTANTS                                                  *
    *                                                             *
    ***************************************************************
    SKIP2
    01  CONSTANTS.
        05  C-ABEND-CODE-0001           PIC X(4)  VALUE '0001'.
        05  C-CLOSED                    PIC X     VALUE 'C'.
        05  C-COBOLIN                   PIC X(7)  VALUE 'COBOLIN'.
        05  C-COMMENT                   PIC X     VALUE '*'.
        05  C-DUMP-OPTION               PIC X(4)  VALUE 'DUMP'.
        05  C-OPEN                      PIC X     VALUE 'O'.
        05  PROGRAM-ID-CONSTANT         PIC X(10) VALUE 'PROGRAM-ID'.
        05  C-READ                      PIC X(7)  VALUE ' READ '.
        05  C-REPORT                    PIC X(7)  VALUE 'REPORT '.
        05  C-SKIP-NO-LINES             PIC X     VALUE '+'.
        05  C-SKIP-1-LINES              PIC X     VALUE SPACE.
        05  C-SKIP-2-LINES              PIC X     VALUE '0'.
        05  C-SKIP-3-LINES              PIC X     VALUE '-'.
        05  C-TOP-OF-PAGE               PIC X     VALUE '1'.
        05  C-WRITTEN                   PIC X(7)  VALUE 'WRITTEN'.
        05  C-YES                       PIC X     VALUE 'Y'.
        05  C-1             COMP SYNC    PIC S9    VALUE +1.
        05  C-2             COMP SYNC    PIC S9    VALUE +2.
        05  C-3             COMP SYNC    PIC S9    VALUE +3.
        05  C-5             COMP SYNC    PIC S9    VALUE +5.
        05  C-100           COMP SYNC    PIC S9(4) VALUE +100.
        05  C-1000          COMP SYNC    PIC S9(4) VALUE +1000.
    SKIP2
    ***************************************************************
    *                                                             *
    *   STATEMENT COUNTS                                           *
    *                                                             *
    ***************************************************************
    SKIP2
    01  STATEMENT-COUNTS.
    SKIP1
    ***************************************************************
    *                                                             *
    *   IDENTIFICATION THROUGH DATA DIVISION COUNTS               *
    *                                                             *
    ***************************************************************
```

248

```
SKIP1
    05  SECURITY-COUNT          COMP   PIC S9(7) VALUE ZERO.
    05  DATA-DIVISION-COUNT     COMP   PIC S9(7) VALUE ZERO.
    05  PIC-COUNT               COMP   PIC S9(7) VALUE ZERO.
    05  COMP-COUNT              COMP   PIC S9(7) VALUE ZERO.
    05  PIC-S9-COUNT            COMP   PIC S9(7) VALUE ZERO.
    05  PIC-9-COUNT             COMP   PIC S9(7) VALUE ZERO.
    05  PIC-X-COUNT             COMP   PIC S9(7) VALUE ZERO.
    05  PROCEDURE-DIVISN-COUNT  COMP   PIC S9(7) VALUE ZERO.
SKIP1
****************************************************************
*                                                              *
*  DECISION COUNTS                                             *
*                                                              *
****************************************************************
SKIP1
    05  IF-COUNT                COMP   PIC S9(7) VALUE ZERO.
    05  UNTIL-COUNT             COMP   PIC S9(7) VALUE ZERO.
    05  VARYING-COUNT           CQMP   PIC S9(7) VALUE ZERO.
    05  WHEN-COUNT              COMP   PIC S9(7) VALUE ZERO.
SKIP1
****************************************************************
*                                                              *
*  FUNCTION  COUNTS                                           *
*                                                              *
****************************************************************
SKIP1
SKIP1
    05  CALL-COUNT              COMP   PIC S9(7) VALUE ZERO.
    05  PERFORM-COUNT           COMP   PIC S9(7) VALUE ZERO.
    05  COMPUTE-COUNT           COMP   PIC S9(7) VALUE ZERO.
    05  COPY-COUNT              COMP   PIC S9(7) VALUE ZERO.
    05  GENERATE-COUNT          COMP   PIC S9(7) VALUE ZERO.
    05  INITIATE-COUNT          COMP   PIC S9(7) VALUE ZERO.
    05  INSPECT-COUNT           COMP   PIC S9(7) VALUE ZERO.
    05  MERGE-COUNT             COMP   PIC S9(7) VALUE ZERO.
    05  SEARCH-COUNT            COMP   PIC S9(7) VALUE ZERO.
    05  SEARCH-ALL-COUNT        COMP   PIC S9(7) VALUE ZERO.
    05  SORT-COUNT              COMP   PIC S9(7) VALUE ZERO.
SKIP1
****************************************************************
*                                                              *
*  ARITHMETIC STATEMENT COUNTS                                *
*                                                              *
****************************************************************
SKIP1
    05  ADD-COUNT               COMP   PIC S9(7) VALUE ZERO.
    05  SUBTRACT-COUNT          COMP   PIC S9(7) VALUE ZERO.
    05  MULTIPLY-COUNT          COMP   PIC S9(7) VALUE ZERO.
    05  DIVIDE-COUNT            COMP   PIC S9(7) VALUE ZERO.
SKIP1
```

```
******************************************************************
*                                                                *
*   INPUT/OUTPUT COUNTS                                           *
*                                                                *
******************************************************************
 SKIP1
        05   IO-COUNT              COMP    PIC S9(7) VALUE ZERO.
        05   IMS-COUNT             COMP    PIC S9(7) VALUE ZERO.
        05   ACCEPT-COUNT          COMP    PIC S9(7) VALUE ZERO.
        05   CLOSE-COUNT           COMP    PIC S9(7) VALUE ZERO.
        05   DISPLAY-COUNT         COMP    PIC S9(7) VALUE ZERO.
        05   OPEN-COUNT            COMP    PIC S9(7) VALUE ZERO.
        05   READ-COUNT            COMP    PIC S9(7) VALUE ZERO.
        05   RELEASE-COUNT         COMP    PIC S9(7) VALUE ZERO.
        05   RETURN-COUNT          COMP    PIC S9(7) VALUE ZERO.
        05   REWRITE-COUNT         COMP    PIC S9(7) VALUE ZERO.
        05   WRITE-COUNT           COMP    PIC S9(7) VALUE ZERO.
 SKIP1
******************************************************************
*                                                                *
*   ENTRY/EXIT COUNTS                                            *
*                                                                *
******************************************************************
 SKIP1
        05   ENTRY-COUNT           COMP    PIC S9(7) VALUE ZERO.
        05   GOBACK-COUNT          COMP    PIC S9(7) VALUE ZERO.
        05   STOP-RUN-COUNT        COMP    PIC S9(7) VALUE ZERO.
 SKIP1
******************************************************************
*                                                                *
*   BAD BRANCH STATEMENT COUNTS                                   *
*                                                                *
******************************************************************
 SKIP1
        05   ALTER-COUNT           COMP    PIC S9(7) VALUE ZERO.
        05   GOTO-COUNT            COMP    PIC S9(7) VALUE ZERO.
 SKIP1
******************************************************************
*                                                                *
*   MISCELLANIOUS COUNTS                                          *
*                                                                *
******************************************************************
 SKIP1
        05   MOVE-COUNT            COMP    PIC S9(7) VALUE ZERO.
        05   SET-COUNT             COMP    PIC S9(7) VALUE ZERO.
 SKIP1
******************************************************************
*                                                                *
*   DESCRIPTIVE AND READABILITY COUNTS                            *
*                                                                *
******************************************************************
```

```
       SKIP1
           05  COMMENT-COUNT              COMP   PIC S9(7) VALUE ZERO.
           05  EJECT-COUNT                COMP   PIC S9(7) VALUE ZERO.
           05  SKIP-COUNT                 COMP   PIC S9(7) VALUE ZERO.
           05  SELECT-COUNT               COMP   PIC S9(7) VALUE ZERO.
       SKIP2
      ****************************************************************
      *                                                              *
      *  STATEMENT STRINGS                                           *
      *                                                              *
      ****************************************************************
       SKIP2
       01  STATEMENT-STRINGS.
       SKIP1
           05  SECURITY-STRING            PIC X(9)  VALUE ' SECURITY'.
       SKIP1
      ****************************************************************
      *                                                              *
      *  DATA DIVISION SEARCH STRINGS                               *
      *                                                              *
      ****************************************************************
       SKIP1
           05  PIC-STRING                 PIC X(4)  VALUE ' PIC'.
           05  COMP-STRING                PIC X(5)  VALUE ' COMP'.
           05  PIC-S9-STRING              PIC X(3)  VALUE ' S9'.
           05  PIC-9-STRING               PIC X(2)  VALUE ' 9'.
           05  PIC-X-STRING               PIC X(2)  VALUE ' X'.
       SKIP1
      ****************************************************************
      *                                                              *
      *  PROCEDURE DIVISION SEARCH STRINGS                          *
      *                                                              *
      ****************************************************************
       SKIP1
           05  PROCEDURE-DIVISN-STRING  PIC X(18)
                                  VALUE 'PROCEDURE DIVISION'.
       SKIP1
      ****************************************************************
      *                                                              *
      *  DECISION COUNT SEARCH STRINGS                              *
      *                                                              *
      ****************************************************************
       SKIP1
           05  IF-STRING                  PIC X(4)  VALUE ' IF '.
           05  UNTIL-STRING               PIC X(7)  VALUE ' UNTIL '.
           05  VARYING-STRING             PIC X(9)  VALUE ' VARYING '.
           05  WHEN-STRING                PIC X(6)  VALUE ' WHEN '.
       SKIP1
           05  DECISION-STRING            PIC X(9)  VALUE 'DECISION'.
           05  DECISION-COMMENT           PIC X(29)
                   VALUE 'TOTAL DECISIONS IN THE MODULE'.
```

```
SKIP1
*****************************************************************
*                                                               *
*   FUNCTION COUNT SEARCH STRINGS                               *
*                                                               *
*****************************************************************
SKIP1
      05  CALL-STRING              PIC X(6)  VALUE ' CALL '.
      05  COMPUTE-STRING           PIC X(9)  VALUE ' COMPUTE '.
      05  COPY-STRING              PIC X(6)  VALUE ' COPY '.
      05  GENERATE-STRING          PIC X(10) VALUE ' GENERATE '.
      05  INITIATE-STRING          PIC X(10) VALUE ' INITIATE '.
      05  INSPECT-STRING           PIC X(9)  VALUE ' INSPECT '.
      05  PERFORM-STRING           PIC X(9)  VALUE ' PERFORM '.
      05  MERGE-STRING             PIC X(7)  VALUE ' MERGE '.
      05  SEARCH-STRING            PIC X(8)  VALUE ' SEARCH '.
      05  SEARCH-ALL-STRING        PIC X(10) VALUE 'SEARCH ALL'.
      05  SORT-STRING              PIC X(6)  VALUE ' SORT '.
SKIP1
      05  FUNCTION-STRING          PIC X(9)  VALUE 'FUNCTIONS'.
      05  FUNCTION-COMMENT            PIC X(25)
                 VALUE 'TOTAL NUMBER OF FUNCTIONS'.
SKIP1
*****************************************************************
*                                                               *
*   ARITHMETIC COUNT SEARCH STRINGS                             *
*                                                               *
*****************************************************************
SKIP1
      05  ADD-STRING               PIC X(5)  VALUE ' ADD '.
      05  SUBTRACT-STRING          PIC X(4)  VALUE ' SUB'.
      05  MULTIPLY-STRING          PIC X(5)  VALUE ' MULT'.
      05  DIVIDE-STRING            PIC X(8)  VALUE ' DIVIDE '.
SKIP1
      05  ARITHMETIC-STRING        PIC X(10) VALUE 'ARITHMETIC'.
      05  ARITHMETIC-COMMENT          PIC X(26)
                 VALUE 'TOTAL ARITHMETIC OPERATORS'.
SKIP1
*****************************************************************
*                                                               *
*   INPUT/OUTPUT SEARCH STRINGS                                 *
*                                                               *
*****************************************************************
SKIP1
      05  ACCEPT-STRING            PIC X(8)  VALUE ' ACCEPT '.
      05  CLOSE-STRING             PIC X(7)  VALUE ' CLOSE '.
      05  DISPLAY-STRING           PIC X(9)  VALUE ' DISPLAY '.
      05  IMS-STRING               PIC X(7)  VALUE 'DLITCBL'.
      05  OPEN-STRING              PIC X(6)  VALUE ' OPEN '.
      05  READ-STRING              PIC X(6)  VALUE ' READ '.
      05  RELEASE-STRING           PIC X(9)  VALUE ' RELEASE '.
```

```
      05  RETURN-STRING           PIC X(8)  VALUE ' RETURN '.
      05  REWRITE-STRING          PIC X(9)  VALUE ' REWRITE '.
      05  WRITE-STRING            PIC X(7)  VALUE ' WRITE '.
  SKIP1
      05  INPUT-OUTPUT-STRING     PIC X(9)  VALUE 'INPUT/OUT'.
      05  INPUT-OUTPUT-COMMENT       PIC X(20)
                   VALUE 'TOTAL I/O STATEMENTS'.
  SKIP1
  **************************************************************
  *                                                            *
  *  ENTRY/EXIT SEARCH STRINGS                                 *
  *                                                            *
  **************************************************************
  SKIP1
      05  ENTRY-STRING            PIC X(7)  VALUE ' ENTRY '.
      05  GOBACK-STRING           PIC X(7)  VALUE ' GOBACK'.
      05  STOP-RUN-STRING         PIC X(9)  VALUE ' STOP RUN'.
  SKIP1
      05  ENTRY-EXIT-STRING       PIC X(10) VALUE 'ENTRY/EXIT'.
      05  ENTRY-EXIT-COMMENT         PIC X(27)
                   VALUE 'TOTAL ENTRY AND EXIT POINTS'.
  SKIP1
  **************************************************************
  *                                                            *
  *  UGLY BRANCH SEARCH STRINGS                                *
  *                                                            *
  **************************************************************
  SKIP1
      05  ALTER-STRING            PIC X(7)  VALUE ' ALTER '.
      05  GOTO-STRING             PIC X(4)  VALUE ' GO '.
  SKIP1
  **************************************************************
  *                                                            *
  *  MISCELLANEOUS SEARCH STRINGS                              *
  *                                                            *
  **************************************************************
  SKIP1
      05  MOVE-STRING             PIC X(6)  VALUE ' MOVE '.
      05  SET-STRING              PIC X(5)  VALUE ' SET '.
  SKIP1
      05  OTHER-STRING            PIC X(5)  VALUE 'OTHER'.
      05  OTHER-COMMENT              PIC X(28)
                   VALUE 'TOTAL OTHER COBOL STATEMENTS'.
  SKIP1
  **************************************************************
  *                                                            *
  *  SELF DOCUMENTATION AND READIBILITY SEARCH STRINGS         *
  *                                                            *
  **************************************************************
  SKIP1
      05  COMMENT-STRING          PIC X(9)  VALUE ' COMMENT '.
```

253

```
        05  COMMENTS-STRING          PIC X     VALUE '*'.
        05  EJECT-STRING             PIC X(7)  VALUE ' EJECT '.
        05  SKIP-STRING              PIC X(5)  VALUE ' SKIP'.
    SKIP1
        05  SELECT-STRING            PIC X(8)  VALUE ' SELECT '.
        05  SELECT-COMMENT            PIC X(19)
                    VALUE 'TOTAL NON IMS FILES'.
    SKIP1
        05  FORMAT-STRING            PIC X(6)  VALUE 'FORMAT'.
        05  FORMAT-COMMENT           PIC X(28)
                    VALUE 'TOTAL CODE FORMAT STATEMENTS'.
    SKIP1
    ****************************************************************
    *                                                              *
    *  SOFTWARE METRIC CRITERIA LITERALS                           *
    *                                                              *
    ****************************************************************
    SKIP1
        05  SOFTWARE-CRITERIA-STRING PIC X(8)  VALUE 'CRITERIA'.
        05  SOFTWARE-CRITERIA-COMMENT PIC X(28)
                        VALUE 'CRITERIA EVOLVED FROM COUNTS'.
    SKIP1
        05  SOFTWARE-METRIC-STRING   PIC X(7)  VALUE 'METRICS'.
        05  SOFTWARE-METRIC-COMMENT   PIC X(30)
                        VALUE 'SOFTWARE METRICS FROM CRITERIA'.
    SKIP2
        05  T-DECISION-COUNT            PIC X(14)
                        VALUE 'DECISION COUNT'.
        05  T-DECISION-DENSITY          PIC X(16)
                        VALUE 'DECISION DENSITY'.
        05  T-FUNCTION-COUNT            PIC X(14)
                        VALUE 'FUNCTION COUNT'.
        05  T-CONCISENESS               PIC X(11)
                        VALUE 'CONCISENESS'.
        05  T-ENTRY-EXIT-RATIO          PIC X(16)
                        VALUE 'ENTRY/EXIT RATIO'.
        05  T-STRUCTUREDNESS            PIC X(14)
                        VALUE 'STRUCTUREDNESS'.
        05  T-SELF-DOCUMENTATION        PIC X(18)
                        VALUE 'SELF DOCUMENTATION'.
        05  T-CORRECTNESS               PIC X(11)
                        VALUE 'CORRECTNESS'.
        05  T-TRACEABILITY              PIC X(12)
                        VALUE 'TRACEABILITY'.
        05  T-CONSISTENCY               PIC X(11)
                        VALUE 'CONSISTENCY'.
        05  T-COMPLETENESS              PIC X(12)
                        VALUE 'COMPLETENESS'.
        05  T-EFFICIENCY                PIC X(10)
                        VALUE 'EFFICIENCY'.
        05  T-FLEXIBILITY               PIC X(11)
```

```
                                     VALUE 'FLEXIBILITY'.
     05  T-MODULARITY                PIC X(10)
                                     VALUE 'MODULARITY'.
     05  T-GENERALITY                PIC X(10)
                                     VALUE 'GENERALITY'.
     05  T-EXPANDABILITY             PIC X(13)
                                     VALUE 'EXPANDABILITY'.
     05  T-INTEGRITY                 PIC X(9)
                                     VALUE 'INTEGRITY'.
     05  T-INTEROPERABILITY          PIC X(16)
                                     VALUE 'INTEROPERABILITY'.
     05  T-MAINTAINABILITY           PIC X(15)
                                     VALUE 'MAINTAINABILITY'.
     05  T-SIMPLICITY                PIC X(10)
                                     VALUE 'SIMPLICITY'.
     05  T-PORTABILITY               PIC X(11)
                                     VALUE 'PORTABILITY'.
     05  T-MACHINE-INDEPENDENCE      PIC X(20)
                                     VALUE 'MACHINE INDEPENDENCE'.
     05  T-SOFTWARE-INDEPENDENCE     PIC X(21)
                                     VALUE 'SOFTWARE INDEPENDENCE'.
     05  T-RELIABILITY               PIC X(11)
                                     VALUE 'RELIABILITY'.
     05  T-ERROR-TOLERANCE           PIC X(15)
                                     VALUE 'ERROR TOLERANCE'.
     05  T-REUSABILITY               PIC X(11)
                                     VALUE 'REUSABILITY'.
     05  T-USABILITY                 PIC X(9)
                                     VALUE 'USABILITY'.
     05  T-PRODUCTIVITY              PIC X(12)
                                     VALUE 'PRODUCTIVITY'.
     05  T-LOC                       PIC X(19)
                                     VALUE 'LINES OF CODE (LOC)'.
     05  T-LOC-100                   PIC X(9)
                                     VALUE 'LOC/100'.
     05  T-LOC-1000                  PIC X(9)
                                     VALUE 'LOC/1000'.
     05  T-TOTAL-COUNT               PIC X(18)
                                     VALUE 'TOTAL SOURCE LINES'.
******************************************************************
*                                                                *
*   SOFTWARE METRIC COUNTS, CRITERIA AND METRICS                 *
*                                                                *
******************************************************************
 01  SOFTWARE-METRICS.
 SKIP1
     05  DECISION-COUNT          COMP PIC S9(5)V99 VALUE ZERO.
     05  DECISION-DENSITY        COMP PIC S9(5)V99 VALUE ZERO.
 SKIP1
     05  FUNCTION-COUNT          COMP PIC S9(5)V99 VALUE ZERO.
     05  CONCISENESS             COMP PIC S9(5)V99 VALUE ZERO.
```

```
        05  ENTRY-EXIT-RATIO        COMP PIC S9(5)V99 VALUE ZERO.
        05  STRUCTUREDNESS          COMP PIC S9(5)V99 VALUE ZERO.
        05  SELF-DOCUMENTATION      COMP PIC S9(5)V99 VALUE ZERO.
        05  CORRECTNESS             COMP PIC S9(5)V99 VALUE ZERO.
        05  TRACEABILITY            COMP PIC S9(5)V99 VALUE ZERO.
        05  CONSISTENCY             COMP PIC S9(5)V99 VALUE ZERO.
        05  COMPLEXITY              COMP PIC S9(5)V99 VALUE ZERO.
        05  STYLE                   COMP PIC S9(5)V99 VALUE ZERO.
        05  COMPLETENESS            COMP PIC S9(5)V99 VALUE ZERO.
        05  EFFICIENCY              COMP PIC S9(5)V99 VALUE ZERO.
        05  FLEXIBILITY             COMP PIC S9(5)V99 VALUE ZERO.
        05  MODULARITY              COMP PIC S9(5)V99 VALUE ZERO.
        05  GENERALITY              COMP PIC S9(5)V99 VALUE ZERO.
        05  EXPANDABILITY           COMP PIC S9(5)V99 VALUE ZERO.
        05  INTEGRITY               COMP PIC S9(5)V99 VALUE ZERO.
        05  INTEROPERABILITY        COMP PIC S9(5)V99 VALUE ZERO.
        05  MAINTAINABILITY         COMP PIC S9(5)V99 VALUE ZERO.
        05  SIMPLICITY              COMP PIC S9(5)V99 VALUE ZERO.
        05  PORTABILITY             COMP PIC S9(5)V99 VALUE ZERO.
        05  MACHINE-INDEPENDENCE    COMP PIC S9(5)V99 VALUE ZERO.
        05  SOFTWARE-INDEPENDENCE   COMP PIC S9(5)V99 VALUE ZERO.
        05  RELIABILITY             COMP PIC S9(5)V99 VALUE ZERO.
        05  ERROR-TOLERANCE         COMP PIC S9(5)V99 VALUE ZERO.
        05  REUSABILITY             COMP PIC S9(5)V99 VALUE ZERO.
        05  USABILITY               COMP PIC S9(5)V99 VALUE ZERO.
        05  PRODUCTIVITY            COMP PIC S9(5)V99 VALUE ZERO.
        05  PROGRAM-SIZE            COMP PIC S9(5)V99 VALUE ZERO.
        05  LOC                     COMP PIC S9(5)V99 VALUE ZERO.
        05  LOC-100                 COMP PIC S9(5)V99 VALUE ZERO.
        05  LOC-1000                COMP PIC S9(5)V99 VALUE ZERO.
        05  TOTAL-COUNT             COMP PIC S9(5)V99 VALUE ZERO.
 ******************************************************************
 *                                                                *
 *   RECORD RECORD AND BALANCE MESSAGES                           *
 *                                                                *
 ******************************************************************
 SKIP2
 01  RECORD-COUNTS SYNC.
        05  FILLER                      PIC X(18)
            VALUE 'FILE RECORD COUNTS'.
        05  COBOLIN-RECORD-COUNT    COMP PIC S9(7) VALUE ZERO.
        05  REPORTO-RECORD-COUNT    COMP PIC S9(7) VALUE ZERO.
 SKIP3
 01  RECORD-COUNT-CONTROLS.
        05  FILLER                      PIC XXX   VALUE SPACES.
        05  METRICS-CONTROLS            PIC X(8) VALUE 'METRICS '.
        05  FILLER                      PIC XX    VALUE SPACES.
        05  PRINT-FD-NAME               PIC X(7) VALUE SPACES.
        05  FILLER                      PIC XX    VALUE SPACES.
        05  PRINT-RECORD-COUNT          PIC ZZZZZZ9.
        05  FILLER                      PIC XX    VALUE SPACES.
```

```
        05  PRINT-ACTION              PIC X(7) VALUE SPACES.
     SKIP2
     ****************************************************************
     *                                                              *
     *   STANDARD 01 LEVELS                                         *
     *                                                              *
     ****************************************************************
     SKIP2
     01  ABEND-FIELDS.        COPY ABNDFLDS.
     SKIP2
     01  METRICS-VERSION-INFORMATION.
        05  FILLER                    PIC XXX  VALUE SPACES.
        05  METRICS-VERSION           PIC X(8) VALUE 'METRICS '
        05  FILLER                    PIC X(15)
              VALUE ' SOURCE LEVEL '.
        05  SOURCE-CODE-LEVEL         PIC X(6) VALUE ' 1.11 '.
        05  FILLER                    PIC XX   VALUE SPACES.
        05  VERSION-DATE              PIC X(8)
               VALUE '07/19/80'.
     SKIP2
     01  START-RUN-MESSAGE.
        05  FILLER                    PIC XXX  VALUE SPACES.
        05  METRICS                   PIC X(4) VALUE 'METRICS'
        05  FILLER                    PIC X(23)
              VALUE ' IS BEGINNING EXECUTION'.
     SKIP2
     01  END-RUN-MESSAGE.
        05  FILLER                    PIC XXX  VALUE SPACES.
        05  METRICS                   PIC X(7) VALUE 'METRICS'
        05  FILLER                    PIC X(20)
              VALUE ' IS ENDING EXECUTION'.
     SKIP3
     ****************************************************************
     *                                                              *
     *   WORKING STORAGE -------- LOCAL VARIABLES                   *
     *                                                              *
     ****************************************************************
     SKIP1
     01  LOCAL-VARIABLES.
        05  DAYS-WORKED      COMP PIC S9(7) VALUE +1.
     01  SWITCHES.
        05  COMMENT-SW            PIC X      VALUE SPACE.
        88  COMMENT-FOUND        VALUE '*'.
     SKIP3
     ****************************************************************
     *                                                              *
     *   WORKING STORAGE -------- REPORT HEADERS AND FOOTERS        *
     *                                                              *
     ****************************************************************
     SKIP1
     01  REPORT-HEADER-1.
```

257

```
        05 FILLER                         PIC X(10) VALUE SPACES.
        05 PROGRAM-NAME                   PIC X(8)  VALUE 'METRICS '.
        05 FILLER                         PIC X(20) VALUE SPACES.
        05 FILLER                         PIC X(31)
                  VALUE 'SOFTWARE METRICS FOR PROGRAM - '.
        05 HEADER-NAME                    PIC X(10) VALUE SPACES.
        05 FILLER                         PIC X(21) VALUE SPACES.
        05 RUNDATE                        PIC X(8)  VALUE SPACES.
        05 FILLER                         PIC X(24) VALUE SPACES.
    SKIP1
    01  REPORT-HEADER-A.
        05 FILLER                         PIC X(10) VALUE SPACES.
        05 FILLER                         PIC X(8)  VALUE '_____'.
        05 FILLER                         PIC X(20) VALUE SPACES.
        05 FILLER                         PIC X(35)
                  VALUE '_____'.
        05 FILLER                         PIC X(5)  VALUE '_____'.
        05 FILLER                         PIC X(21) VALUE SPACES.
        05 FILLER                         PIC X(8)  VALUE '_____'.
        05 FILLER                         PIC X(24) VALUE SPACES.
    SKIP1
    01  REPORT-HEADER-2.
        05 FILLER                         PIC X(10) VALUE SPACES.
        05 FILLER                         PIC X(11)
                  VALUE 'MEASUREMENT'.
        05 FILLER                         PIC X(21) VALUE SPACES.
        05 FILLER                         PIC X(5)  VALUE 'VALUE'.
        05 FILLER                         PIC X(15) VALUE SPACES.
        05 FILLER                         PIC X(8)  VALUE 'COMMENTS'.
        05 FILLER                         PIC X(72) VALUE SPACES.
    SKIP1
    01  REPORT-HEADER-B.
        05 FILLER                         PIC X(10) VALUE SPACES.
        05 FILLER                         PIC X(11)
                  VALUE '_____'.
        05 FILLER                         PIC X(21) VALUE SPACES.
        05 FILLER                         PIC X(5)  VALUE '_____'.
        05 FILLER                         PIC X(15) VALUE SPACES.
        05 FILLER                         PIC X(8)  VALUE '_____'.
        05 FILLER                         PIC X(72) VALUE SPACES.
    SKIP1
    01  DETAIL-LINE.
        05 FILLER                         PIC X(10) VALUE SPACES.
        05 MEASUREMENT                    PIC X(21) VALUE SPACES.
        05 FILLER                         PIC X(9) VALUE SPACES.
        05 STATEMENT-COUNT                PIC ZZZZ9.99-.
        05 STATEMENT-FILLER REDEFINES STATEMENT-COUNT PIC X(9).
        05 FILLER                         PIC X(10) VALUE SPACES.
        05 COMMENT                        PIC X(40) VALUE SPACES.
        05 FILLER                         PIC X(41) VALUE SPACES.
    SKIP3
```

```
******************************************************************
*                                                                *
*   WORKING STORAGE  -----  RECORD STRUCTURES                    *
*                                                                *
******************************************************************
 SKIP2
 *        ***************************
 *        *                         *
 *        *  END OF FILE SWITCHES    *
 *        *                         *
 *        *  'O' THE FILE IS OPEN    *
 *        *  'C' THE FILE IS CLOSED  *
 *        *                         *
 *        ***************************
 SKIP2
 01  EOF-SWITCHES.
     05  COBOLIN-EOF-SW           PIC X VALUE 'C'.
         88  COBOLIN-OPEN              VALUE 'O'.
         88  COBOLIN-CLOSED           VALUE 'C'.
         88  COBOLIN-FILE-AT-EOF      VALUE 'C'.
 SKIP3
 01  COBOLIN-REC.
     05  FILLER              PIC X(6)  VALUE SPACES.
     05  COMMENT-SPACE       PIC X     VALUE SPACE.
     05  PROGRAM-ID-LITERAL  PIC X(10) VALUE SPACE.
     05  FILLER              PIC X(2)  VALUE SPACE.
     05  PROGRAM-ID-NAME     PIC X(10) VALUE SPACE.
     05  FILLER              PIC X(51) VALUE SPACE.
 SKIP3
 01  W-REPORTO-REC.
     05  CARRAIGE-CONTROL    PIC X.
     05  REPORT-REC          PIC X(132).
 EJECT
 COPY COBSTAND.
 EJECT
 PROCEDURE DIVISION.
 SKIP2
     DISPLAY START-RUN-MESSAGE.
     DISPLAY METRICS-VERSION-INFORMATION.
     MOVE CURRENT-DATE TO RUNDATE OF REPORT-HEADER-1.
 SKIP2
******************************************************************
*                                                                *
*   OPEN STATEMENTS                                              *
*                                                                *
******************************************************************
 SKIP2
     OPEN
         INPUT   COBOLIN
         OUTPUT  REPORTO.
     MOVE C-OPEN TO COBOLIN-EOF-SW.
```

```
      SKIP2
 ********************************************************************
 *                                                                *
 *  USE INSPECT TALLYING TO COUNT OCCURANCES OF STRINGS           *
 *  FIRST IN THE ID THRU DATA DIVISIONS COUNT COMMENTS AND        *
 *  COPY'S, THEN COUNT ALL OF THEM FOR THE PROCEDURE DIVISION.*
 *                                                                *
 ********************************************************************
      SKIP2
           PERFORM SEARCH-ID-THRU-DATA-DIVISION
               UNTIL PROCEDURE-DIVISN-COUNT > ZERO.
           COMPUTE DATA-DIVISION-COUNT = COBOLIN-RECORD-COUNT -
                     COMMENT-COUNT.
           PERFORM SEARCH-PROCEDURE-DIVISION
               UNTIL COBOLIN-REC = HIGH-VALUES.
           PERFORM COMPUTE-PRIMITIVE-METRICS.
           PERFORM COMPUTE-METRIC-CRITERIA.
           PERFORM COMPUTE-MANAGMENT-METRICS.
           PERFORM CREATE-METRIC-REPORT.
      SKIP3
 ********************************************************************
 *                                                                *
 *  CLOSE OPENED FILES, PRINT RECORD COUNTS AND EXIT.            *
 *                                                                *
 ********************************************************************
      SKIP2
           CLOSE COBOLIN
                 REPORTO.
      SKIP2
           PERFORM DISPLAY-RECORD-COUNTS.
      SKIP2
 ***************************************************
 *                                               *
 *                 EXIT METRICS                  *
 *                                               *
 ***************************************************
      SKIP3
           DISPLAY END-RUN-MESSAGE.
           MOVE ZERO TO RETURN-CODE.
      SKIP2
           GOBACK.
      EJECT
 *    *******************************************
 *    *                                        *
 *    *  IF NOT AT END OF FILE, READ A RECORD  *
 *    *      OTHERWISE DONT BUMP RECORD COUNT..*
 *    *   AT END, SET EOF SWITCH, FILL THE     *
 *    *         RECORD AND AVOID BUMPING THE   *
 *    *         RECORD COUNT.                  *
 *    *                                        *
 *    *******************************************
```

260

```
      SKIP1
      READ-COBOLIN.
      SKIP1
          IF COBOLIN-OPEN THEN
              READ COBOLIN
                  INTO COBOLIN-REC
                  AT END
                      MOVE C-CLOSED TO COBOLIN-EOF-SW
                      MOVE HIGH-VALUES TO COBOLIN-REC
                      SUBTRACT C-1 FROM COBOLIN-RECORD-COUNT
          ELSE
              SUBTRACT C-1 FROM COBOLIN-RECORD-COUNT.
      SKIP1
          ADD C-1 TO COBOLIN-RECORD-COUNT.
      SKIP1
 **** EXIT.
      WRITE-REPORT.
          WRITE REPORTO-RECORD
              FROM W-REPORTO-REC
              AFTER POSITIONING CARRAIGE-CONTROL LINES.
      SKIP1
          ADD C-1 TO REPORTO-RECORD-COUNT.
          MOVE SPACES TO MEASUREMENT, STATEMENT-FILLER, COMMENT.
      SKIP1
 **** EXIT
      SKIP3
 *    *******************************************
 *    *                                         *
 *    *    DISPLAY THE ACTION TAKEN AGAINST EACH *
 *    *    FILE AND THE NUMBER OF RECORDS READ,  *
 *    *    UPDATED OR WRITTEN.                   *
 *    *                                         *
 *    *******************************************
      SKIP1
      DISPLAY-RECORD-COUNTS.
      SKIP2
          MOVE C-READ TO PRINT-ACTION.
          MOVE COBOLIN-RECORD-COUNT TO PRINT-RECORD-COUNT.
          MOVE C-COBOLIN TO PRINT-FD-NAME.
          DISPLAY RECORD-COUNT-CONTROLS.
      SKIP2
          MOVE C-REPORT TO PRINT-FD-NAME.
          MOVE REPORTO-RECORD-COUNT TO PRINT-RECORD-COUNT.
          DISPLAY RECORD-COUNT-CONTROLS.
      SKIP1
 **** EXIT
      EJECT
 ******************************************************************
 *                                                                *
 * FIND COPY STATEMENTS IN FIRST THREE DIVISIONS (COMMENTS)       *
 *                                                                *
```

```
*****************************************************************
SKIP2
SEARCH-ID-THRU-DATA-DIVISION.
    PERFORM READ-COBOLIN.
    IF COBOLIN-REC = HIGH-VALUES THEN
        PERFORM CALL-ABEND
    ELSE
        PERFORM COMMENT-COUNT-CHECK
        IF COMMENT-FOUND THEN
            NEXT SENTENCE
        ELSE
            INSPECT COBOLIN-REC
                TALLYING PIC-COUNT
                    FOR ALL PIC-STRING
            INSPECT COBOLIN-REC
                TALLYING PIC-S9-COUNT
                    FOR ALL PIC-S9-STRING
            INSPECT COBOLIN-REC
                TALLYING PIC-9-COUNT
                    FOR LEADING PIC-9-STRING
            INSPECT COBOLIN-REC
                TALLYING PIC-X-COUNT
                    FOR LEADING PIC-X-STRING
            INSPECT COBOLIN-REC
                TALLYING COMP-COUNT
                    FOR ALL COMP-STRING
            INSPECT COBOLIN-REC
                TALLYING SECURITY-COUNT
                    FOR ALL SECURITY-STRING
            INSPECT COBOLIN-REC
                TALLYING SELECT-COUNT
                    FOR ALL SELECT-STRING
            INSPECT COBOLIN-REC
                TALLYING COPY-COUNT
                    FOR ALL COPY-STRING
            INSPECT COBOLIN-REC
                TALLYING PROCEDURE-DIVISN-COUNT
                    FOR ALL PROCEDURE-DIVISN-STRING
            IF PROGRAM-ID-LITERAL = PROGRAM-ID-STRING THEN
                MOVE PROGRAM-ID-NAME TO HEADER-NAME.
SKIP2
SEARCH-PROCEDURE-DIVISION.
SKIP1
    PERFORM READ-COBOLIN.
SKIP1
    IF COBOLIN-REC = HIGH-VALUES THEN
        NEXT SENTENCE
    ELSE
        PERFORM COMMENT-COUNT-CHECK
        IF COMMENT-FOUND THEN
            NEXT SENTENCE
```

```
            ELSE
                INSPECT COBOLIN-REC
                    TALLYING IF-COUNT
                        FOR ALL IF-STRING
                INSPECT COBOLIN-REC
                    TALLYING UNTIL-COUNT
                        FOR ALL UNTIL-STRING
                INSPECT COBOLIN-REC
                    TALLYING VARYING-COUNT
                        FOR ALL VARYING-STRING
                INSPECT COBOLIN-REC
                    TALLYING WHEN-COUNT
                        FOR ALL WHEN-STRING
    SKIP1
                INSPECT COBOLIN-REC
                    TALLYING CALL-COUNT
                        FOR ALL CALL-STRING
                INSPECT COBOLIN-REC
                    TALLYING COMPUTE-COUNT
                        FOR ALL COMPUTE-STRING
                INSPECT COBOLIN-REC
                    TALLYING COPY-COUNT
                        FOR ALL COPY-STRING
                INSPECT COBOLIN-REC
                    TALLYING GENERATE-COUNT
                        FOR ALL GENERATE-STRING
                INSPECT COBOLIN-REC
                    TALLYING INITIATE-COUNT
                        FOR ALL INITIATE-STRING
                INSPECT COBOLIN-REC
                    TALLYING INSPECT-COUNT
                        FOR ALL INSPECT-STRING
                INSPECT COBOLIN-REC
                    TALLYING MERGE-COUNT
                        FOR ALL MERGE-STRING
                INSPECT COBOLIN-REC
                    TALLYING PERFORM-COUNT
                        FOR ALL PERFORM-STRING
                INSPECT COBOLIN-REC
                    TALLYING SEARCH-COUNT
                        FOR ALL SEARCH-STRING
                INSPECT COBOLIN-REC
                    TALLYING SEARCH-ALL-COUNT
                        FOR ALL SEARCH-ALL-STRING
                INSPECT COBOLIN-REC
                    TALLYING SORT-COUNT
                        FOR ALL SORT-STRING
                INSPECT COBOLIN-REC
    SKIP1
                INSPECT COBOLIN-REC
                    TALLYING ADD-COUNT
```

```
                              FOR ALL ADD-STRING
                   INSPECT COBOLIN-REC
                      TALLYING SUBTRACT-COUNT
                              FOR ALL SUBTRACT-STRING
                   INSPECT COBOLIN-REC
                      TALLYING MULTIPLY-COUNT
                              FOR ALL MULTIPLY-STRING
                   INSPECT COBOLIN-REC
                      TALLYING DIVIDE-COUNT
                              FOR ALL DIVIDE-STRING
          SKIP1
                   INSPECT COBOLIN-REC
                      TALLYING ACCEPT-COUNT
                              FOR ALL ACCEPT-STRING
                   INSPECT COBOLIN-REC
                      TALLYING CLOSE-COUNT
                              FOR ALL CLOSE-STRING
                   INSPECT COBOLIN-REC
                      TALLYING DISPLAY-COUNT
                              FOR ALL DISPLAY-STRING
                   INSPECT COBOLIN-REC
                      TALLYING IMS-COUNT
                              FOR ALL IMS-STRING
                   INSPECT COBOLIN-REC
                      TALLYING OPEN-COUNT
                              FOR ALL OPEN-STRING
                   INSPECT COBOLIN-REC
                      TALLYING READ-COUNT
                              FOR ALL READ-STRING
                   INSPECT COBOLIN-REC
                      TALLYING RELEASE-COUNT
                              FOR ALL RELEASE-STRING
                   INSPECT COBOLIN-REC
                      TALLYING RETURN-COUNT
                              FOR ALL RETURN-STRING
                   INSPECT COBOLIN-REC
                      TALLYING REWRITE-COUNT
                              FOR ALL REWRITE-STRING
                   INSPECT COBOLIN-REC
                      TALLYING WRITE-COUNT
                              FOR ALL WRITE-STRING
          SKIP1
                   INSPECT COBOLIN-REC
                      TALLYING ALTER-COUNT
                              FOR ALL ALTER-STRING
                   INSPECT COBOLIN-REC
                      TALLYING GOTO-COUNT
                              FOR ALL GOTO-STRING
                   INSPECT COBOLIN-REC
                      TALLYING MOVE-COUNT
                              FOR ALL MOVE-STRING
```

264

```
                INSPECT COBOLIN-REC
                    TALLYING SET-COUNT
                        FOR ALL SET-STRING
    SKIP1
                INSPECT COBOLIN-REC
                    TALLYING EJECT-COUNT
                        FOR ALL EJECT-STRING
                INSPECT COBOLIN-REC
                    TALLYING SKIP-COUNT
                        FOR ALL SKIP-STRING.
    SKIP1
    EJECT
****************************************************************
*                                                              *
*   CHECK FOR COMMENTS ON THE CURRENT LINE                     *
*                                                              *
****************************************************************
    SKIP1
    COMMENT-COUNT-CHECK.
    SKIP1
        IF COMMENT-SPACE = C-COMMENT THEN
            ADD C-1 TO COMMENT-COUNT
            MOVE C-COMMENT TO COMMENT-SW
        ELSE
            MOVE SPACES TO COMMENT-SW.
    EJECT
****************************************************************
*                                                              *
*   COMPUTE PRIMITIVE METRICS                                  *
*                                                              *
****************************************************************
    SKIP1
    COMPUTE-PRIMITIVE-METRICS.
    SKIP1
****************************************************************
*                                                              *
*   LINES OF CODE COUNTS AND VARIATIONS                        *
*                                                              *
****************************************************************
    SKIP1
        COMPUTE LOC = IF-COUNT + PERFORM-COUNT +
                SEARCH-COUNT + CALL-COUNT + COMPUTE-COUNT +
                GENERATE-COUNT + INITIATE-COUNT +
                INSPECT-COUNT + MERGE-COUNT + SORT-COUNT +
                ADD-COUNT + SUBTRACT-COUNT + MULTIPLY-COUNT +
                DIVIDE-COUNT + ACCEPT-COUNT + CLOSE-COUNT +
                DISPLAY-COUNT + OPEN-COUNT + READ-COUNT +
                RELEASE-COUNT + RETURN-COUNT + REWRITE-COUNT +
                WRITE-COUNT + ENTRY-COUNT + GOBACK-COUNT +
                STOP-RUN-COUNT + ALTER-COUNT + GOTO-COUNT +
                MOVE-COUNT + SET-COUNT.
```

```
      SKIP1
          COMPUTE LOC-100 = LOC / C-100.
          IF LOC-100 < C-1 THEN
              MOVE C-1 TO LOC-100.
          COMPUTE LOC-1000 = LOC / C-1000.
          IF LOC-1000 < C-1 THEN
              MOVE C-1 TO LOC-1000.
      SKIP1
          COMPUTE PROGRAM-SIZE = LOC-100 ** C-2.
      SKIP1
          COMPUTE TOTAL-COUNT = COBOLIN-RECORD-COUNT.
      SKIP1
**********************************************************************
*                                                                    *
*   DECISION COUNTS AND VARIATIONS                                   *
*                                                                    *
**********************************************************************
      SKIP1
          COMPUTE DECISION-COUNT = IF-COUNT + UNTIL-COUNT +
                                   WHEN-COUNT.
      SKIP1
          COMPUTE DECISION-DENSITY = DECISION-COUNT / LOC-100.
      SKIP1
**********************************************************************
*                                                                    *
*   FUNCTIONS, CONCISENESS, ETC                                      *
*                                                                    *
**********************************************************************
      SKIP1
          COMPUTE FUNCTION-COUNT = CALL-COUNT + COMPUTE-COUNT +
                  COPY-COUNT + GENERATE-COUNT + INITIATE-COUNT +
                  INSPECT-COUNT + MERGE-COUNT + SORT-COUNT +
                  PERFORM-COUTN + SEARCH-COUNT.
      SKIP1
          COMPUTE CONCISENESS = FUNCTION-COUNT / LOC-100.
      SKIP1
**********************************************************************
*                                                                    *
*   INPUT OUTPUTS AND COMBINATIONS                                   *
*                                                                    *
**********************************************************************
      SKIP1
          COMPUTE IO-COUNT = ACCEPT-COUNT + CLOSE-COUNT +
                  DISPLAY-COUNT + OPEN-COUNT + READ-COUNT +
                  RELEASE-COUNT + RETURN-COUNT + REWRITE-COUNT +
                  WRITE-COUNT.
      SKIP1
**********************************************************************
*                                                                    *
*   STRUCTUREDNESS, MODULARITY, ETC                                  *
*                                                                    *
```

```
****************************************************************
SKIP1
    IF ENTRY-COUNT > 0 THEN
        IF GOBACK-COUNT > ZERO OR STOP-RUN-COUNT > 0 THEN
            COMPUTE ENTRY-EXIT-RATIO = ENTRY-COUNT /
                (GOBACK-COUNT + STOP-RUN-COUNT)
        ELSE
            COMPUTE ENTRY-EXIT-RATIO = ENTRY-COUNT
    ELSE
        IF GOBACK-COUNT > ZERO OR STOP-RUN-COUNT > 0 THEN
            COMPUTE ENTRY-EXIT-RATIO = ENTRY-COUNT /
                (GOBACK-COUNT + STOP-RUN-COUNT)
        ELSE
            COMPUTE ENTRY-EXIT-RATIO = C-1.
EJECT
****************************************************************
*                                                              *
*   METRIC CRITERIA                                            *
*                                                              *
****************************************************************
SKIP1
COMPUTE-METRIC-CRITERIA.
    COMPUTE STRUCTUREDNESS =
        (((C-5 * ALTER-COUNT) + GOTO-COUNT) / LOC-100) ** C-2.
SKIP1
    COMPUTE MODULARITY = CALL-COUNT + CONCISENESS -
                PROGRAM-SIZE - STRUCTUREDNESS.
SKIP1
    IF SELECT-COUNT > 2 THEN
        COMPUTE COMPLEXITY =
                (SELECT-COUNT - C-3) + DECISION-DENSITY
    ELSE
        COMPUTE COMPLEXITY = DECISION-DENSITY.
SKIP1
****************************************************************
*                                                              *
*   PROGRAMMING STYLE AND DOCUMENTATION                        *
*                                                              *
****************************************************************
SKIP1
    COMPUTE STYLE = (EJECT-COUNT + SKIP-COUNT +
                    COMMENT-COUNT) / (LOC / 10).
SKIP1
    COMPUTE SELF-DOCUMENTATION = COMMENT-COUNT / LOC-100.
SKIP1
****************************************************************
*                                                              *
*   COMPUTE EFFICIENCY                                         *
*                                                              *
****************************************************************
SKIP1
```

```
    IF PIC-S9-COUNT > 0 OR PIC-9-COUNT > 0 THEN
        IF SEARCH-ALL-COUNT > 0 THEN
            COMPUTE EFFICIENCY =
                    ((PIC-S9-COUNT + COMP-COUNT) /
                    (PIC-S9-COUNT + PIC-9-COUNT)) +
                    (SEARCH-ALL-COUNT / SEARCH-COUNT) -
                    ((OPEN-COUNT + CLOSE-COUNT) / C-5)
        ELSE
            COMPUTE EFFICIENCY =
                    ((PIC-S9-COUNT + COMP-COUNT) /
                    (PIC-S9-COUNT + PIC-9-COUNT)) +
                    ((OPEN-COUNT + CLOSE-COUNT) / C-5)
SKIP1
    COMPUTE TRACEABILITY = ENTRY-EXIT-RATIO +
                          SELF-DOCUMENTATION.
SKIP1
    COMPUTE CONSISTENCY = STYLE + SELF-DOCUMENTATION.
SKIP1
    COMPUTE COMPLETENESS = SELF-DOCUMENTATION.
SKIP1
    COMPUTE GENERALITY = (COPY-COUNT / (LOC-1000)) +
                CONCISENESS.
SKIP1
    COMPUTE SIMPLICITY = DECISION-DENSITY + PROGRAM-SIZE +
                ENTRY-EXIT-RATIO - LOC-100 - STRUCTUREDNESS.
SKIP1
    COMPUTE MACHINE-INDEPENDENCE = SELECT-COUNT.
SKIP1
    COMPUTE SOFTWARE-INDEPENDENCE = GENERATE-COUNT +
                INITIATE-COUNT + IO-COUNT + IMS-COUNT.
EJECT
****************************************************************
*                                                              *
*   COMPUTE METRIC CRITERIA                                    *
*                                                              *
****************************************************************
SKIP1
COMPUTE-METRIC-CRITERIA.
SKIP1
    COMPUTE CORRECTNESS = ENTRY-EXIT-RATIO + STYLE -
                STRUCTUREDNESS.
SKIP1
    COMPUTE FLEXIBILITY = MODULARITY + GENERALITY +
                SELF-DOCUMENTATION.
SKIP1
    COMPUTE INTEGRITY = SECURITY-COUNT.
SKIP1
    COMPUTE INTEROPERABILITY = SELECT-COUNT.
SKIP1
    COMPUTE MAINTAINABILITY = CONSISTENCY + SIMPLICITY +
                MODULARITY.
```

```
       SKIP1
           COMPUTE PORTABILITY = MODULARITY + SELF-DOCUMENTATION -
                   MACHINE-INDEPENDENCE - SOFTWARE-INDEPENDENCE.
       SKIP1
           COMPUTE RELIABILITY = CONSISTENCY + SIMPLICITY.
       SKIP1
           COMPUTE REUSABILITY = GENERALITY + MODULARITY +
                   SELF-DOCUMENTATION -
                   MACHINE-INDEPENDENCE - SOFTWARE-INDEPENDENCE.
       SKIP1
           COMPUTE PRODUCTIVITY = TOTAL-COUNT / DAYS-WORKED.
       EJECT
      ****************************************************************
      *                                                             *
      *  DUMP-CODE AND DUMP-OPTION OF ABEND FIELDS MUST BE SET       *
      *  BEFORE CALLING THIS ROUTINE.                               *
      *                                                             *
      ****************************************************************
       SKIP2
       CALL-ABEND.
           PERFORM DISPLAY-RECORD-COUNTS.
           MOVE C-ABEND-CODE-0001 TO ABEND-CODE.
           MOVE C-DUMP-OPTION TO DUMP-OPTION.
       EJECT
      ****************************************************************
      *                                                             *
      *  WRITE REPORT HEADERS                                       *
      *                                                             *
      ****************************************************************
       SKIP2
       WRITE-HEADERS.
       SKIP2
           MOVE C-TOP-OF-PAGE TO CARRAIGE-CONTROL.
           MOVE REPORT-HEADER-1 TO REPORT-REC.
           PERFORM WRITE-REPORT.
           MOVE C-SKIP-NO-LINES TO CARRAIGE-CONTROL.
           MOVE REPORT-HEADER-A TO REPORT-REC.
           PERFORM WRITE-REPORT.
           MOVE C-SKIP-3-LINES TO CARRAIGE-CONTROL.
           MOVE REPORT-HEADER-2 TO REPORT-REC.
           PERFORM WRITE-REPORT.
           MOVE C-SKIP-NO-LINES TO CARRAIGE-CONTROL.
           MOVE REPORT-HEADER-B TO REPORT-REC.
           PERFORM WRITE-REPORT.
       EJECT
      ****************************************************************
      *                                                             *
      *  WRITE SOFTWARE METRIC REPORT                              *
      *                                                             *
      ****************************************************************
       SKIP2
```

269

```
CREATE-METRIC-REPORT.
SKIP2
    PERFORM WRITE-HEADERS.
SKIP1
    MOVE C-SKIP-2-LINES TO CARRAIGE-CONTROL.
SKIP1
    MOVE DECISION-STRING TO MEASUREMENT OF DETAIL-LINE.
    MOVE DECISION-COMMENT TO COMMENT OF DETAIL-LINE.
    MOVE DETAIL-LINE TO REPORT-REC.
    PERFORM WRITE-REPORT.
SKIP1
    MOVE IF-STRING TO MEASUREMENT OF DETAIL-LINE.
    MOVE IF-COUNT TO STATEMENT-COUNT OF DETAIL-LINE.
    MOVE DETAIL-LINE TO REPORT-REC.
    PERFORM WRITE-REPORT.
SKIP1
    MOVE VARYING-STRING TO MEASUREMENT OF DETAIL-LINE.
    MOVE VARYING-COUNT TO STATEMENT-COUNT OF DETAIL-LINE.
    MOVE DETAIL-LINE TO REPORT-REC.
    PERFORM WRITE-REPORT.
SKIP1
    MOVE UNTIL-STRING TO MEASUREMENT OF DETAIL-LINE.
    MOVE UNTIL-COUNT TO STATEMENT-COUNT OF DETAIL-LINE.
    MOVE DETAIL-LINE TO REPORT-REC.
    PERFORM WRITE-REPORT.
SKIP1
    MOVE WHEN-STRING TO MEASUREMENT OF DETAIL-LINE.
    MOVE WHEN-COUNT TO STATEMENT-COUNT OF DETAIL-LINE.
    MOVE DETAIL-LINE TO REPORT-REC.
    PERFORM WRITE-REPORT.
SKIP1
    MOVE FUNCTION-STRING TO MEASUREMENT OF DETAIL-LINE.
    MOVE FUNCTION-COMMENT TO COMMENT OF DETAIL-LINE.
    MOVE DETAIL-LINE TO REPORT-REC.
    PERFORM WRITE-REPORT.
SKIP1
    MOVE PERFORM-STRING TO MEASUREMENT OF DETAIL-LINE.
    MOVE PERFORM-COUNT TO STATEMENT-COUNT OF DETAIL-LINE.
    MOVE DETAIL-LINE TO REPORT-REC.
    PERFORM WRITE-REPORT.
SKIP1
    MOVE SEARCH-STRING TO MEASUREMENT OF DETAIL-LINE.
    MOVE SEARCH-COUNT TO STATEMENT-COUNT OF DETAIL-LINE.
    MOVE DETAIL-LINE TO REPORT-REC.
    PERFORM WRITE-REPORT.
SKIP1
    MOVE CALL-STRING TO MEASUREMENT OF DETAIL-LINE.
    MOVE CALL-COUNT TO STATEMENT-COUNT OF DETAIL-LINE.
    MOVE DETAIL-LINE TO REPORT-REC.
    PERFORM WRITE-REPORT.
SKIP1
```

```
          MOVE COMPUTE-STRING TO MEASUREMENT OF DETAIL-LINE.
          MOVE COMPUTE-COUNT TO STATEMENT-COUNT OF DETAIL-LINE.
          MOVE DETAIL-LINE TO REPORT-REC.
          PERFORM WRITE-REPORT.
      SKIP1
          MOVE COPY-STRING TO MEASUREMENT OF DETAIL-LINE.
          MOVE COPY-COUNT TO STATEMENT-COUNT OF DETAIL-LINE.
          MOVE DETAIL-LINE TO REPORT-REC.
          PERFORM WRITE-REPORT.
      SKIP1
          MOVE GENERATE-STRING TO MEASUREMENT OF DETAIL-LINE.
          MOVE GENERATE-COUNT TO STATEMENT-COUNT OF DETAIL-LINE.
          MOVE DETAIL-LINE TO REPORT-REC.
          PERFORM WRITE-REPORT.
      SKIP1
          MOVE INITIATE-STRING TO MEASUREMENT OF DETAIL-LINE.
          MOVE INITIATE-COUNT TO STATEMENT-COUNT OF DETAIL-LINE.
          MOVE DETAIL-LINE TO REPORT-REC.
          PERFORM WRITE-REPORT.
      SKIP1
          MOVE INSPECT-STRING TO MEASUREMENT OF DETAIL-LINE.
          MOVE INSPECT-COUNT TO STATEMENT-COUNT OF DETAIL-LINE.
          MOVE DETAIL-LINE TO REPORT-REC.
          PERFORM WRITE-REPORT.
      SKIP1
          MOVE MERGE-STRING TO MEASUREMENT OF DETAIL-LINE.
          MOVE MERGE-COUNT TO STATEMENT-COUNT OF DETAIL-LINE.
          MOVE DETAIL-LINE TO REPORT-REC.
          PERFORM WRITE-REPORT.
      SKIP1
          MOVE SORT-STRING TO MEASUREMENT OF DETAIL-LINE.
          MOVE SORT-COUNT TO STATEMENT-COUNT OF DETAIL-LINE.
          MOVE DETAIL-LINE TO REPORT-REC.
          PERFORM WRITE-REPORT.
      SKIP1
          MOVE ARITHMETIC-STRING TO MEASUREMENT OF DETAIL-LINE.
          MOVE ARITHMETIC-COMMENT TO COMMENT OF DETAIL-LINE.
          MOVE DETAIL-LINE TO REPORT-REC.
          PERFORM WRITE-REPORT.
      SKIP1
          MOVE ADD-STRING TO MEASUREMENT OF DETAIL-LINE.
          MOVE ADD-COUNT TO STATEMENT-COUNT OF DETAIL-LINE.
          MOVE DETAIL-LINE TO REPORT-REC.
          PERFORM WRITE-REPORT.
      SKIP1
          MOVE SUBTRACT-STRING TO MEASUREMENT OF DETAIL-LINE.
          MOVE SUBTRACT-COUNT TO STATEMENT-COUNT OF DETAIL-LINE.
          MOVE DETAIL-LINE TO REPORT-REC.
          PERFORM WRITE-REPORT.
      SKIP1
          MOVE MULTIPLY-STRING TO MEASUREMENT OF DETAIL-LINE.
```

```
        MOVE MULTIPLY-COUNT TO STATEMENT-COUNT OF DETAIL-LINE.
        MOVE DETAIL-LINE TO REPORT-REC.
        PERFORM WRITE-REPORT.
SKIP1
        MOVE DIVIDE-STRING TO MEASUREMENT OF DETAIL-LINE.
        MOVE DIVIDE-COUNT TO STATEMENT-COUNT OF DETAIL-LINE.
        MOVE DETAIL-LINE TO REPORT-REC.
        PERFORM WRITE-REPORT.
SKIP1
        PERFORM WRITE-HEADERS.
        MOVE C-SKIP-2-LINES TO CARRAIGE-CONTROL.
SKIP1
        MOVE INPUT-OUTPUT-STRING TO MEASUREMENT OF DETAIL-LINE.
        MOVE INPUT-OUTPUT-COMMENT TO COMMENT OF DETAIL-LINE.
        MOVE DETAIL-LINE TO REPORT-REC.
        PERFORM WRITE-REPORT.
SKIP1
        MOVE SELECT-STRING TO MEASUREMENT OF DETAIL-LINE.
        MOVE SELECT-COUNT TO STATEMENT-COUNT OF DETAIL-LINE.
        MOVE SELECT-COMMENT TO COMMENT OF DETAIL-LINE.
        MOVE DETAIL-LINE TO REPORT-REC.
        PERFORM WRITE-REPORT.
SKIP1
        MOVE ACCEPT-STRING TO MEASUREMENT OF DETAIL-LINE.
        MOVE ACCEPT-COUNT TO STATEMENT-COUNT OF DETAIL-LINE.
        MOVE DETAIL-LINE TO REPORT-REC.
        PERFORM WRITE-REPORT.
SKIP1
        MOVE CLOSE-STRING TO MEASUREMENT OF DETAIL-LINE.
        MOVE CLOSE-COUNT TO STATEMENT-COUNT OF DETAIL-LINE.
        MOVE DETAIL-LINE TO REPORT-REC.
        PERFORM WRITE-REPORT.
SKIP1
        MOVE DISPLAY-STRING TO MEASUREMENT OF DETAIL-LINE.
        MOVE DISPLAY-COUNT TO STATEMENT-COUNT OF DETAIL-LINE.
        MOVE DETAIL-LINE TO REPORT-REC.
        PERFORM WRITE-REPORT.
SKIP1
        MOVE OPEN-STRING TO MEASUREMENT OF DETAIL-LINE.
        MOVE OPEN-COUNT TO STATEMENT-COUNT OF DETAIL-LINE.
        MOVE DETAIL-LINE TO REPORT-REC.
        PERFORM WRITE-REPORT.
SKIP1
        MOVE READ-STRING TO MEASUREMENT OF DETAIL-LINE.
        MOVE READ-COUNT TO STATEMENT-COUNT OF DETAIL-LINE.
        MOVE DETAIL-LINE TO REPORT-REC.
        PERFORM WRITE-REPORT.
SKIP1
        MOVE RELEASE-STRING TO MEASUREMENT OF DETAIL-LINE.
        MOVE RELEASE-COUNT TO STATEMENT-COUNT OF DETAIL-LINE.
        MOVE DETAIL-LINE TO REPORT-REC.
```

```
      PERFORM WRITE-REPORT.
SKIP1
      MOVE RETURN-STRING TO MEASUREMENT OF DETAIL-LINE.
      MOVE RETURN-COUNT TO STATEMENT-COUNT OF DETAIL-LINE.
      MOVE DETAIL-LINE TO REPORT-REC.
      PERFORM WRITE-REPORT.
SKIP1
      MOVE REWRITE-STRING TO MEASUREMENT OF DETAIL-LINE.
      MOVE REWRITE-COUNT TO STATEMENT-COUNT OF DETAIL-LINE.
      MOVE DETAIL-LINE TO REPORT-REC.
      PERFORM WRITE-REPORT.
SKIP1
      MOVE WRITE-STRING TO MEASUREMENT OF DETAIL-LINE.
      MOVE WRITE-COUNT TO STATEMENT-COUNT OF DETAIL-LINE.
      MOVE DETAIL-LINE TO REPORT-REC.
      PERFORM WRITE-REPORT.
SKIP1
      MOVE ENTRY-EXIT-STRING TO MEASUREMENT OF DETAIL-LINE.
      MOVE ENTRY-EXIT-COMMENT TO COMMENT OF DETAIL-LINE.
      MOVE DETAIL-LINE TO REPORT-REC.
      PERFORM WRITE-REPORT.
SKIP1
      MOVE ENTRY-STRING TO MEASUREMENT OF DETAIL-LINE.
      MOVE ENTRY-COUNT TO STATEMENT-COUNT OF DETAIL-LINE.
      MOVE DETAIL-LINE TO REPORT-REC.
      PERFORM WRITE-REPORT.
SKIP1
      MOVE GOBACK-STRING TO MEASUREMENT OF DETAIL-LINE.
      MOVE GOBACK-COUNT TO STATEMENT-COUNT OF DETAIL-LINE.
      MOVE DETAIL-LINE TO REPORT-REC.
      PERFORM WRITE-REPORT.
SKIP1
      MOVE STOP-RUN-STRING TO MEASUREMENT OF DETAIL-LINE.
      MOVE STOP-RUN-COUNT TO STATEMENT-COUNT OF DETAIL-LINE.
      MOVE DETAIL-LINE TO REPORT-REC.
      PERFORM WRITE-REPORT.
SKIP1
      MOVE OTHER-STRING TO MEASUREMENT OF DETAIL-LINE.
      MOVE OTHER-COMMENT TO COMMENT OF DETAIL-LINE.
      MOVE DETAIL-LINE TO REPORT-REC.
      PERFORM WRITE-REPORT.
SKIP1
      MOVE GOTO-STRING TO MEASUREMENT OF DETAIL-LINE.
      MOVE GOTO-COUNT TO STATEMENT-COUNT OF DETAIL-LINE.
      MOVE DETAIL-LINE TO REPORT-REC.
      PERFORM WRITE-REPORT.
SKIP1
      MOVE ALTER-STRING TO MEASUREMENT OF DETAIL-LINE.
      MOVE ALTER-COUNT TO STATEMENT-COUNT OF DETAIL-LINE.
      MOVE DETAIL-LINE TO REPORT-REC.
      PERFORM WRITE-REPORT.
```

```
SKIP1
     MOVE MOVE-STRING TO MEASUREMENT OF DETAIL-LINE.
     MOVE MOVE-COUNT TO STATEMENT-COUNT OF DETAIL-LINE.
     MOVE DETAIL-LINE TO REPORT-REC.
     PERFORM WRITE-REPORT.
SKIP1
     MOVE SET-STRING TO MEASUREMENT OF DETAIL-LINE.
     MOVE SET-COUNT TO STATEMENT-COUNT OF DETAIL-LINE.
     MOVE DETAIL-LINE TO REPORT-REC.
     PERFORM WRITE-REPORT.
SKIP1
     MOVE FORMAT-STRING TO MEASUREMENT OF DETAIL-LINE.
     MOVE FORMAT-COMMENT TO COMMENT OF DETAIL-LINE.
     MOVE DETAIL-LINE TO REPORT-REC.
     PERFORM WRITE-REPORT.
SKIP1
     MOVE EJECT-STRING TO MEASUREMENT OF DETAIL-LINE.
     MOVE EJECT-COUNT TO STATEMENT-COUNT OF DETAIL-LINE.
     MOVE DETAIL-LINE TO REPORT-REC.
     PERFORM WRITE-REPORT.
SKIP1
     MOVE SKIP-STRING TO MEASUREMENT OF DETAIL-LINE.
     MOVE SKIP-COUNT TO STATEMENT-COUNT OF DETAIL-LINE.
     MOVE DETAIL-LINE TO REPORT-REC.
     PERFORM WRITE-REPORT.
SKIP1
     MOVE COMMENT-STRING TO MEASUREMENT OF DETAIL-LINE.
     MOVE COMMENT-COUNT TO STATEMENT-COUNT OF DETAIL-LINE.
     MOVE DETAIL-LINE TO REPORT-REC.
     PERFORM WRITE-REPORT.
SKIP1
     PERFORM WRITE-HEADERS.
SKIP1
     MOVE C-SKIP-2-LINES TO CARRAIGE-CONTROL.
     MOVE SOFTWARE-CRITERIA-STRING TO MEASUREMENT OF DETAIL-LINE
     MOVE SOFTWARE-CRITERIA-COMMENT TO COMMENT OF DETAIL-LINE.
     MOVE DETAIL-LINE TO REPORT-REC.
     PERFORM WRITE-REPORT.
SKIP1
     MOVE T-COMPLETENESS TO MEASUREMENT OF DETAIL-LINE.
     MOVE COMPLETENESS TO STATEMENT-COUNT OF DETAIL-LINE.
     MOVE DETAIL-LINE TO REPORT-REC.
     PERFORM WRITE-REPORT.
SKIP1
     MOVE T-CONCISENESS TO MEASUREMENT OF DETAIL-LINE.
     MOVE CONCISENESS TO STATEMENT-COUNT OF DETAIL-LINE.
     MOVE DETAIL-LINE TO REPORT-REC.
     PERFORM WRITE-REPORT.
SKIP1
     MOVE T-CONSISTENCY TO MEASUREMENT OF DETAIL-LINE.
     MOVE CONSISTENCY TO STATEMENT-COUNT OF DETAIL-LINE.
```

```
        MOVE DETAIL-LINE TO REPORT-REC.
        PERFORM WRITE-REPORT.
SKIP1
        MOVE T-DECISION-COUNT TO MEASUREMENT OF DETAIL-LINE.
        MOVE DECISION-COUNT TO STATEMENT-COUNT OF DETAIL-LINE.
        MOVE DETAIL-LINE TO REPORT-REC.
        PERFORM WRITE-REPORT.
SKIP1
        MOVE T-DECISION-DENSITY TO MEASUREMENT OF DETAIL-LINE.
        MOVE DECISION-DENSITY TO STATEMENT-COUNT OF DETAIL-LINE.
        MOVE DETAIL-LINE TO REPORT-REC.
        PERFORM WRITE-REPORT.
SKIP1
        MOVE T-ENTRY-EXIT-RATIO TO MEASUREMENT OF DETAIL-LINE.
        MOVE ENTRY-EXIT-RATIO TO STATEMENT-COUNT OF DETAIL-LINE.
        MOVE DETAIL-LINE TO REPORT-REC.
        PERFORM WRITE-REPORT.
SKIP1
        MOVE T-FUNCTION-COUNT TO MEASUREMENT OF DETAIL-LINE.
        MOVE FUNCTION-COUNT TO STATEMENT-COUNT OF DETAIL-LINE.
        MOVE DETAIL-LINE TO REPORT-REC.
        PERFORM WRITE-REPORT.
SKIP1
        MOVE T-GENERALITY TO MEASUREMENT OF DETAIL-LINE.
        MOVE GENERALITY TO STATEMENT-COUNT OF DETAIL-LINE.
        MOVE DETAIL-LINE TO REPORT-REC.
        PERFORM WRITE-REPORT.
SKIP1
        MOVE T-MACHINE-INDEPENDENCE TO MEASUREMENT OF DETAIL-LINE.
        MOVE MACHINE-INDEPENDENCE TO STATEMENT-COUNT OF DETAIL-LINE.
        MOVE DETAIL-LINE TO REPORT-REC.
        PERFORM WRITE-REPORT.
SKIP1
        MOVE T-MODULARITY TO MEASUREMENT OF DETAIL-LINE.
        MOVE MODULARITY TO STATEMENT-COUNT OF DETAIL-LINE.
        MOVE DETAIL-LINE TO REPORT-REC.
        PERFORM WRITE-REPORT.
SKIP1
        MOVE T-SELF-DOCUMENTATION TO MEASUREMENT OF DETAIL-LINE.
        MOVE SELF-DOCUMENTATION TO STATEMENT-COUNT OF DETAIL-LINE.
        MOVE DETAIL-LINE TO REPORT-REC.
        PERFORM WRITE-REPORT.
SKIP1
        MOVE T-SIMPLICITY TO MEASUREMENT OF DETAIL-LINE.
        MOVE SIMPLICITY TO STATEMENT-COUNT OF DETAIL-LINE.
        MOVE DETAIL-LINE TO REPORT-REC.
        PERFORM WRITE-REPORT.
SKIP1
        MOVE T-SOFTWARE-INDEPENDENCE TO MEASUREMENT OF DETAIL-LINE.
        MOVE SOFTWARE-INDEPENDENCE TO STATEMENT-COUNT OF DETAIL-LINE.
        MOVE DETAIL-LINE TO REPORT-REC.
```

```
      PERFORM WRITE-REPORT.
  SKIP1
      MOVE T-STRUCTUREDNESS TO MEASUREMENT OF DETAIL-LINE.
      MOVE STRUCTUREDNESS TO STATEMENT-COUNT OF DETAIL-LINE.
      MOVE DETAIL-LINE TO REPORT-REC.
      PERFORM WRITE-REPORT.
  SKIP1
      MOVE T-TRACEABILITY TO MEASUREMENT OF DETAIL-LINE.
      MOVE TRACEABILITY TO STATEMENT-COUNT OF DETAIL-LINE.
      MOVE DETAIL-LINE TO REPORT-REC.
      PERFORM WRITE-REPORT.
  SKIP1
      MOVE T-LOC-1000 TO MEASUREMENT OF DETAIL-LINE.
      MOVE LOC-1000 TO STATEMENT-COUNT OF DETAIL-LINE.
      MOVE DETAIL-LINE TO REPORT-REC.
      PERFORM WRITE-REPORT.
  SKIP1
      MOVE T-LOC-100 TO MEASUREMENT OF DETAIL-LINE.
      MOVE LOC-100 TO STATEMENT-COUNT OF DETAIL-LINE.
      MOVE DETAIL-LINE TO REPORT-REC.
      PERFORM WRITE-REPORT.
  SKIP1
      MOVE T-LOC TO MEASUREMENT OF DETAIL-LINE.
      MOVE LOC TO STATEMENT-COUNT OF DETAIL-LINE.
      MOVE DETAIL-LINE TO REPORT-REC.
      PERFORM WRITE-REPORT.
  SKIP1
      MOVE T-TOTAL-COUNT TO MEASUREMENT OF DETAIL-LINE.
      MOVE TOTAL-COUNT TO STATEMENT-COUNT OF DETAIL-LINE.
      MOVE DETAIL-LINE TO REPORT-REC.
      PERFORM WRITE-REPORT.
  SKIP1
      PERFORM WRITE-HEADERS.
  SKIP1
      MOVE C-SKIP-2-LINES TO CARRAIGE-CONTROL.
      MOVE SOFTWARE-METRIC-STRING TO MEASUREMENT OF DETAIL-LINE.
      MOVE SOFTWARE-METRIC-COMMENT TO COMMENT OF DETAIL-LINE.
      MOVE DETAIL-LINE TO REPORT-REC.
      PERFORM WRITE-REPORT.
  SKIP1
      MOVE C-SKIP-2-LINES TO CARRAIGE-CONTROL.
      MOVE T-CORRECTNESS TO MEASUREMENT OF DETAIL-LINE.
      MOVE CORRECTNESS TO STATEMENT-COUNT OF DETAIL-LINE.
      MOVE DETAIL-LINE TO REPORT-REC.
      PERFORM WRITE-REPORT.
  SKIP1
      MOVE T-EFFICIENCY TO MEASUREMENT OF DETAIL-LINE.
      MOVE EFFICIENCY TO STATEMENT-COUNT OF DETAIL-LINE.
      MOVE DETAIL-LINE TO REPORT-REC.
      PERFORM WRITE-REPORT.
  SKIP1
```

```
          MOVE T-FLEXIBILITY TO MEASUREMENT OF DETAIL-LINE.
          MOVE FLEXIBILITY TO STATEMENT-COUNT OF DETAIL-LINE.
          MOVE DETAIL-LINE TO REPORT-REC.
          PERFORM WRITE-REPORT.
SKIP1
          MOVE T-EXPANDABILITY TO MEASUREMENT OF DETAIL-LINE.
          MOVE EXPANDABILITY TO STATEMENT-COUNT OF DETAIL-LINE.
          MOVE DETAIL-LINE TO REPORT-REC.
          PERFORM WRITE-REPORT.
SKIP1
          MOVE T-INTEGRITY TO MEASUREMENT OF DETAIL-LINE.
          MOVE INTEGRITY TO STATEMENT-COUNT OF DETAIL-LINE.
          MOVE DETAIL-LINE TO REPORT-REC.
          PERFORM WRITE-REPORT.
SKIP1
          MOVE T-INTEROPERABILITY  TO MEASUREMENT OF DETAIL-LINE.
          MOVE INTEROPERABILITY TO STATEMENT-COUNT OF DETAIL-LINE.
          MOVE DETAIL-LINE TO REPORT-REC.
          PERFORM WRITE-REPORT.
SKIP1
          MOVE T-MAINTAINABILITY TO MEASUREMENT OF DETAIL-LINE.
          MOVE MAINTAINABILITY TO STATEMENT-COUNT OF DETAIL-LINE.
          MOVE DETAIL-LINE TO REPORT-REC.
          PERFORM WRITE-REPORT.
SKIP1
          MOVE T-PORTABILITY TO MEASUREMENT OF DETAIL-LINE.
          MOVE PORTABILITY TO STATEMENT-COUNT OF DETAIL-LINE.
          MOVE DETAIL-LINE TO REPORT-REC.
          PERFORM WRITE-REPORT.
SKIP1
          MOVE T-RELIABILITY  TO MEASUREMENT OF DETAIL-LINE.
          MOVE RELIABILITY TO STATEMENT-COUNT OF DETAIL-LINE.
          MOVE DETAIL-LINE TO REPORT-REC.
          PERFORM WRITE-REPORT.
SKIP1
          MOVE T-REUSABILITY TO MEASUREMENT OF DETAIL-LINE.
          MOVE REUSABILITY TO STATEMENT-COUNT OF DETAIL-LINE.
          MOVE DETAIL-LINE TO REPORT-REC.
          PERFORM WRITE-REPORT.
SKIP1
          MOVE T-USABILITY TO MEASUREMENT OF DETAIL-LINE.
          MOVE USABILITY TO STATEMENT-COUNT OF DETAIL-LINE.
          MOVE DETAIL-LINE TO REPORT-REC.
          PERFORM WRITE-REPORT.
```

Index